HISTORY'S GREATEST

AUTOMOTIVE MYSTERIES MYTHS AND RUMORS REVEALED

HISTORY'S GREATEST

AUTOMOTIVE
MYSTERIES
MYTHS
AND RUMORS
REVEALED

JAMES DEAN'S **KILLER** PORSCHE
NASCAR's **FASTEST** MONKEY
BONNIE AND CLYDE'S
GETAWAY CAR

AND MORE

Preston Lerner and Matt Stone

First published in 2012 by Motorbooks, an imprint of MBI Publishing
Company, 400 First Avenue North, Suite 300, Minneapolis, MN 55401 USA

Motorbooks titles are also available at discounts in bulk quantity for industrial
or sales-promotional use. For details write to Special Sales Manager at MBI
Publishing Company, 400 First Avenue North, Suite 300, Minneapolis, MN
55401 USA.

To find out more about our books, visit us online at www.motorbooks.com.

ISBN-13: 978-0-7603-4260-2

Editor: Darwin Holmstrom
Design Manager: Brad Springer
Layout: Helena Shimizu
Cover designer: Matthew Simmons
Background image credit: Sebastian Kaulitzki/Shutterstock.com

About the Authors

Matt Stone, former executive editor of *Motor Trend* magazine, has been a profes-
sional journalist and photographer since 1985. He is a member of SPEED TV's
Barrett-Jackson Auction broadcast team and has authored and photographed
several books for Motorbooks, including *My First Car* (2011), *McQueen's
Machines* (2010), *Winning: The Racing Life of Paul Newman* (2009), and *365 Cars
You Must Drive* (2006). He lives in Pasadena, California.

Preston Lerner, a regular contributor to *Automobile* magazine, has written
about motorsports for publications ranging from *Sports Illustrated* to *The New
York Times Magazine* and has authored two books for Motorbooks: *Winning:
The Racing Life of Paul Newman* (2009), which he co-authored with Matt Stone,
and *Scarab* (2003). He lives in Burbank, California.

Printed in China

10 9 8 7 6 5 4 3 2 1

CONTENTS

ACKNOWLEDGMENTS

No piece of journalism is the work of a writer alone. By definition, journalism requires sources to provide information and insights, color and perspective.

Because our book covers so many disparate subjects from so many different locales and eras, our list of sources is necessarily long—so long that it seems to marginalize the contributions of the many people who helped us. Yet each one of them provided an essential piece of the puzzle, and without their generosity, we couldn't have tackled a project this large. At the same time, since we were covering ground that had already been surveyed by other journalists and historians, we stood on the shoulders of those who came before us. Most of them are explicitly credited in the chapters, but we've included a partial bibliography for those who'd like to conduct their own research. That said, we're to blame for any errors of fact or mistakes in judgment. The following is a partial list of all the people who contributed to this project:

Eric Ahlstrom
Mario Andretti
David Audley
Martha Baer
Stan Barrett
Don Baumea
Warren Beath
Burt Boeckmann
Craig Breedlove
Don Capps
Bud Chatterley
Phil Conley
Hugh Conway

Carrick Cook
John Craft
Donald Davidson
Doug Duncan
Bill Ellis
John Ficarra
John Fitch
The Henry Ford
Elliott Forbes-Robinson
Frances Flock
Michael Frazier
Peter Garrison
Jannelle Grigsby

Charles Haynes
Katrina Heron
David Hobbs
Phil Hutchinson
Russell Jaslow
Kevin Jeannette
Dean Jeffries
Gordon Johncock
Junior Johnson
Allan Kam
Sean Kane
Dick Keller
Leslie Kendall
Peter Kurth
Richard Lane
Marty Lorentzen
Brian Lyons
Barry Maiten
Tom McDonald
Hershel McGriff
Mike Michels
Mark and Linda Mountanos
Peter Mullin
Jack Ong

Cotton Owens
Dick Passwater
Michael Pecht
Jim and Jack Petty
Paige Plant
Lee Raskin
Andrew Reilly
David Reinholz
Sam Posey
L. Spencer Riggs
Mike Salisbury
Adam Savage
Bob Sharp
Tom Shelton
Paul Skilleter
Gary Smith
Richard Smith
The Smolinski family
Jack Styles
T. A. Toomes
Paul Vixie
Dean Webber
Bill Wolf
Trish Yunick

Our special gratitude goes to those good Samaritans who graciously provided photographs from their personal collections, asking nothing in return: Thank you, Stan Barrett, Burt Boeckmann, Bruce Canepa, Doug Duncan, Frances Flock, Richard Lane, Jim and Jack Petty, Lee Raskin, Mike Salisbury, Paul Skilleter, Richard Smith, Tom Strongman, and Trish Yunick. We appreciate your help more than you'll ever know.

INTRODUCTION

This is a book about cars, but it was inspired by a movie—a Western, no less—director John Ford's subversive masterpiece, *The Man Who Shot Liberty Valance*. Ford's critics condemn him as an apologist who was blind to the cruel realities of how the West was won. But in *Liberty Valance*, Ford deconstructed and ultimately demolished the creation myth that he himself had done so much to nurture.

In an extended flashback, the movie tells the story of a naïve attorney, Ransom Stoddard, played by James Stewart, who believes that the rule of law can tame the Wild West. Shortly after arriving on the frontier, he's beaten and robbed by Liberty Valance, a psychopathic outlaw brought to lurid life by Lee Marvin. Later, Stewart finds a protector in a fearless rancher, Tom Doniphon, embodied by John Wayne. The movie climaxes with the overmatched attorney miraculously killing the gunfighter in a shoot-out. Known thereafter as "the man who shot Liberty Valance," Stewart's character soars to political stardom and marries the woman whom Wayne had loved.

Near the end of the movie, during the newspaper interview that's the pretext for the flashback, the elderly Stoddard—now a U.S. Senator—reveals the true story behind the shooting. The gunfight with Liberty Valance is staged again, but from a different angle. This time, movie-goers see that it was John Wayne's character, not Jimmy Stewart's, who shot Liberty Valance. So Ford shows us that the senator's entire career—a metaphor for how the frontier was civilized—was based not merely on a lie but on a cold-blooded murder. After hearing this, the newspaper editor burns his young reporter's notes rather than debunk the cherished myth. "When the legend becomes fact," he declares, "print the legend."

This advice has been taken to heart by writers at least since the time of Herodotus, the ancient Greek who's known as both the "Father of

Liberty Valance, played by Lee Marvin—in the black hat, naturally—confronts Jimmy Stewart and John Wayne while henchman Lee Van Cleef looks on in a still image from *The Man Who Shot Liberty Valance*. Moviestore Collection Ltd/Alamy

History" and the "Father of Lies." It's not hard to understand why: some stories are too good to be subjected to a rigorous reality check. In fact, the more incredible they are, the more people want to believe and share them. So they get passed from friend to friend, and magazine to magazine, and book to book, and now website to website. And before too long, the sheer volume of sources that can be cited for a particular story becomes "proof" that it has to be true, despite logic and all evidence to the contrary. And that's fine. After all, who doesn't enjoy a genuinely imaginative urban legend, the more outlandish the better? But the mash-up of fact and fiction cheapens the value of the stories that really are true. And that's just not right.

There are already plenty of people who devote plenty of time to debunking myths, hoaxes, and urban legends—*Skeptic* magazine, the snopes.com website, and so on. But our peculiar interest is the world of automobiles. So we rounded up the most popular and far-fetched car-related myths and legends, and we took a fresh look at everything that's been said and written about them. We interviewed participants. We rooted around in archives. We studied period photos. We dug up old videos. When we finished our research, we made a good faith effort to determine whether the legend was true: Did some yahoo really strap JATO rockets to the roof of his '64 Impala and fly it into a cliff in the Arizona desert at 350 miles per hour? Who won the first Indy 500—Ray Harroun or Ralph Mulford? Unintended acceleration—mysterious vehicle flaw or simple driver error?

Some of the most unbelievable myths turned out to be absolutely true. Others proved to be nothing more than figments of overheated imaginations. But in every case, we had fun exploring the stories behind the stories—how they were born, burnished, and circulated. So like the newspaper editor in *The Man Who Shot Liberty Valance*, we're printing the legends. But we're also sharing all the facts. Decide for yourself what you want to believe.

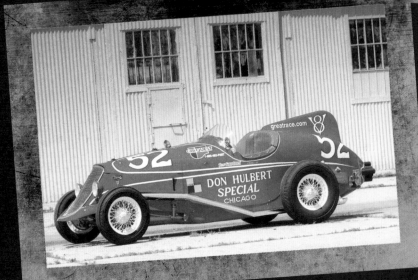

1
URBAN LEGENDS

THE ROCKET CAR VS. THE MOUNTAIN

LEGEND: A Chevrolet Impala fitted with solid-fuel rockets flew off the road, climbed 125 feet into the air, and crashed at 350 mph into a cliff in the Arizona desert.

Have you heard the one about the yahoo who strapped a set of JATO rockets to the roof of his Impala and lit the fuse? As the story goes, when Arizona Highway Patrol officers arrived on the scene, they found a smoldering Chevy telescoped into the side of a cliff, with a long, fresh set of tire streaks on the highway nearby. Seems that everything was hunky-dory as long the road went straight. But when it curved suddenly to the left, the poor sucker behind the wheel was going way too fast to turn or stop. The Impala skidded off the highway, took off like a bat out of hell, and flew into the cliff at 350 mph.

You haven't heard this one before? Seriously? What rock have you been living under? Besides being one of the oldest car-related urban legends on record, it's probably the most beloved, and it's without question the most inventive. The legend comes in more flavors than Baskin-Robbins ice cream, from a Plymouth Road Runner fitted with an ICBM motor to a Ford Pinto packing an F-16 jet engine with full afterburners. In one form or another, this was one of the first Internet memes to emerge during the formative years of the World Wide Web. Later, the unknown driver won one of the inaugural Darwin Awards, which honor especially creative examples of intractable stupidity. Later still, the tale was the subject of the first episode of *MythBusters*, the TV show that applies the scientific method and a kids-don't-try-this-at-home ethic to popular legends. Even today, the Arizona Department of Public Safety continues to field inquiries about the deadly rocket car. "We get calls all the time," says Officer Carrick Cook. "I just heard from a retired deputy who wanted to know if it was true."

For the record, rocket cars have been around for nearly a century. Way back in 1928, German industrialist Fritz von Opel used 24 small solid-fuel rockets to power his generously winged RAK 2 to a speed of 143 mph, a remarkable feat during a period when rocketry was still getting off the ground—literally. In 1970, Gary Gabelich set a land-speed record of 630.388 mph on the Bonneville Salt Flats with his rocket-powered *Blue*

The pioneering Aerojet company was the first American firm to launch an airplane using JATO boosters, and it supplied rockets to the military during World War II. Here, an Aerojet glider takes off with JATO rocket power. Time & Life Pictures/Getty Images

Flame. Meanwhile, rocket-powered funny cars were a regular sight on American dragstrips until a spate of fatal wrecks blunted their popularity in the mid-1970s. Then, in 1979, Hollywood stunt man Stan Barrett went more than 736 mph and probably broke the sound barrier during a heroic but controversial run at Edwards Air Force Base in his Budweiser Rocket.

Of course, before anybody could start telling stories about JATO-powered cars, first the JATO rocket itself had to be invented. The jet-assisted take-off booster is a small cylinder filled with liquid or solid fuel and an oxidizer. When the fuel ignites, it expands and escapes out a small nozzle at the rear. The thrust produced by the escaping gas can be harnessed to allow airplanes to take off much faster, on much shorter runways, than would otherwise be the case. Although the first JATO booster appeared in Germany in 1935, similar technology was developed subsequently at the California Institute of Technology and adapted by the military. JATO bottles were used extensively on American airplanes and seaplanes during World War II and the decades that followed. In fact, a JATO-equipped C-130T cargo plane dubbed *Fat Albert* flew as part of the Navy's Blue Angels air show routine until 2009.

Some urban legend hounds say the JATO rocket car story first started making the rounds at military bases during this era, which makes sense. But those looking for a car-centric origin of the myth may prefer an

Perhaps the best-known and most visible JATO vehicle of all time was the C-130T cargo plane, dubbed *Fat Albert*, that flew as part of the Navy's Blue Angels air show routine until 2009. Paul Drabot/Shutterstock.com

alternative source in the unlikely person of Andy Granatelli. Best known as the supersized face of STP engine oil additives and the author of the grandiloquently titled autobiography *They Call Me Mister 500*, Granatelli suffered late-race heartbreaks at Indianapolis with his star-crossed turbine cars in 1967 and 1968 before finally winning the 500 with Mario Andretti in 1969. But back in 1946, Granatelli and his brothers, Joe and Vince, were ambitious young hot-rodders in Chicago who were trying to make a name for themselves. So when a local race promoter asked them if they could fashion a rocket car out of some military-surplus JATO rockets that he'd supply, they signed on the dotted line before bothering to consider the technical challenges they faced.

In May 1946, West Coast hot dog Duke Nalon had pushed a rocket-assisted race car to 140 mph at the Indianapolis Motor Speedway. Although the test served no practical purpose, the car generated plenty of smoke and publicity, which is exactly what the Granatellis were looking for. At the time, they owned a large, Ford-based, open-wheel Indy car with a giant tailfin that had raced without distinction during the 1930s as the *Don Hulbert Special*. They fitted steel casings for eight JATO rockets at the rear, wired them to a single button on the dashboard and dubbed the contraption the *Firebug*. There was no budget for racetrack testing. So at

4 o'clock in morning, keeping their eyes peeled for cops, they drove the beast out to Highway 83, a lonely stretch of ruler-straight road on the southern fringe of Chicago where local hot-rodders often met to street race. Granatelli wound up the flathead Ford until the Firebug was screaming along at 125 mph. Then, not knowing what to expect, he hit the button on the dashboard.

"There was a God-awful explosion," he wrote. "Wham! Then a sudden thrust of acceleration, and our necks snapped back until we were half-pulled out of the seats and thrust against the cowling. And the sky lit up, bright yellow and vermilion. Fantastic! I thought we were on our way to the moon. The sheet of fire fanned out about 75 feet wide and then up as high as the tops of the telephone poles on either side of the highway; it tapered back about 300 feet, burning brightly. And we took off—like an Apollo rocket headed for outer space."

Granatelli said the Firebug reached 180 mph—and ran an elderly couple in an old Chevrolet off the road—before he finally got the car whoa-ed down. Billing himself as Antonio the Great, he drove the *Firebug* during the summer on a barnstorming tour of dirt ovals throughout the Midwest, not as a race car but as an exhibition attraction. To make sure that everybody in the stands got to see a JATO rocket being lit—and to avoid killing himself—Granatelli rewired the system so he could fire a single bottle at a time. After dozens of performances, he retired the *Firebug* and set his sights on Indy. But tales of the JATO rocket car continued to percolate by word of mouth. And with the dawn of the Information Age, the legend was poised to go viral.

In the days before the World Wide Web revolutionized the online space, the principal medium for computer-to-computer communication was a system known as the Usenet. Although the underlying architecture was different, the Usenet operated much like contemporary online forums, with posts being passed between users and archived in discussion threads. Users coalesced in groups with shared interests such as recreation (e.g., rec.arts.movies) and science (sci.psychology).

In 1990, software engineer Charles Haynes read what might be called the first modern version of the JATO rocket car story. He says now that he can't remember where he came across it, possibly on an internal mailing list. Even then, it was known to be an urban legend and a nominee for the Darwin Awards, which hadn't yet been formalized into an official institution. But he thought it was clever enough to pass on to his friend and fellow programmer, Paul Vixie. "I used to sit at a crossroads between various pre-Internet communities," Vixie recalls, "and I would see stuff that was funny and forward it on. So it was in this case."

Vixie posted the text from Haynes on rec.humor.funny. The post quickly spread to all tentacles of the Usenet. But as it did, the headers identifying Haynes and Vixie were stripped, along with material identifying the story as a nominee for the mythical Darwin Award. What was left was a brief account that, like a Raymond Carver short story, was a compact, self-contained masterpiece. The prose wasn't as flat as a police report, but there was no obvious sign that the post was a joke. On the contrary, it was studded with just enough technical detail to make it seem plausible. The core of the post is worth quoting in its entirety:

"The facts, as best could be determined, are that the operator of the 1967 Impala hit JATO ignition at a distance of approximately 3.0 miles from the crash site. This was established by the prominent scorched and melted asphalt at that location. The JATO, if operating properly, would have reached maximum thrust within five seconds, causing the Chevy to reach speeds well in excess of 350 MPH, continuing at full power for an additional 20–25 seconds. The driver, soon to be pilot, most likely would have experienced G-forces usually reserved for dog-fighting F-14 jocks under full afterburners, basically causing him to become insignificant for the remainder of the event. However, the automobile remained on the straight highway for about 2.5 miles (15–20 seconds) before the driver applied and completely melted the brakes, blowing the tires and leaving thick rubber marks on the road surface, then becoming airborne for an additional 1.4 miles and impacting the cliff face at a height of 125 feet, leaving a blackened crater 3 feet deep in the rock. Most of the driver's remains were not recoverable; however, small fragments of bone, teeth and hair were extracted from the crater, and fingernail and bone shards were removed from a piece of debris believed to be a portion of the steering wheel."

Of course, the same details that made the story seem credible quickly undermined it when they couldn't be verified. (No police records, no photos, etc.) By 1991, the legend had been debunked so thoroughly that it was listed in the FAQ on the alt.folklore.urban Usenet group. But this was about the time that the Internet, still known as the World Wide Web, starting taking mature shape, and as it did, the JATO rocket car story found new acolytes. It hit the big time in 1995 when it was named the winner of a Darwin Award.

By this point, the Darwin Awards had graduated from an apocryphal tongue-in-cheek honor passed around on the Usenet to a curated website with official judges and formal rules. ("Nominees significantly improve the gene pool by eliminating themselves from the human race in an obviously stupid way.") According to the Darwin Award website, the JATO rocket car is the most popular Darwin Award winner of all time. It got

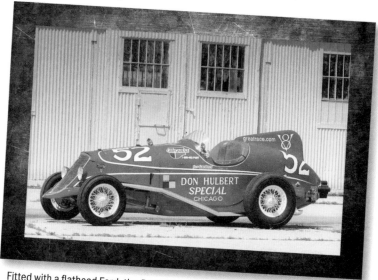

Fitted with a flathead Ford, the *Don Hulbert Special* failed to qualify at Indy in 1934. But it later ended up in the hands of the Granatelli brothers, who fitted it with JATO rockets and terrorized fans at fairground dirt tracks shortly after World War II. Tom Strongman

so much publicity, in fact, that the Arizona Department of Public Safety felt compelled to issue a press release declaring that the event had never happened. The Darwin Awards website now acknowledges that the story was a hoax. Although this should have disqualified the driver from being nominated, he's been grandfathered in as a Darwin Award winner anyway.

While the Darwin Award heightened the visibility of the JATO car story, the increased scrutiny also spotlighted its essential implausibility. So the tale seemed doomed to become another popular but demonstrably bogus urban legend like the kidney heist (business traveler wakes up in his hotel room missing a kidney that's been harvested by an unscrupulous stranger) or the head-scratcher about Mr. Rogers being a Navy SEAL and/ or a decorated sniper during the Vietnam War. Then, in 1998, a brilliant deconstruction, and reconstruction, of the rocket car myth appeared on a thought-proving but obscure website—cardhouse.com—devoted to quirky literature and what would now be called blogs on a variety of subjects.

The unnamed author described himself as a highschool biology teacher with a wife and two kids. His piece was an inspired, hilarious, and exhaustively detailed tale that ran nearly 25,000 words. (For comparison, Jack London's novella, *The Call of the Wild*, is about 27,000 words in its entirety.) Following the exploits of four young men in their early 20s, the story read like a cross between *The Little Rascals* and *Mad Max 2: The Road*

The *Don Hulbert Special* was restored to its original Indy configuration by Stan Betz. Now owned by Gary Kuck of Lincoln, Nebraska, it features eight metal rocket tubes. But JATO boosters are no longer part of its inventory. Tom Strongman

Warrior. Or as the author put it: "The only thing missing was a sign saying 'He-Man Rocket Kar Klub' over a treehouse door." It began with a brief, bald recap of the JATO car story.

"I'm sure this sounds pretty ridiculous if it's the first time you've heard the Legend of the Rocket Car," the author wrote, "but that's because I didn't go out of my way to make it sound good. Most people do try to make it sound convincing, embellishing the story with all sorts of little facts and details to make it easier to swallow. I've personally heard a dozen versions of this story over the past 20 years, and I'm constantly amazed at how the story grows, shrinks, and generally mutates with each retelling. Maybe I notice these changes more than most people because I've always paid close attention to this particular rumor. Oh, I'm not a car expert or an aerospace engineer or anything, and I really don't have much interest in urban legends. Even if I did, from an intellectual point of view, this story isn't as entertaining as some of the others that have come and gone. . . . I only pay attention to the Rocket Car legend because I'm 99% sure that I started the whole thing in the spring of 1978."

The story unfolded in an undisclosed location in the Mojave Desert. The writer said his father owned a junkyard and often bought military-surplus goods sight unseen from nearby auctions at a "major U.S. Army storage facility"—unidentified, naturally. After one such auction, the author was shocked to find a lot containing four JATO bottles, "each in a long, hay-filled crate with 'BARREL ASSEMBLY' stenciled on the side." He cooked up a wacky idea to mount them to a car, and to put his plan into motion, he enlisted three old friends—one who was studying mechanical engineering at a nearby but unnamed university and two knuckleheads with access to a four-wheel-drive pickup truck packing a big-block Chevy motor.

The would-be engineer immediately nixed the idea of running a JATO-powered sedan on the highway. Way too dangerous, he said, because there'd be no way to keep the car on the road no matter how straight it was. Instead, he proposed using a set of derelict narrow-gauge railroad tracks that dated back to the turn of the century. So the Gang of Four commandeered the pickup to snag a pair of twin-axle bucket cars out of an abandoned silver mine. They cut down the bucket car bodies until they had two small, rolling flatbeds. Next, they took a 1959 Chevrolet Impala—bone-white with a red interior—that was sitting on cinderblocks and welded it to the chopped bucket cars. Stopping the contraption promised to be a challenge. After ruling out a parachute, a tailhook, and an anchor, they rigged a Rube Goldberg–esque brake system out of air shocks and wood beams that would be lowered against the railroad tracks. Then, a single JATO bottle was shoved into a five-foot length of water pipe that had been fabricated to house it.

The rocket car was ready to roll.

On the day before Easter Sunday, the JATO team returned to the desert, loaded their baby on a set of abandoned railroad tracks that ran parallel to the highway, and lit the fuse for an unmanned test run. "When I touched the wire to the battery post, we heard a little fizz from the JATO. I knew what it was, since I'd heard it before. The igniter going off. I didn't expect to hear it, since I figured the rocket would light instantly. Instead, it hissed for a second, then stopped. But before I could start to worry if the rocket was a dud, there was a massive eruption of orange flame from the ass of the Chevy, as if it had just laid the worst fart in history. Along with the flame was a huge, howling roar, something nobody had counted on. We'd all seen the Apollo launches on TV, and we *knew* that rockets were noisy, but nothing had prepared us for this. It sounded like . . . I don't know what. Like a solid-fuel rocket igniting, I suppose. And the noise and smoke continued for what seemed like a long time before the Rocket Car took off. No, scratch that. It didn't take off, it JUMPED. I've been trying to figure out a way to put it into words, but the sight is almost impossible to describe. Think of this: You know what it looks like when you shoot a paper clip with a rubber band? One second the clip is between your fingers, and the next it's just . . . gone. You can't track it with your eyes, because it moves too fast. All you can do is hope to shift your eyes to where it was going, so you can see where it hits. Think of the same thing happening with a 1500-pound car."

The brake system deployed automatically, as planned, but it wasn't robust enough to stop the car. Instead, it ran off the rails and crashed at an angle into the mine entrance. "After a very short pause, the timber collapsed, immediately followed by the overhead timber it supported. Those timbers must have been under considerable stress, because a second later the entire entrance to the mine collapsed on top of the Rocket Car with a huge grinding rumble and a cloud of dust. I just gawked. I remember that part clearly, standing there looking at the car in the distance, just before dust obscured the picture. My Rocket Car was sitting there like a busted Tonka truck while a mountain fell on it. I almost cried."

They couldn't move the car or remove the JATO bottle. So they headed home and hoped nobody would find out what they'd done. Providentially, a big windstorm blew in that night, covering most of the railroad tracks, though not the back end of the car or the JATO bottle. But there were still skid marks on the highway that seemed to point directly to the site of the accident. So a passerby might reasonably have concluded that some yahoo had stuck a rocket in his car, skidded off the road and crashed his fool ass into the mine-shaft. "Anyway, that's my story, take it or leave it," the author wrote. "And even if everyone who sees it thinks it's bullshit, I'm glad I told it."

The story was an Internet sensation. Besides being showcased on the cardhouse.com website, it also appeared in December 1998 in the pioneering ezine published by Cult of the Dead Cow. (It's still archived, with its original dot-matrix-style graphics, on the cDc website.) But Internet traffic was relatively light in those days, so the piece was fated to remain a cult classic. It wasn't until an edited version—running "only" 16,000 words—was featured in the August 2000 issue of *Wired* that the legend hit the mainstream in a big way.

Wired was the hippest, hottest, and boldest of the new breed of maga-zines that had sprung up to chronicle the culture of the Information Age, and the JATO rocket car tale fit squarely in its strike zone. "That was one of my favorite stories," says Katrina Heron, who was the editor-in-chief at the time. Neither she nor anybody else can remember who found the story on the cardhouse.com website, but Martha Baer was assigned to edit it. Although the writer was now calling himself John Pelligrino, Baer assumed that this was a pseudonym. As for the story itself, she says, "I thought he was pulling my leg." *Wired* ran the story with a brief, cautionary editor's note: "According to its author, the story has garnered thousands

The world's first rocket car—known as the RAK1 to distinguish it from the later and more powerful RAK2—was created by Fritz von Opel. It featured a propulsion system from German rocketry pioneer Friedrich Sander. UK History/Alamy

of emails, some filled with praise, others with doubt, delight, sympathy, or suspicion. After a series of cagey communications with the writer, we reprint the piece here in the spirit of 'all of the above.'"

Is the story true? Extremely dubious. Nobody has come forward to confirm it. Nobody ever reported finding any wreckage. Then again, the story seems technically feasible. Basically, what Pelligrino described was a shade-tree, desert-rat car-guy version of a rocket sled, which was used by the military to test ejection seats and other equipment. And it didn't really amount to much—one run, no faster than highway speed, ending in a harmless crash. It's hard to imagine Pelligrino's account being the original source of the JATO rocket car story. First of all, the legend dated back farther than 1978. More damning, his version didn't feature the you're-shitting-me elements that made the story so memorable—the car taking off, splattering against a cliff, and being stuck there as a smoking monument to stupidity.

So when Adam Savage and Jamie Hyneman were lining up material for the pilot episode of *MythBusters*, they went back to the early, more fantastic version of the legend. They tried to procure JATO rockets from the military, but they were firmly and repeatedly rebuffed. Instead, they mounted three hobby rocket motors—with more combined thrust than a single JATO bottle—to the roof of an Impala and took the *Death Race 2000*-style vehicle out to the Mojave Desert. "We were so fresh that we really didn't know what to expect," Savage admits. Fresh, yes. Stupid, no. So Hyneman rigged up a remote-control system, and he fired the rockets while flying chase in a helicopter.

Ignition produced a satisfying profusion of smoke and noise, and the Impala leapt forward so fiercely that it nearly outdistanced the chopper. But the car quickly topped out at 160 mph without ever looking as though it intended to leave the ground. (Shades of Antonio the Great, a.k.a. Andy Granatelli, and his *Firebug*.) So the myth was definitively busted. But the legend lives on, and rightfully so. As Savage puts it: "It's a *damn* good story, and it always bears retelling." A century from now, no doubt, it will still be making the rounds, maybe featuring a spacecraft instead of a car, powered by an ion thruster rather than a JATO rocket, ending up in a smoking heap on a distant exoplanet instead of a cliff in the Arizona desert. Because as long as men strive to go where no man has gone before, there will always be a place for a comically cautionary tale about an epic mismatch of ambition and intelligence.

VERDICT: False.
But more memorable than a true story. –*Preston Lerner*

RODNEY KING'S 115-MILES-PER-HOUR HYUNDAI

LEGEND: Rodney King was doing 115 mph in his 3-year-old Hyundai Excel before the beating that sparked the Los Angeles riots in 1992.

You know the old adage about there being no such thing as bad publicity? Executives at Hyundai would beg to differ.

On March 3, 1991, KTLA led the Sunday night news with exclusive footage of white Los Angeles Police Department police officers brutally beating African American motorist Rodney King. Although the video was amateurishly shot and poorly lit, it clearly showed King being kicked like a soccer ball and whacked repeatedly with metal batons. Also visible in the background was a forlorn-looking white subcompact that eagle-eyed observers could identify as a Hyundai Excel. And that was a problem for the Korean carmaker trying to establish a foothold in the United States. Because as the Rodney King beating mushroomed into a national outrage, its humble little Excel reluctantly joined O.J.'s Ford Bronco and JFK's Lincoln limousine in the pantheon of cars rendered infamous by media coverage.

Four LAPD police officers were tried for assaulting King—with 56 baton blows, several kicks, and two jolts with a Taser—after a freeway chase that allegedly reached speeds of 115 mph. Anybody who'd so much as glanced at the videotape was skeptical of the official claim that the officers had used reasonable force to subdue King. And anybody with even a vague understanding of how an internal combustion engine worked doubted that a 3-year-old Excel could have been wound up to 115 mph. Disbelief morphed into cynicism after an all-white jury acquitted all four officers of the most serious charges. And in South Central L.A., cynicism gave way to anger that sparked one of the worst episodes of civic violence in twentieth century American history.

During a six-day spree of looting, arson, assault, and murder in 1992 known collectively as the Los Angeles riots, 53 people were killed, 2,000 were injured, and nearly $1 billion in property was destroyed. Order wasn't restored until a curfew was enforced and 4,000 National Guard

This press kit photo shows off the smart Giugiaro-styled lines and utilitarian character of the 1988 Hyundai Excel. Strong initial sales gave way to customer dissatisfaction, and the association with Rodney King didn't help the company's reputation. Hyundai Motor America.

troops arrived to quell the violence. Besides exposing the racial fault lines dividing Los Angeles, the riots also trashed the reputation of a police department that had often been held up as a national model. The LAPD was overhauled, starting with the forced resignation of combative Police Chief Daryl Gates, and Rodney King eventually won a $3.8 million settlement with the City of L.A. And it all began with a speeding Hyundai.

The events that led inexorably to the torching of Los Angeles started unfolding shortly before midnight on Saturday, March 2, 1991. Melanie Singer, a three-year veteran of the California Highway Patrol, was working her shift in the San Gabriel and San Fernando valleys in northern Los Angeles County. She was at the wheel of a marked cruiser while her husband, Timothy, who'd been with the CHP for 12 years, rode shotgun. They were based in nearby Altadena, so this was very much their home turf.

Meanwhile, elsewhere in Altadena, Rodney King and two friends—Bryant "Pooh" Allen and Freddie Helms—were knocking back bottles of malt liquor and watching basketball on the tube. King had been released from prison several months earlier on parole after serving a brief sentence for second-degree robbery. But despite his record, the 25-year-old King was said to be, according to most accounts, a gentle giant. Around 11:30 p.m., he told his friends that he wanted to go to Hansen Dam Recreation Center, near Pacoima. So they piled into King's car—a 1988

Hyundai Excel—and embarked on what should have been a 20-mile drive west across L.A.'s northernmost suburbs.

What happened next was recorded in detail in the report filed the next day by Timothy Singer. At 12:30 a.m.—now Sunday morning—the Singers were westbound on Interstate 210, also known as the Foothill Freeway. As Melanie Singer descended toward Sunland, her rearview mirror showed a pair of headlights approaching at a rapid clip. The white Hyundai Excel driven by Rodney King swept past, then slowed down, presumably after the driver realized that he'd just blown by a CHP car. Melanie Singer pulled off at the next exit and immediately climbed back onto the 210 — a common ploy to catch speeders. As she'd expected, King had sped back up. Singer put the hammer down and started chasing him, eventually activating her emergency lights and sirens. Inside the Hyundai, rap music was booming out the speakers while Allen repeatedly told King to pull over. (Helms supposedly slept through the whole thing.) King himself later told a parole officer that he didn't stop because he thought a speeding ticket would violate his parole and send him back to prison. He exited the freeway about six miles after the chase began, and the pursuit continued on local streets until King stopped in front of a sprawling apartment complex in the city of Lakeview Terrace. That's where the beating took place—with local resident George Holliday shooting video from his nearby terrace.

How fast was King going at the height of the chase? CHP officers don't typically carry radar guns. Instead, they're trained to estimate speed by pacing other cars—that is, matching the pace of suspect vehicles and then evaluating their own speed. This, evidently, was the technique Melanie Singer used. "As I reached the bottom of the hill, down on the bottom of Sunland itself, my vehicle was reading on the display at 115, and bouncing about 115 to 117 miles per hour," she testified during the first trial of the officers charged with beating King. Speaking to reporters three days after being beaten, King told a different story. "There was no chase," he insisted. "I may have been speeding just a little bit."

Nowadays, of course, it's not hard to imagine a Hyundai clocking 115 mph during a high-speed chase. The company's current hot rod, the Genesis R-Spec, maxes out at close to 150 mph, and even its mainstream family sedan, the Sonata, can be optioned with 274 horsepower. But back in 1991, Hyundai was very much the new kid on the block. The upstart Korean manufacturer didn't even develop its first car until 1975. In fact, the first-generation Excel—the Rodney King commemorative model, so to speak—was the first Hyundai imported to the United States. It arrived in 1986 with attractive styling by Giorgetto Giugiaro, a spunky ad campaign, and one of the lowest sticker prices in America.

"Our guess is that Hyundai will be a major force in the U.S. car market almost from the moment it opens its door," Michael Jordan wrote presciently in *Car and Driver*. "This car company seems to be in the right place at precisely the right time." In line with Jordan's forecast, the Excel shattered first-year sales records for an import. Unfortunately, it later broke the hearts of many of its owners thanks to gruesome reliability and dreadful quality, and before long, the substandard subcompact was being bought only by desperate consumers who couldn't afford anything better. *Popular Mechanics* recently named it to its list of "10 Cars that Deserved to Fail" alongside such epic losers as the exploding Pinto, the homely Aztec, and the notoriously abysmal Yugo.

That said, the Excel sold primarily on the basis of price, and if you didn't factor reliability into the equation, it offered excellent value. In reviews, most writers understandably made allowances for the car's inherent cheapness. But the one criticism found in virtually all road tests of the 1986 to 1990 Excel was anemic performance. "Dog-slow," "Needs more power!" and "Faster than speeding molasses" were three of the comments in *Car and Driver*. And these were found in generally flattering stories.

The engine was a 1.5-liter four-banger with an iron block and one of the last carburetors sold in America. It strained to put out 68 horsepower at 5500, which was only 300 rpm short of redline. Sixty-eight horsepower! To put that in perspective, today's teeny-tiny Fiat 500 makes 101 horses. Although the Excel was extremely light, weighing a mere 2,220 pounds, it had trouble getting out of its own way. *Car and Driver* measured the 0–60 time of the 1986 model at 16.3 seconds. *Motor Trend*, testing a 1988 Excel with slightly shorter gear ratios, managed 0–60 in 14.9 seconds. *Car and Driver* got the quarter-mile time in 20.0 seconds with a terminal velocity of 67 mph, while *Motor Trend* clocked 20.08 seconds at 69 mph. *Motor Trend* didn't provide a number for maximum speed, but Patrick Bedard wrote in *Car and Driver* that the car "will wind out to a top speed of 90 if you're patient." Two years later, in *Car and Driver*'s long-term test, the car went slightly faster—a whopping 91 mph.

Obviously, though, a freeway chase could conceivably produce different results than a track test. Sgt. Stacey Koon, one of the two LAPD officers convicted of beating King in a second trial held in federal court, insisted that there was no reason to doubt Singer's testimony. "The speedometer in King's Hyundai was pegged at 120 miles per hour, indicating that the manufacturer, at least, believed 115 was an attainable velocity," he wrote in his book about the case, *Presumed Guilty*.

Actually, Hyundai officials were no less surprised than other Angelenos about the astonishing performance of their feeble subcompact.

Most Americans fixated with disgust and horror on the images of Rodney King being beaten by Los Angeles Police Department officers. But car experts couldn't help but notice the Hyundai Excel serving as a backdrop for the action. Getty Images.

"My first reaction was, 'One hundred miles an hour in an Excel? You've got to be kidding me,'" says Bill Wolf, who was then the public relations chief of Hyundai Motor America. As soon as the story broke, he was deluged with calls from journalists. So he turned around and asked Hyundai engineers whether the Excel could have gone 100 mph. "The engineers said it was impossible," he recalls. "Our official response was that the top speed of the Excel was 85 miles per hour. We used to joke around the office that the only way it could have gone 100 miles per hour was off a cliff."

All joking aside, there were those who argued that the speed of the car could have been affected by factors such as a tailwind and driving downhill. As it happens, sections of the Foothill Freeway are reasonably hilly. In fact, there's a particularly steep grade on the stretch of road approaching the Sunland Boulevard exit, where King passed the CHP cruiser before slowing down. This is where Melanie Singer says she saw 115 to 117 mph on her speedometer, which seems plausible. Her husband's police report, however, offers a different version of events. He wrote that King slowed after passing the patrol car on the long descent and that speeds of 110 to 115 mph weren't reached until his wife "exited the fwy. at Sunland Blvd. & immediately re-entered in an attempt to pace the veh." According to the police report, Melanie Singer was able to overtake and pace the Hyundai.

Rodney King, shown testifying in federal court in 1993, inadvertently became the celebrity most closely associated with Hyundai after leading police on a chase in his Excel and being victimized by the beating that ultimately sparked the Los Angeles Riots. AFP/Getty Images

At that point, she flipped on her lights and siren, and King slowed to about 80 mph.

In its entirety, the chase covered about eight miles, most of it at speeds well above the posted limit. But the ultra-high-speed portion of it was more like four miles. Say King was doing 70 mph when the Singers exited the freeway, and he firewalled the throttle when he saw the CHP cruiser pull off. Even if the Excel were capable of going 115 mph, did King have enough time to reach that sort of velocity? According to *Car and Driver*, the Hyundai needed 23.6 seconds to go from 30 to 50 mph. To go from 50 to 70 mph took nearly three times as long—64.8 seconds, or more than a minute. Going from 70 to 90 surely would have taken 2 or 3 minutes, by which time Singer's lights and sirens would have been on, and King would have slowed back down to 80 mph. Even in the unlikely event that a 3-year-old car with 68 horsepower in its heyday had been capable of going 115 mph—24 more than *Car and Driver* managed in two instrumented tests and 30 more than the official top speed cited by Hyundai—King couldn't have reached that sort of velocity before the chase ended.

Still, it's hard to fault Melanie Singer for what was surely an honest mistake. King was hauling ass when he blew by her the first time, and there's no reason to doubt that she hit speeds north of 115 mph while she was hustling to catch him. In a rare interview conducted by CNN anchor Don Lemon in 2012, King belatedly admitted that he'd obliterated the speed limit before pulling over. "I was doing 100," he said. "I did every bit of 100, and I'm not proud of it." Moreover, he was weaving between three lanes during the freeway portion of the chase, and he ran through red lights and stop signs after exiting the 210, so the Singers were justifiably eager to pull him over.

The events that transpired after King stopped belong to the realm of nightmare. (For the record, neither of the Singers was involved in the beating, and both of them testified for the prosecution.) But anybody who believes that King's Hyundai was doing 115 mph during the chase is dreaming.

VERDICT: False.
Rodney King's 115-mph Hyundai Excel is an urban legend. *–Preston Lerner*

THE EDSEL, A.K.A. THE MONGOOSE CIVIQUE

LEGEND: The Edsel could have been named Pluma Piluma. Or the Pastelogram. Or even the Mongoose Civique.

The Edsel was the worst product/brand marketing failure in American history. Ford had confidently forecast sales of 200,000 cars annually after the Edsel launched in 1957. In fact, only 63,100 cars were produced the first year, and sales went downhill from there. By the time the car was euthanized in 1959, Ford reportedly had lost at least $250 million on the Edsel, which translates into a bath of nearly $2 billion in current dollars. Even worse, the flop turned the company that had pioneered the modern automobile industry into a national laughingstock. "What does the ultimate loser look like?" went a joke from the period. "Richard Nixon driving an Edsel." Although half a century has passed since production ceased, the Edsel remains an enduring icon of disaster and a potent symbol of failure.

What went wrong? As with any catastrophe of this magnitude, there wasn't one single mistake that doomed the Edsel. On the contrary, it was the victim of a perfect storm of factors ranging from corporate hubris to plain old bad luck. The most glaring problem was its signature horse-collar grills, which critics likened to a toilet seat and which prompted the wicked remark that Edsel "looked like an Oldsmobile sucking on a lemon." That said, the Edsel doesn't appear especially gruesome to modern eyes. And, in truth, it was quite conventional by the standards of the day—which was another problem. The Edsel had been the subject of the most aggressive and extensive pre-release publicity campaign in American history. So when it was finally unveiled and car buyers realized it was basically a Ford or a Mercury in different clothing, they were disappointed. At the same time, consumers were confused by the Edsel's place in the Ford hierarchy: Was it supposed to be above or below Mercury on the corporate totem pole?

One of the wounds was self-inflicted. The Edsel was introduced earlier than most new cars in an effort to monopolize the interest of car buyers. This captured a lot of attention. But since the Edsel was carrying 1958 model-year pricing, it seemed expensive compared with year-end

The Edsel made a glamorous debut in 1957 after the most elaborate pre-release publicity campaign in automotive history. But sales spluttered after an initial spike, and the car was quickly—and mercifully—pulled from production.
Popperfoto/Getty Images

'57 models. Timing, it's said, is everything in life, and the Edsel couldn't have been much less auspicious. Its debut roughly coincided with the Automobile Manufacturers Association's horsepower ban, which blunted Ford's ability to brag about one of the car's most sellable features. Meanwhile, Detroit's chrome-laden gas hogs were coming under fire for the first time in books such as *The Insolent Chariots*, and a new generation of compact cars was poised to revolutionize the market. The Edsel also had the misfortune of arriving just as the country was slipping into a recession that savaged the automobile industry. It's no coincidence that the Packard, Desoto, Hudson, and Nash nameplates all disappeared during this period.

But the name was the final nail in the coffin. Within the company, Edsel Ford remained a beloved figure even though he'd been overshadowed by his father, and naming a car after a corporate legend certainly hadn't hurt Buick, Dodge, Chevrolet, Oldsmobile, Chrysler, et al. Still, the idea of celebrating the Ford dynasty seemed out of touch with the forward-looking American zeitgeist of the 1950s. Ironically, the name was detested most especially by the Ford family, with president Henry II famously declaring that he didn't want to see his father's name spinning on thousands of hubcaps. At the same time, Edsel sounded both alien and hoity-toity. During consumer research tests when the car was being developed, common associations included "Edsel-smedsel," "pretzel," and "diesel," which obviously didn't augur well for the brand. The challenge of coming up with something better prompted what may have been the most elaborate and belabored product name search in history. Besides Ford's vast in-house effort, its advertising agency came up with no fewer than 18,000 possibilities. Finally, in desperation, Ford executives enlisted the aid of a celebrated New York City poet. Although she served the Edsel team strictly in an unofficial capacity, she produced a list of what are unquestionably the most inspired, most inventive, and most wildly inappropriate names ever suggested for American automobiles. In the end, though, nothing could save the Edsel from its fate.

The roots of the Edsel date back to 1945, when an out-of-touch Henry Ford was forced into retirement and succeeded by his grandson, Henry Ford II. The company he inherited desperately needed new products and modern management. To restore Ford to its former glory, Hank the Deuce shamelessly raided the executive ranks of GM and hired a new breed of buttoned-down managers armed with MBAs and a bottom-line mentality. Two of them—Robert McNamara (yes, that Robert McNamara) and Arjay Miller—later served as company president, and several others climbed to the top of the corporate ladder. Known collectively as the Whiz Kids, this team of executives—many with little or no experience in the automobile industry—rejuvenated Ford's product lineup and revitalized its corporate culture.

By the early 1950s, Ford had clawed its way back to parity with GM in the volume sales battle at the low end of the market. But there was plenty of room for growth in the medium-priced segment, where Mercury lagged far behind GM's B-O-P triumvirate of Buick, Oldsmobile, and Pontiac. In April 1955, the board of directors unanimously approved a plan to reorganize the company into three separate divisions. Ford would be the sales leader at the bottom, while Lincoln-Mercury-Continental would focus on luxury cars. Occupying the middle ground between the two would be a new division, with its own dealer network, selling a series of as-yet-undesigned coupes and sedans based on existing Ford and Mercury bodies.

A so-called Special Products Division was formed to create the new car. From the beginning, the new vehicle—slated to come in four distinct models—was known as the E-Car. (Actually, the styling team referred to it as the Ventura, but this was an internal designation.) Although Ford insisted that the E stood for Experimental, it was widely assumed that the car had already been dubbed the Edsel. The name resonated especially

Edsel Ford, Henry Ford's only child, was named president of Ford when he was barely 26. But he was marginalized by his domineering father, and his brief career, cut short by stomach cancer, is often seen as a study in what might have been. Time & Life Pictures/Getty Images

well with Ford lifers, who remembered Edsel as the affable and progressive counterweight to his autocratic and reactionary father. "Edsel Ford was a hero among product planners," Richard H. Stout wrote in his history of Ford, *Make 'Em Shout Hooray.* "They envisioned him as the white knight who could cut through power struggles, committees, bypass financial men, and casually bring a whole new car program through to resounding success. To them Edsel was a name filled with class, style, elegance, and meaning."

Alas, Edsel's widow and four children were united in their opposition to prostituting his name, and it never got any serious consideration from the people running the E-Car program. "From the start, then, it was clearly understood by all in the new division that whatever the car's name might

Edsel Ford's three sons—William Clay, Benson, and Henry II, left to right—sit in an Edsel Citation Convertible at the national press introduction. All three of them initially opposed naming the car after their late father. Bettman/Corbis

be, the one it would *not* be was Edsel," wrote David Wallace, the manager of marketing research of product planning and merchandising for the Special Products Division. "On the inside, we were delighted with such rumors and did nothing to halt their spreading. So long as people were sure that the car would be called the Edsel, the more they could be distracted from whatever the name might be."

The Edsel was one of the first major products to be developed in concert with an ambitiously conceived and rigorously applied program of motivational research. Wallace, fresh from a stint as a market researcher at *Time*, was an outlier in Dearborn, neither a died-in-the-wool car guy nor a Whiz Kid–style bean counter. In his book *The Fate of the Edsel and Other Business Adventures*, author John Brooks described him as "a lean, craggy-jawed pipe puffer with a soft, slow, thoughtful way of speaking, [who] gives the impression of being the Platonic ideal of the college professor—the very steel die from which the breed is cut."

In addition to his other duties, Wallace was charged with spear-heading the search for a name for the E-Car. According to an exquisite article he wrote for *Automobile Quarterly* shortly before his death, "The name we were seeking was one that would bring to people's mind an association with elegance, fleetness and grace. It was to be clean, lithesome, supple, of strength and durability, such as the delicate steel cables of a great suspension bridges." To achieve this lofty goal, he and his team came up with six criteria for selecting a winner:

The name should be short, so it will display well on dealer signs.

It should have two, or at the most three, syllables to give it cadence.

Its sound should be clear and distinct, to aid in radio and television identifications.

It should start with the letters C, S, J, or others subject to calligraphic sweep for ornaments and advertisement signatures. Heavy-footed letters such as M, W, and K would be out—too rooted.

It should not, of course, be prone to obscene double entendres or jokes. And it should not translate into anything objectionable.

It should be American; foreign expressions were taboo.

By the middle of 1955, names were being reviewed at the executive level on almost a weekly basis. "The meeting took place in a small, inside room used . . . for storing banks of useless files," C. Gayle Warnock, the Edsel Division's resourceful public relations chief, recalled later in his history, *The Edsel Affair*. "With no windows and without artificial light, it was as dark as a coal mine. Into this room, Wallace would lug an old, bulky magic lantern, the latest prepared glass slides, and a portable screen. For about 30 minutes, he would project the latest batch of names, one at a time, for the group's study."

Several executives had their own favorites. Warnock, for example, preferred Altair. Edsel Division general manager Dick Krafve liked Arrow. Sales and marketing manager Larry Doyle lobbied for Phoenix. Lewis Crusoe, who outranked all of them as Ford's vice president for vehicle operations, pushed Simplex. This was a name that Wallace despised. But Crusoe had famously named the Thunderbird—universally regarded as one of the all-time-great car names—on the spur of the moment, and Wallace was afraid that he might choose Simplex if nobody could agree on anything better. So even as he continued soliciting opinions from executives, Wallace hired a market research firm to conduct man-in-the-street interviews with passengers at Willow Run Airport. And by the fall of 1955, Wallace and his team had focused their attention on four choices—Corsair, Citation, Pacer, and Ranger.

Meanwhile, Foote, Cone & Belding had been hired as the Edsel's advertising agency after a marathon selection process. The company was understandably eager to make a good impression, so it announced an internal contest to come up with potential names, with the winner getting a brand-new E-Car. Some 18,000 names were proposed by employees in the New York, Chicago, and London offices. Black binders containing an

"What's in a Name?"

By all measures and accounts, Edsel was a rotten name for a car. But it could have been much, much worse. Consider, for example, the sad fate of the Chevy Nova, the durable and long-lived GM product that bombed in Central and South America because the name translated as "no go" in Spanish.

Enshrined in international business textbooks, the Nova story ought to be remembered as a cautionary tale for two reasons: First, it teaches brand strategists who plan to market their goods in foreign countries that they have to be sensitive to the local culture. Second, it provides more proof that you can't believe everything you read.

The myth of the Nova's failure is one of the automotive world's most enduring urban legends. But it's not true, and neither are most of the other accounts of cars that supposedly failed because their names got lost in translation. So enough already with the whopper about how Mitsubishi executives named their sports car the Starion because that's how the Japanese mispronounce "stallion."

edited list were presented to Krafve by beaming FC&B account executives—no fewer than 6,000 names, arranged in alphabetical order. Krafve customarily wore a somewhat puzzled expression, but never more so than now. "But, my god, we don't want 6,000 names," he protested. "We only want one!"

FC&B went back to the drawing board. The New York and Chicago offices came back with short lists of 10 candidates. Both of them contained Corsair, Pacer, Ranger, and Citation. Wallace claimed that a statistician later calculated the odds of this happening at 1 in 3.5 million. "All fitted, in more or less acceptable degree, our early specification of elegance, dash, clean polysyllabic pronunciation, good positive and minimum negative association, a beginning initial subject to styling ornamentation," he wrote. "But none gave us that gutty feeling that IT, and IT alone, was the perfect one."

This was the moment when Wallace was touched with a form of genius that verges dangerously close to madness. He recalled that the wife of his assistant, Bob Young, had attended readings at Mount Holyoke College given by poet Marianne Moore. Wallace was intrigued not only by her credentials, which included a Pulitzer Prize and a National Book Award, but also her interest in popular culture. She attended prizefights and baseball games, and she'd even written a paean to her beloved Bums,

Although the Edsel was hyped as a groundbreaking car, it was actually a conventional piece of engineering with unconventional—and unfortunate—styling. One exception was the unusual—and problematic—steering wheel-mounted push-button transmission. iStockphoto.com/Terry J. Alcorn

as the Brooklyn Dodgers were known back then. So on October 19, 1955, Wallace mailed her a letter. "Over the past weeks," he wrote, "this office has confected a list of three-hundred-odd candidates which, it pains me to relate, are characterized by an embarrassing pedestrianism. We are miles short of our ambition. And so we are seeking the help of one who knows more about this sort of magic than we do."

Wallace really didn't expect a reply, and he didn't provide Moore with any guidelines, much less the six bullet points that his team had crafted to guide the name search. But to his astonishment, she was sufficiently intrigued to take on the unofficial and unpaid assignment. Ten days later, she wrote back with several suggestions—Ford Silver Sword, Aerundo, Hurricane Aquila, and Hurricane Accipiter. This was merely the first trickle of what was to become a torrent of poetic invention. In one letter came Resilient Bullet, Intelligent Bullet, Bullet Cloisonne, Bullet Lavolta, Ford Faberge, and Arcenciel (rainbow). The next, gathering strength, contained Mongoose Civique, Anticipator, Regna Racer, Aeroterre, Tonnerre Alifere (winged thunder), Aliforme Alifere (wing-slender), Turbotorc, Thunderbird Allie (Cousin Thunderbird), Thunder Crester, Dearborn Diamante, Magigravure, and Pastelogram. And a week later: Regina (or Rex), Taper Racer, Taper Acer, Varsity Stroke, Angleastro, Astranaut, Chaparral, Tir a l'arc (bull's eye), Cresta Lark, Triskelion, Pluma Piluma, and Adante con Moto. And as a postscript, she added, "I

Pulitzer Prize-winning poet Marianne Moore, shown in her signature tricorn hat, was unofficially enlisted to come up with names for what would ultimately be sold as the Edsel rather than—as she suggested—the Utopian Turtletop. Hulton Archive/ Getty Images

cannot resist the temptation to disobey my brother and submit Turcotinga (turquoise cotinga—the cotinga being a solid indigo South American finch or sparrow)."

This appeared to be the end of Moore's correspondence. But two days later, a final sally arrived with a single suggestion that served as a fitting cadenza to her E-Car concerto: Utopian Turtletop. "Young and I were in stitches," Wallace wrote later. "If we were failing to find an acceptable name for our car, we were at least accumulating more exotic impossibilities than anybody else in the business."

Wallace never seriously considered any of Moore's submissions. In fact, none of them were ever run up the corporate flagpole, and Moore's compensation consisted of nothing more than a bouquet of flowers mailed at Christmas. Moore, for her part, quickly moved on, and the episode barely rates a mention in any of the many books about her.

By the spring of 1956, it was decision time, and the issue went before Ford's executive committee. Dozens of potential names were printed on 40-by-60-inch cards and displayed to the company's top brass. Chairman of the board Ernest Breech, who was presiding in the absence of the vacationing Henry Ford II, growled that he didn't like any of them. For lack of any alternatives, the committee decided to reconsider some previous rejects, among them Benson (one of Edsel Ford's three sons) and Drof (try spelling it backward). When Edsel was mentioned, Breech perked up. "Edsel," he declared. "Let's call it that." Henry II, reached in Nassau, reluctantly agreed, and he persuaded the rest of the family to withdraw their objections. "There go 200,000 sales," Warnock muttered when he heard the news.

The Edsel was formally unveiled on September 4, 1957. The initial response was almost universally positive, and not even the most hardened pessimist could have imagined the calamity that awaited. In retrospect, it's clear that a different name—whether Citation or Corsair or Pluma Piluma or Mongoose Civique—couldn't have saved the Edsel. Ironically, it's often said that the motivational research that went into the search for a name was one of the factors that sank the automotive *Titanic*. According to this line of thought, all that touchy-feely stuff investigated by Wallace and his team led product planners down the wrong path and created a car that Americans didn't want. In fact, as author Thomas E. Bonsall pointed out, motivational research played only a marginal role in the car's gestation. "The Edsel was, in all important particulars, developed in the same way cars had always been developed in Detroit: by the seat-of-the-pants intuition of those calling the shots," he wrote in his Edsel history, *Disaster in Dearborn*. In this particular case, the car guys got it dead wrong, and McNamara—who'd opposed the Edsel—consolidated power after its failure. As Bonsall put it: "The Whiz Kids had vanquished the product men, and Ford Motor Company would never be the same."

Still, when it comes to the name, Wallace deserves the last word. In late 1956, shortly before the name was about to be divulged publicly, he sent a final note to Moore. "We have chosen a name out of the more than six-thousand-odd candidates that we gathered," he wrote. "It has a certain ring to it. An air of gaiety and zest. At least, that's what we keep saying. Our name, dear Miss Moore, is — Edsel.

"I know you will share your sympathies with us."

VERDICT: False.
But the Edsel could hardly have fared any worse as the Utopian Turtletop. –*Preston Lerner*

THE NEW 70 MPG DALE

DALE 1

DOLLAR FOR DOLLAR, THE BEST CAR EVER BUILT!

2
CRIME

SHAKEN, STIRRED, AND DUMPED IN THE OCEAN

LEGEND: One of the four Aston Martin DB5 sports cars built and modified for the filming and promotion of James Bond movies *Goldfinger* and *Thunderball* was stolen as part of an insurance fraud scheme and may have been dumped out of an airplane off the Florida coast.

As "Q" might say: "Now pay attention, Double O Seven; one of your Aston Martin DB5s is missing."

How could one of the most famous and recognizable cars in movie motoring history just disappear from sight and remain missing more than 15 years later? Two Aston DB5s were employed for the filming of *Goldfinger* in 1964, one of them reserved as the "beauty," or "star," car for close-up shots with Sean Connery as Bond at the wheel and fully customized and weaponized with all of 007's trick hardware—oil slick dispenser, revolving license plates, machine guns hidden behind the front turn signal lights, and the legendary ejector seat. The second, dubbed the "stunt" car, was unmodified during filming and was used primarily for action driving sequences.

Why two cars? Adding all of the Bond gear increased the weight of the so-named star car, thus diminishing its handling and accelerative performance. The unmodified stunt car was lighter and better performing, so it was employed in the action scenes. The stunt car later received all of the Bond gadgetry.

A further two cars were constructed for deployment during the promotion of the follow-up film, 1965's *Thunderball*—important pieces of the film's American publicity tour, making appearances at the film's premier, on television, and in numerous photo shoots. Once the cars had done their duty for the production and filming of *Goldfinger* and after appearing in *Thunderball*, they ended up in private hands and took on lives of their own. Debates began about which was the "real" Bond DB5, and the entire story was well sorted out by Bond enthusiast and author David Worrall in his book *The Most Famous Car In The World—The Complete History of the James Bond Aston Martin DB5*. Worrall categorized each car's story by chassis number: The star car, chassis DP/216/1 (originally

The man, the car: the original movie James Bond (Sir Sean Connery, of course) with arguably the coolest James Bond car ever, the oil-spraying, gun-toting, car-tracking, ejector-seated Aston Martin DB5. Could this photo depict the actual car that has since gone missing? Aston Martin publicity photo

built up out of an Aston Martin DB4 model, also serving as one of the prototype DB5s, hence the DP designation in its serial number); the originally unmodified stunt, or action, car, chassis DB5/1486/R; PR Car #1, bearing chassis DB5/2008/R; and PR car #2, numbered DB52017/R. Each car has been sold and resold over time and has led its own interesting life. All four Silver Birch–colored DB5s have a legit connection to the Bond legacy, although their roles and provenance in Bond history vary slightly. The most mysterious among them is DP/216/1, the original star car.

In 1986, the star car was sold at auction to Floridian Anthony V. Pugliese III for $250,000. Pugliese and then brother-in-law Robert Luongo soon put the car on the road in an aggressive promotional tour in what seemed an attempt to greatly increase its value, the effort led primarily by Luongo. The financial arrangements between these two men is somewhat unclear as to whether Luongo was acting in Pugliese's employ or doing so with the understanding that he would reap some financial benefit upon the car's ultimate resale.

In June of 1997, its private public relations tour now over, the atar DB5—now insured for $4.2 million—was stored in a warehouse in Boca

Perhaps if Bond hadn't been out chasing birds with his jet pack, the car might not have gone missing. Michael Ochs Archive/Getty Images

Raton, Florida. According to police reports and well documented in *Motor Trend Classic* magazine's May/June 2006 issue in an article by journalist Mary Seelhorst, the car was stolen from its hibernation in Boca. Analysis of tire tracks left at the scene indicated that DP/216/1 was taken against its will, and literally dragged out of the warehouse. Further analysis indicated that it was loaded into a light aircraft at or near that point. A furious search of nearby airports ensued under the theory that a modest-sized plane with this heavy a cargo aboard, couldn't fly all that far. The car or such an aircraft was never located.

The theory is that while the plane was in midflight, the car was dumped into the ocean, the obvious motive being insurance fraud. Pugliese invested about a quarter of a million dollars in the car, plus the costs of parading it around the country to car shows, movie screenings, and other Bond-related events. Recent appraisals and his $4 million–plus insurance policy indicated he stood to make a substantial return on his investment if he could collect.

Investigations continued and lawsuits brewed, but in the end, Pugliese's insurance company paid up on his $4.2 million claim, and to this day, the case is still technically unsolved and the original James Bond star car Aston Martin DB5, remains missing in action, perhaps lost forever, possibly corroding in warm salt water somewhere off the Florida coast.

VERDICT:
Maybe. Has one of the original James Bond Aston Martins become a man-made reef in the Atlantic Ocean? It's quite possible.
–Matt Stone

TRANSSEXUAL LIZ CARMICHAEL AND THE DECEPTIVE DALE

LEGEND: The car of the future, circa 1974, was a composite-bodied three-wheeler powered by a two-cylinder motor and $6 million fraudulently raised by a transvestite con man.

The more automobile design has changed, the more it has remained the same. A century after the Model T Ford debuted, the vast majority of the cars on the road still feature steel bodies, chassis suspended on four wheels, and four-stroke internal combustion engines. Not that would-be revolutionaries haven't tried to "improve" the automobile with a host of innovations: Bodies made of carbon-fiber. Bodies fitted with wings. Bodies that float on water. Three-wheelers. Six-wheelers. Steam engines. Jet turbines. For a while, there was even talk of nuclear power.

Back in 1974, when the country was still reeling from the fuel embargo and painful memories of long lines at gas stations were fresh in everyone's minds, the vehicle anointed as "the car of the future" had one rear wheel, two cylinders, and a space age composite body that appeared to have been inspired by *The Jetsons*. The relevant specs were 70 miles per gallon, a top speed of 85 mph, and a bargain-basement price of $1,995. Before long, the car was featured not only in daily newspapers and national magazines but also on talk shows and as a prize on *The Price is Right*.

The Dale, as the car was dubbed, was promoted relentlessly by a larger-than-life character named Liz Carmichael. Built and sounding more like a linebacker than the widowed mother of five she claimed to be, she told the world that she was going to crush the hidebound manufacturers in Detroit and "rule the auto industry as a queen." It didn't happen exactly the way she planned it. But Carmichael ended up playing a starring role on a stage far from the car business, first in Los Angeles County Superior Court and later as a convicted felon on the lam featured on *Unsolved Mysteries*.

"I was 15 when the Dale came out, and I saw it at the L.A. Auto Show," recalls Leslie Kendall, curator of the Petersen Automotive Museum, which owns a mock-up of the car. "I remember thinking, *Man, that is something!* I also remember seeing a picture of Liz and thinking, *Holy moly, that is not*

Dale Clifft is the forgotten man of the Dale saga. The Southern California inventor built the three-wheeler that inspired the car that bears his name. But he had nothing to do with the fraud that followed, and he earned nothing but heartache from his association with Liz Carmichael.
Richard Smith

a woman! It was the perfect scam for L.A. First, you had someone bilking people out of money. And that somebody was doing it with an imaginary car. And that someone was a transsexual. It was a movie of the week waiting to happen."

The Dale was based on a three-wheel vehicle developed by Southern California inventor Dale Clifft. In addition to working for the electronics giant/military contractor Litton Industries, Clifft tinkered mechanically on various personal projects. He later founded the Dale Development Co. and earned patents for items ranging from a bicycle motor to a device designed to blow insulation into an existing wall. "He specialized in making things simple and more efficient," his friend Richard Smith says. "That's what he was all about."

In 1973, after the OPEC fuel embargo, Clifft turned his attention to creating a more efficient form of transportation. With the help of a friend from Litton and working out of his garage in suburban Los Angeles, Clifft built a clever motorcycle-based three-wheeler. According to Smith, the frame consisted of half-inch electrical conduit with the joints brazed together. Most of the mechanical components came from the motorcycle world. The engine, for example, was a robust 305cc twin from a Honda CB77 Super Hawk. And while there were two front wheels, they were suspended with motorcycle-style forks. The whole thing was covered with Naugahyde in a metalflake maroon. "This actually made for a good-looking

This magnificent portrait of Liz Carmichael gazing imperiously at the camera with a cigarette in her hand was the work of crack *Car and Driver* photographer Mike Salisbury, who went to the Dale "factory" looking for a new car and instead found a transvestite con artist. Mike Salisbury

skin on the vehicle," Smith wrote in his self-published tribute to Clifft, *The Dale Automobile: An American Dream.*

Some reports suggest that Clifft dubbed his vehicle the Commutercycle, but Smith doesn't remember it having a name. And while the three-wheeler was registered for street use as a motorcycle, it was strictly a one-off vehicle with all the flaws and compromises inherent in homebuilt creations. Carbon monoxide could leak into the cockpit. Stopping power from the cable-actuated brakes and tiny tires was negligible, and crash safety was pretty much nil. Nevertheless, Clifft often commuted to work in his creation, and Smith recalls riding as a passenger in it on several occasions. "The ride was a little rough," he says. "But it got down the road pretty good."

Clifft didn't have the resources to develop the car into a production vehicle. But he got plenty of attention from the locals when he zipped around in the vehicle. In 1974, while eating dinner in a restaurant on Ventura Boulevard, he was approached by a stranger who told him he knew somebody who might be willing to put the three-wheeler into production. In retrospect, Smith says he's convinced the meeting was planned—that Clifft had been set up from the start. But that didn't become clear until months later. And by that time, despite the name of the vehicle, the story of the Dale focused not on Clifft but on its remarkably resourceful promoter.

Geraldine Elizabeth Carmichael was a huge woman, anywhere from 6 feet tall and 175 pounds to 6 foot 2 and 225 pounds, depending on the account, and she had a voice to match. At various times, she claimed to be an Indiana farm girl who'd wrenched on tractors, a one-time stock car racer, an entrepreneur with an MBA from the University of Miami, a mechanical engineer with a degree from Ohio State University, the mother of five children, the widow of a NASA structural engineer, the former owner of a company that modified cars, the builder of custom and experimental vehicles, and the patent holder on a "self-skinning foam." She romanced Clifft by telling him that she planned to put his three-wheel design into mass production then sealed the deal by offering him a royalty payout that could total as much as $3 million.

In August 1974, the Twentieth Century Motor Car Company was incorporated in Nevada. Liz Carmichael set up shop in a posh office suite on Ventura Boulevard in Encino while production commenced in an industrial building on Deering Avenue in Canoga Park. She amassed a sales team and began aggressively marketing the Dale. "We'll either be fabulously wealthy," she told company associates, "or we'll go to jail."

Twentieth Century produced a slick, six-page, full-color brochure showcasing a futuristic-looking car in banana-yellow livery. "The new 70 mpg Dale," read the copy on the cover. "Dollar for dollar, the best car ever built!" Inside the brochure, the claims were even more extravagant: "The most exciting new car of this century." "The first Space Age automobile." "Designed and built like it's ready to be driven to the moon." "The most exciting idea that ever happened to personal transportation." Nor did the hype stop there. "The eyes of the world are on the amazing new Dale," a creative copywriter began. "A masterpiece in automotive design and engineering. A whole new standard of performance, economy and safety available in no other car in the world today."

The unibody two-seater featured a shell made of a "rocket structural resin" that "will absorb over four times the impact of a Cadillac without serious damage." The windows were made of a material called Rigidex, which "has 70 times the impact resistance of safety glass. Only the force of a bullet could penetrate it." There were no pesky wiring looms to malfunction. "The car is operated electronically through a printed-circuit dashboard. All accessories (radio, heater, air conditioner) are simply plugged in." Carmichael said she chose the three-wheel layout because it saved 300 pounds and knocked $350 off the price, bringing the curb weight down to 1,000 pounds and the sticker price below $2,000. Powered by a 40-horsepower 850cc horizontally opposed twin from a BMW motorcycle, the Dale supposedly maxed out at 85 mph. The car even came with a 15-month/15,000-mile warranty. For an additional $100, buyers could extend it to 30 months and 30,000 miles.

Before long, a mock-up was placed on display—behind stanchions so nobody could get too close—in the Twentieth Century office. (It featured front wheels nailed to a 4x4 that served as the front axle.) There was also a barely functional prototype, but it ran so poorly that Carmichael used film footage of Clifft scampering around the dry lake at El Mirage in his original three-wheeler. And the Dale sports car was supposed to be just the beginning. Next, Carmichael said, would come a sedan called the Revelle, and then a station wagon called the Vanagen. Already, she claimed, she had 100 employees working in a 150,000-square-foot factory in Burbank. Her projections called for 88,000 cars to be sold during the first year of production—and 250,000 during the second—through 100 dealerships and 210 distributors. The initial investment, she claimed, was $33 million. "We're going to revolutionize personal transportation," she told Dan Jedlicka, the respected car writer for the *Chicago Sun-Times*. "Sure, Detroit will try to hurt me. That's why I'm talking about my autos so far in advance. If we're hurt by the big automakers, I want it out in the open. I want the world to know."

Jedlicka's story was slyly skeptical, but most of the coverage in newspapers and magazines and on TV and radio accepted Carmichael's grandiose claims at face value. (The prestigious *Columbia Journalism Review* later published an article castigating the media for its credulous reporting.) Throughout 1974, millions of dollars flowed into Twentieth Century's coffers as investors, would-be dealers, and prospective customers put down deposits for a piece of the pie. The first intimation that all wasn't what it seemed came in September when the California Corporation Commission issued a cease and desist order prohibiting the company from continuing to sell stock in the corporation. But Carmichael was unrepentant. "I don't want to sound like an egomaniac, but I am a genius," she told the Associated Press. "I believe 100 percent that this car would revolutionize the industry."

Toward the end of the year, *Car and Driver* dispatched photographer Mike Salisbury to see Carmichael and her plant in person. A yellow,

The Dale brochure was filled with what might be called magical realism, which is a euphemistic way of saying that it was a complete fantasy. The claims made on the cover were emblematic of the big lies that followed inside. Petersen Automotive Museum

egg-like car—the Dale—was parked in a corner. There was no gas pedal or steering wheel. Ringed around the car, a couple of guys wearing Clark Kent glasses were scribbling on clipboards. Salisbury was convinced that they were performing a pantomime for his benefit. As soon as they left, he opened the engine compartment and found it occupied by a Briggs & Stratton lawnmower motor. "It didn't take much to realize that the whole thing was a scam," he says. But the best was yet to come.

Accompanied by the honking of an air horn, a big Lincoln rolled up. It was a twin to Elvis Presley's personal car except that it had gold monograms. The door opened and a large woman stepped out. She was wearing a pale yellow pants suit, open-toed high-heeled pumps, and a long Shirley Temple wig. With a cigarette in one hand, she walked around the Lincoln to greet Salisbury. "Hello, I'm Elizabeth," she said in a voice that he likened to Broderick Crawford's. *Yes*, he thought, *and I'm 'enery the Eighth I am, I am.*

Richard Smith was skeptical about the project virtually from the start. He worked at the General Motors assembly plant in Van Nuys, so he understood the logistics of mass production, and it didn't take him long to realize that Twentieth Century had neither the manpower nor the wherewithal

CRIME

to build thousands of vehicles a year. Looking back, Smith believes that Clifft's enthusiasm for the project blinded him to Carmichael's shenanigans. Clifft finally opened his eyes when Carmichael claimed that she'd crashed a Dale into a wall at 30 mph without being hurt. "They didn't even have a car that could *go* 30 miles per hour," Smith says. Clifft left his personal papers with Smith and started carrying a handgun in his pickup truck.

Despite Liz Carmichael's personal magnetism and oversize drive, the project quickly spun out of control. In December, the California Corporation Commission filed a second cease and desist order. The next month, even as a Dale was being displayed at the L.A. Auto Show, the company's public relations man was shot to death by another employee in the corporate office. Meanwhile, state and federal investigators were taking a closer look at Twentieth Century's books and products. In January 1975, the company quietly slipped out of California and opened a new office in Dallas, off Stemmons Freeway, but this provided only a brief respite. In March, Twentieth Century's assets were seized, and indictments were handed down after officials realized that there were no cars, no factory, and no prospects for future production. Carmichael again got out while the getting was good. But in April, she was spotted and arrested in Miami. And then came the biggest revelation of all:

"When dream-car hypester Liz Carmichael went on the lam, charged with defrauding her investors, police were puzzled to discover wigs, hair remover and well-padded bras in the abandoned $100,000 home the self-styled 'widow' had shared with five children in Dallas," *People Weekly* breathlessly reported. "Now the mystery has been dramatically cleared up. Liz was nabbed by the FBI climbing through the window of a rented Miami house clad in a pink checked pants suit. The fingerprints clinched it: She was a he. Liz was disclosed to be one Jerry Dean Michael, 47, a fugitive from justice since 1961."

Initial reports, based on Carmichael's own comments, stated that she'd undergone a sex-change operation. It later became clear that no surgery had been performed. But Carmichael dressed and acted like a woman, and she ingested hormones powerful enough—in the pungent recollection of L.A. deputy district attorney Robert Youngdahl—"to put tits on a boar." During her trial, Carmichael petitioned for and was granted the right to be referred to as a woman. (She was called "Miss" rather than "Mrs. Carmichael," apparently because Michael had gotten divorced from his wife after the Dale fiasco unraveled.)

Not that Carmichael's legal woes had anything to do with her gender. In addition to an existing federal charge for jumping bail for a

In the brochure, the Dale looked like a car. In person, it looked more like a shop class project gone awry. Three vehicles were built, but two were just mock-ups, and only one of them actually ran—very, very briefly. Petersen Automotive Museum

counterfeiting conviction that was subsequently dismissed, she also faced more than two dozen charges of conspiracy, stock fraud, and grand theft in Los Angeles County Superior Court. Nobody can say exactly how much money was involved in the fraud because Twentieth Century's bookkeeping was so shoddy—criminally lax, you might say. "Everything was cash. There were no books," Youngdahl later told Mark Lisheron, an investigative reporter for the *Austin American-Statesman*. "Carmichael always hired bodyguards to carry away the money." Investigators found receipts for $2 million in orders for cars that had never been built. Youngdahl estimated that more than 5,000 customers had been bilked out as much as $6 million. Dale Clifft, who had nothing to do with Carmichael's scheme besides providing the initial inspiration, received $1,001 of his promised $3 million in royalties, plus a $2,000 check that bounced.

Carmichael, typically dressed in miniskirts, represented herself at trial. A legal axiom holds that anybody who defends himself in court has a fool for a client, but even Youngdahl acknowledged that the clever, articulate, and persuasive Carmichael did a fine job. Her defense was that the Dale was not merely a viable car but also a potential game-changer, and she likened herself to Preston Tucker and other automotive rebels who were persecuted for

CRIME

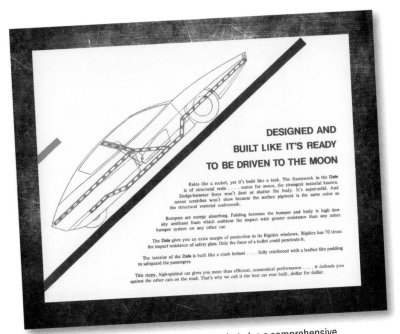

DESIGNED AND
BUILT LIKE IT'S READY
TO BE DRIVEN TO THE MOON

Rides like a rocket, yet it's built like a tank. The framework in the Dale is of structural resin . . . . ounce for ounce, the strongest material known. Sledge-hammer force won't dent or shatter the body. It's super-solid. And minor scratches won't show because the surface pigment is the same color as the structural material underneath.

Bumpers are energy absorbing. Padding between the bumper and body is high density urethane foam which cushions the impact with greater resistance than any other bumper system on any other car.

The Dale gives you an extra margin of protection in its Rigidex windows. Rigidex has 70 times the impact resistance of safety glass. Only the force of a bullet could penetrate it.

The interior of the Dale is built like a crash helmet . . . . fully reinforced with a leather like padding to safeguard the passengers.

This zippy, high-spirited car gives you more than efficient, economical performance . . . . it defends you against the other cars on the road. That's why we call it the best car ever built, dollar for dollar.

The brochure touted not only detailed specs but also a comprehensive warranty that guaranteed free towing to the nearest Twentieth Century Motor Car Corporation dealer. Of course, first you had to *find* a dealership. Petersen Automotive Museum

daring to challenge the powers that be. "Look, this is a private war between me and Detroit's Big Three," she said the day after warrants were issued. "I'm going to beat the hell out of them, and I never expected them to take it lying down." During the trial, she argued that, given time, the Dale would have thrived. "In 1903, the Ford Motor Company was described as the dream of a mad man," she testified. "In financial circles, they said there was no company, no assets and no prospects. But Henry Ford found a few people to invest in his company . . . and one of them made $39.5 million out of that investment."

Of course, Henry Ford had a car. Liz Carmichael had a monstrosity. "It had an Onan portable generator engine fed by a lawnmower carburetor stuck on the end of a sloppily welded lead pipe," Steven Cole Smith wrote in a hilarious recap published in *Car and Driver*. "The rear end was an old Ford differential, cut in half, mounted to one wheel. The transmission—a Toyota automatic—was stuck into the rear end, with no driveshaft." Smith then quoted John Michael Power, a Dallas automotive engineer who testified for the prosecution in Carmichael's trial. "It was literally held together with baling wire and coat hangers," Power said. "It was just really gross."

After a long and contentious trial that required 16 days of jury deliberations, Carmichael was convicted of 26 counts. A local TV station posted bail of $50,000 on her behalf, and she fought her conviction with the same resourcefulness she'd demonstrated while promoting the Dale. In 1980, after exhausting her appeals, Carmichael was ordered to begin serving her sentence. Instead, she skipped bail and eluded authorities for nine years. In 1989, she was featured on an episode of *Unsolved Mysteries*, the hokey NBC true-crime show starring Robert Stack. In it, Youngdahl said he suspected that Carmichael was now living as a man, and that he'd never be seen again. In fact, she was now known as Katherine Elizabeth Johnson and living in a small Texas town near Austin with an ironically familiar name—Dale. She was arrested two weeks after the show aired, and she was subsequently sent to prison in California. She later returned to Austin, where she was the mastermind behind a lucrative scheme that employed a team of homeless men to sell roses on street corners. She reportedly died in 2004.

Naturally, there was an odd postscript to the Dale story. Around the same time that Carmichael was indicted, Southern California hot-rod icon Dean Moon paid $8,000 at an Internal Revenue Service auction to buy a full-scale model of the Dale and the molds used to form its body parts. At a press conference in Hollywood, Moon disclosed that he'd been serving

The similarities between the Dale and the Davis were uncanny. Both were three wheelers built in Southern California. Both were touted as cars of the future. Both cost investors more than a million dollars. And both landed their creators in jail. Petersen Automotive Museum

"Three-Wheel Prequel"

Believe it or not, the Dale wasn't the first futuristic three-wheeler built in the San Fernando Valley to end up sending its creator to jail.

Shortly after World War II, long before Liz Carmichael arrived on the scene with her baritone voice and fraudulent business plan, an automotive visionary with a creative approach to bookkeeping named Gary Davis bought an odd little three-wheeled vehicle known as the Californian.

The car had been designed and built by Frank Kurtis—later of Kurtis-Kraft Indy car and midget fame—as a toy for playboy racer Joel Thorne. But Davis was convinced that the three-wheel layout—one wheel for steering in front and two driven wheels in back—was the perfect basis for an inexpensive runabout that would take postwar America by storm. So he established the Davis Motor Car Company and began production of the Divan sedan.

The cleverly engineered car featured a lozenge-shaped aluminum body, four-across seating, covered headlights, and a removable hardtop. Powered initially by a 47-horsepower four-cylinder Hercules engine—later a 63-horsepower Continental four—the car was said to reach an implausible top speed of 100 mph while making 35 miles per gallon. Company brochures described the Divan as a "three-wheel engineering triumph" and, much like the Dale that would follow in its tire tracks, "the car of tomorrow."

The folks at the Davis Registry believe that 16 to 18 cars came off the assembly line, including 2 prototypes and 3 military vehicles. Along the way, Davis raised $1.2 million, primarily by pre-selling 350 franchises. Unfortunately, production never reached the point where income exceeded expenses, with predictable results. In 1948, ex-employees sued for back wages, and in 1950, the assets of the company were sold to satisfy tax claims.

Although his advocates insist that Davis himself was guilty only of excessive optimism, prosecutors argued that he never intended to deliver cars in any appreciable number, and a Los Angeles jury convicted him in 1951 of 20 counts of fraud. After being released from prison, he worked in the amusement car industry, and he continued to promote the three-wheel concept until his death.

as an agent for "Speedy" Bill Smith, a prominent oval-track racing figure who ran a mail-order business selling performance parts out of Lincoln, Nebraska. Smith told the *Los Angeles Times* that he saw "a little potential" in all the publicity surrounding the Dale and said he planned to sell dune buggy-style kits for $800. "That went over like a wicker bed pan," Kendall says.

Three Dales survive. The crudest, a design study with no interior, is in Smith's Museum of American Speed. Although he declines to talk about it, he wrote in his memoir, *Fast Company*, that he'd liberated it from atop a rotating pole in front of a radiator shop. A mock-up with an interior but no drivetrain—the car that was housed in the Twentieth Century offices in Encino—is owned by the Petersen Automotive Museum in Los Angeles. Although it's occasionally displayed, it's usually parked in the basement. The lone Dale prototype was held as evidence by the Los Angeles County District Attorney's office until 1987, when it was sold at auction. It was subsequently bought by Los Angeles classic car collector Barry Maiten, who's also amassed an extensive collection of Dale paraphernalia and literature. The car hasn't moved for years, and while Maiten insists that he intends to restore it, it now sits in his private museum as a forlorn monument to greed and gullibility. As for Clifft's original three-wheeler, it was falling to pieces by the late 1970s, and Smith lost track of it after Clifft died in 1981. That's not much to show for the investment of the better part of $6 million. But in the car industry, dreams are always expensive. And very few of them ever come true.

VERDICT: True.
The Dale was an out-and-out fraud, but its creator— transvestite bunco artist Liz Carmichael—was a real piece of work. –*Preston Lerner*

SWIMMING WITH THE FISHES

LEGEND: A rare 1925 Bugatti was tethered to chains and sunk into Italy's Lake Maggiore as penalty for the nonpayment of duty taxes. It was rescued from the bottom of the lake in 2009 to be sold for charity and now sits decrepit and unrestored in a museum in Southern California.

Most any Bugatti is a special automobile for numerous reasons. Bugatti is a prestigious French marque. Many Bugattis are spectacular examples of great automotive design. Various Bugattis were successful race cars, and one particular 1925 Bugatti Type 22 "Brescia" Roadster is best known for having been allegedly won in a card game and then seized by Swiss authorities for the nonpayment of duty taxes. Obscure and somewhat Byzantine laws at the time required that the seized property be destroyed, so those in charge felt the best way to effectively yet mercifully do the job was to sink it into Lake Maggiore, a large and beautiful resort lake that borders Italy and Switzerland.

According to the lore and legend of the day, the French Blue sports roadster was owned by Bugatti team racing driver and several times grand prix race winner Rene Dreyfus, who came in contact with a Swiss national named Adalbert Bode. Bode's history is somewhat cloudy, with his interests and occupations variously noted as bartender, racing driver, and gambler. No matter, in or around 1934 in Paris, France, Bode and the ever-gentlemanly Dreyfus (who after retiring from racing as a professional owned a famous French restaurant in Manhattan, named Le Chanteclair) reportedly consumed several bottles of fine champagne and then engaged in an impromptu game of poker with the rare Bugatti two seater as the stakes. Dreyfus lost the game, and thus the car, in the process.

When Bode attempted to bring his newly won car into Switzerland, he was unable to pay the duty taxes on his winnings. He reportedly left the car parked in a private garage near the small town of Ascona. Swiss law required destruction of the property at issue in order to avoid unjust enrichment of the guilty party due to the nonpayment of the taxes. The authorities, for reasons not entirely clear, chose to sink the car into Lake Maggiore, as opposed to merely impounding it, or perhaps disassembling or consigning it to a dismantler. No matter, sometime in 1934 the car was tethered to 35-foot-long steel chains and suspended off the shore into the water. The reason for the chains was that in the event the owner wished to pay his taxes and reclaim the car, it could theoretically be done. To further complicate this somewhat murky situation, there is also information leading to another possible owner, an architect named Marco Schmuklerski, who moved to Ascona from France at about the same time.

What seemed like the proverbial good idea at the time proved not to be, at least from the car's perspective. Time and corrosion ultimately fatigued the chains and the hapless Bugatti broke loose of those reins, sinking to the lake bottom approximately 170 feet down. It came to rest on its left side, the wheels, fenders, and some portions of the bodywork compressing into the soft silt and mud on the lake bottom. Locals had never forgotten the story of the "The Lady in the Lake," and once it was located, it became a popular attraction for recreational divers. Among them was a young local named Damiano Tamagni.

Tamagni was attending the Carnival festival in Locarno, Switzerland, on February 1, 2008, when he was set upon by at least three thugs who beat him severely. The 23-year-old Tamagni died as the result of his injuries from that savage attack. The motives for this murderous crime are not fully known; it may have been a robbery gone awry, and some speculate the act may have been hate related for Tamagni either being gay or perceived as such. No matter, local divers and Tamagni's family began taking steps to rescue the Bugatti from the depths of Lake Maggiore with intent to auction it off to benefit the charitable foundation established in Tamagni's name, its mission being to combat youth violence.

Bringing the car to the surface of the lake proved to be a complex engineering and logistical undertaking that ultimately took nearly a year, with the goal of the car to be sold by Bonhams auction house at its annual sale at the Retromobile classic car event in Paris in early 2010. The three prime protagonists in the rescue and exhumation effort were local diver/ adventurers Jens Boerlin, Nicola Sussigan, and Stefano Mattei. Despite occasional bouts with bad weather, and the sinking of a floating platform built to work from and help guide it back to the surface, the team got the job done on July 12, 2009, to the cheers, tears, and applause of several thousand spectators. Although the car had certainly suffered from decades of submersion, a fair amount of the car remained intact; far more than if it had been in the ocean; Lake Maggiore is a freshwater lake, and the corrosive effects of ocean saltwater would have been dramatically more destructive. Oddly enough, the left side of the car, which had been pressed into the silty lake bed, was relatively well preserved. But the right side of the car, exposed to the open water and to any bacteria choosing to feast on the metal, wood, rubber, and other components of the car, suffered considerably more decay.

Bonhams Auctioneers catalog photos of the Lake Maggiore Bugatti.
Bonhams publicity photo

Note the steel-framed dolly on which it rolls. Considering how many years it languished under water, and the fact that it broke loose of the chains that held it at a certain depth above the lakebed, it is somewhat amazing that the car is as complete as it is and more damage wasn't done as it tumbled to the bottom of the lake. Bonhams publicity photo

The hapless Bugatti's headlight lenses were broken out, and the enameled Bugatti logo badge has been missing from the top of its trademark horseshoe-shaped grille for many years, likely the result of visiting divers helping themselves to souvenirs of their dive to the car. Bonhams publicity photo

One of the more delicate aspects of bringing the waterlogged Bugatti roadster to the surface was to extricate it from the lakebed, where it had been semi-buried in the muddy silt. The next task was to right it off its side and strap it with nylon tow straps robust enough to carry its weight as it was winched to the surface. A bit of daylight lights the car from above. Bonhams publicity photo

Once divers discovered and marked the location of the Bugatti on the Lake Maggiore lakebed, it became a popular spot for adventurous drivers, who often travelled from foreign countries to visit the "Lady in the Lake." Some likely took bits and pieces from the car as mementos of their dive, but most tended to leave it alone as a piece of local history to be respected. Bonhams publicity photo

A fair bit of the engine remains, although the iron exhaust manifold corroded through in several places. Although a Herculean task, the car could be rebodied and restored, but ultimate purchaser Peter Mullin felt it would be a crime against history to do so. Matt Stone

Even after being rescued from the lake, voluminous amounts of water hid in places such as the instruments. Much of this has since been drained, in the name of preserving the car and preventing additional degradation or corrosion. Matt Stone

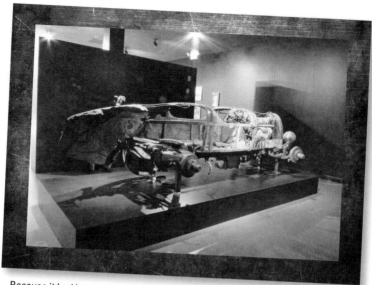

Because it had been exposed to the waters of Lake Maggiore for decades, the Brescia's right side suffered the worst damage and effects of corrosion, with much of the body eaten away; the left side fared a bit better, somewhat preserved by the dirt and mud of the lakebed. Matt Stone

The Bugatti was rebodied at least once in its life, perhaps for racing purposes. The bodywork currently wears this badge, identifying perhaps the company that built the new body or the name of a previous owner. Matt Stone

This is the intake side of the engine, with the carburetor and some of the throttle linkage clearly visible in the middle and the remains of several of the spark plug wires amazingly still intact. A portion of the steering column is seen to the right of this photo, with the radiator core visible on the left. Matt Stone

The tidy, sporty Brescia lives in dry, quiet retirement at the Mullin Automotive Museum in Oxnard, California, in a display gallery area dedicated solely to the car and its story. While it is difficult to recreate the exact look of being underwater, the soft light is intended to convey that feeling, to great effect. Matt Stone

The original steel-spoke wire wheels are deeply corroded, and it is doubtful they are structurally sound enough to be driven on, but that's no longer an issue, as this car will likely remain in a preserved, as-found state, never to be driven again. Matt Stone

The car's right side has suffered the most damage and is not brightly lighted, giving the Lady In the Lake a most ghostly appearance from this angle. Matt Stone

Damaged wheels and missing tires prevented the car from being moved easily around, so Bonhams constructed a relatively simple metal-framed dolly so the fragile chassis could be moved and transported without risking further damage. The car was also washed in order to remove the worst of the mud and silt impacted into the chassis and minimize their potentially corrosive effects.

Bonhams and the Foundazione Damiano Tamagni were besieged with requests about the car, how and when would it be sold, what was the real story, how much was it worth, and such. Even Bonhams' best automotive experts didn't really know for sure, as selling this type of vehicle was new territory for everyone. Restorers, collectors, and potential buyers speculated as to whether the car could, or should, be restored. Fortunately, Californians Merle and Peter Mullin and Andrew Reilly (founders and benefactors of the Mullin Automotive Museum in Oxnard, California, and the museum's curator, respectively) were of the strong opinion that to restore the car would be a crime against its history. The Mullins, a couple of considerable taste and means, are known for one of finest collections of art deco–era French cars in the world, and while they have many concours, winning cars in their museum, they felt the only proper way to respect the car's history and pay fitting tribute to young Tamagni was to preserve, conserve, and present the car in its as-found condition.

Bonhams consigned and auctioned the car in Paris, as planned, and Mullin was the winning bidder, paying $366,367, including purchase price and commissions.

Curator Reilly acknowledged that his role, as it relates to this car, is now more that of preservationist, needing to protect the car in its current condition and prevent further degradation without any actions or process that could be deemed "restoration." The closer Reilly inspected the car, the more of its secrets were revealed. Many of the glass-covered instruments were filled with water. The manual transmission, apparently tightly sealed when built, still held transmission oil from when the car roamed the roads and racecourses of Europe. The car is now on permanent display at the Mullin Automotive Museum, the star of its own special exhibit, bathed in an eerily soft and soothing light—designed to the extent possible to mimic its appearance while submerged—and surrounded by photography of the car while it lived at the bottom of Lake Maggiore. The major difference is that the car sits upright, rather than on its left side, as it did when on the lake bottom.

VERDICT: Absolutely true.
And a stunning example of how badly government bureaucrats can screw up virtually anything.
–Matt Stone

CHAPTER 2

THANKS FOR THE GREAT GETAWAY CARS, HENRY

LEGEND: Notorious bank robbers Clyde Barrow and John Dillinger wrote letters to Henry Ford thanking him for producing such fast, reliable automobiles—that were often used to attempt to outrun police chasing them after various bank robberies in the early 1930s.

It's a very simple letter, written by hand on plain white paper, dated April 10, 1934, Tulsa, Okla. It reads:

> *Mr. Henry Ford*
> *Detroit Mich*
>
> *Dear Sir –*
>
> *While I still have got breath in my lungs I will tell you what a dandy car you make. I have drove Fords exclusively when I could get away with one. For sustained speed and freedom from trouble, the Ford has got every other car skinned, and even if my business hasn't been strickly (sic) legit it don't hurt anything to tell you what a fine car you got in the V8 –*
>
> *Yours Truly,*
> *Clyde Champion Barrow*

The letter also bears a date stamp from Henry Ford's secretary's office, "Received April 13, 1934." The Henry Ford Museum remains in possession of this letter and has never suggested that it isn't authentic. Biographers have, for years, suggested that Barrow may or may not have written this letter.

Researchers Barbara and David Mikkelson present the best evidence that the letter is authentic, although based on handwriting analysis by at least one Barrow biographer, it may have been penned by Bonnie Parker, Barrow's girlfriend and accomplice. The Internet contains many samples of Mr. Barrow and Miss Parker's handwriting, and any cursory inspection reveals that the penmanship is much more like Bonnie's than Clyde's.

Clyde Barrow poses in front of his getaway car of choice: a V-8 Ford.
Hulton Archive/Getty Images

This is similar to the Fords that Bonnie and Clyde used during their crime spree.
Ford publicity photo

Tulsa Okla
10th April
Mr. Henry Ford
Detroit Mich.

RECEIVED APR 13 1934

Dear Sir:—
While I still have got
breath in my lungs I
will tell you what a dandy
car you make. I have drove
Fords exclusively when I could
get away with one. For sustained
speed and freedom from
trouble the Ford has got ever
other car skinned and even if
my business hasn't been
strictly legal it don't hurt eny
thing to tell you what a fine
car you got in the V8 -

Yours truly
Clyde Champion Barrow

From the collections of The Henry Ford (64.167.285.3/THF22011)

May 16 - 34

RECEIVED MAY 17 1934

Hello Old Pal:-
Arrived here at 10 A.M. today.
Would like to drop in and see you awhile.
You have a wonderful car. Been driving
it for three weeks. It's a treat to drive one.
Your slogan should be,
Drive a Ford and watch the other cars
fall behind you. I can make any other
car take a Fords dust.

Bye - Bye.
John Dillinger

From the collections of The Henry Ford (64.167.1.27/THF22013)

WANTED

JOHN HERBERT DILLINGER

On June 23, 1934, HOMER S. CUMMINGS, Attorney General of the United States, under the
authority vested in him by an Act of Congress approved June 6, 1934, offered a reward of

$10,000.00

for the capture of John Herbert Dillinger or a reward of

$5,000.00

for information leading to the arrest of John Herbert Dillinger.

DESCRIPTION

Age, 32 years; Height, 5 feet 7-1/8 inches;
Weight, 153 pounds; Build, medium; Hair,
medium chestnut; Eyes, grey; Complexion,
medium; Occupation, machinist; Marks and
scars, 1/2 inch scar back left hand, scar
middle upper lip, brown mole between eye-
brows.

All claims to any of the aforesaid rewards and all questions and disputes that may
arise as among claimants to the foregoing rewards shall be passed upon by the Attorney
General and his decisions shall be final and conclusive. The right is reserved to divide and allocate portions of any of said rewards as between several claimants. No
part of the aforesaid rewards shall be paid to any official or employee of the Department of Justice.

If you are in possession of any information concerning the whereabouts of John
Herbert Dillinger, communicate immediately by telephone or telegraph collect to the
nearest office of the Division of Investigation, United States Department of Justice,
the local addresses of which are set forth on the reverse side of this notice.

JOHN EDGAR HOOVER, DIRECTOR,
DIVISION OF INVESTIGATION,
UNITED STATES DEPARTMENT OF JUSTICE,
WASHINGTON, D. C.

June 23, 1934

One particular eye raiser is that Barrow's legal middle name was actually Chestnut, but that he once used Champion as his middle name when he was booked into a Texas jail, and perhaps his reputedly impish sense of humor allowed him to appropriate the name Champion how and when he felt compelled to do so. Barrow biographer Jeff Guinn notes that the grammatical errors and misspellings within the letter are consistent with his level (lack of?) education.

No matter, Henry Ford's great V-8 wasn't enough to save Barrow's life, as about six weeks after this letter was date stamped into Mr. Ford's office, Bonnie and Clyde were gunned down in Louisiana by the FBI, and possibly local police, at the wheel of a stolen Ford after another bank robbery.

About a month after Barrow's letter was date stamped into Henry Ford's office, the company announced that another infamous, wanted bank robber had also contacted Mr. Ford to pay his compliments about the company's fine products. It reads:

Hello Old Pal,

Arrived here at 10:00 AM today. Would like to drop in and see you.
You have a wonderful car. Been driving it for three weeks. It's a treat to drive one. Your slogan should be, drive a Ford and watch the other cars fall behind you. I can make any other car take a Ford's dust!

Bye-bye,
John Dillinger

This letter is also handwritten and is in the possession of The Henry Ford Museum. It also bears a date stamp from Mr. Ford's secretarial office that is very similar to the one found on the Barrow letter, dated May 12, 1934. Barbara and David Mikkelson call this letter out as a fake based on period handwriting analysis and the fact that Dillinger wasn't in Michigan in May 1934. Dillinger was gunned down in Chicago a few months later, not at the wheel of a Ford, but simply walking on the street.

VERDICT:
Clyde Barrow's letter to Henry Ford is authentic, but John Dillinger's isn't. –*Matt Stone*

3

RACING

WHO WON THE FIRST INDIANAPOLIS 500?

LEGEND: Ralph Mulford, not Ray Harroun, won the first Indianapolis 500.

Ray Harroun winning the inaugural Indianapolis 500 in 1911 is probably the most famous victory in the history of motorsports. Sure, you could make a case for some other memorable races, both here and in Europe. But as trifectas go, "Harroun," "1911" and "Indy 500" are tough to beat. On the strength of that single triumph, Harroun became a household name and his car—a taxi-cab-yellow Marmon Wasp with a stinger-like tail and spindly rearview mirror—was elevated to the status of American icon. (It was featured in 2011 on a postage stamp commemorating the 100th anniversary of the victory.) Ironically, Harroun retired immediately after winning Indy. Marmon, better known for building elegant production cars than racing thoroughbreds, folded in 1933 after improvidently unveiling a V-16 luxury car during the Great Depression. Both car and driver would be forgotten today were it not for their epic victory in May 1911, which demonstrates the power of the event justifiably billed as "The Greatest Spectacle in Racing." And which raises an intriguing question:

What if Ralph Mulford, who was officially credited with finishing 2nd to Harroun, actually won the race in a largely stock Lozier?

"Smiling" Ralph Mulford, a.k.a. The Gumdrop Kid, was one of the most celebrated drivers of the pioneering days of American racing. Retroactively crowned national champion on two occasions, he won everything from soul-killing 24-hour enduros to dizzying sprint races on treacherous board tracks to hard-fought road races against titans such as Barney Oldfield, Ralph DePalma, and David Bruce-Brown. In 1911, he drove his white Lozier race car—essentially a street machine with the fenders removed—to Indianapolis from the factory in Detroit (with his stalwart wife riding shotgun). Although he was among the fastest drivers in the race, he was hamstrung by being forced to pit repeatedly to change tires. At least, that was the official version of events. But in later years, Mulford claimed that, thanks to a well documented scoring snafu, race officials failed to record one of his laps. So according to him, he was the real winner of the first Indy 500.

To be sure, the first Indy 500 was the site of a scoring disaster of epic proportions. An elaborate timing system built around a device dubbed the

One of the most iconic images in the history of racing—Ray Harroun winning the inaugural 500-miler at the Indianapolis Motor Speedway in a Marmon Wasp equipped with a rearview mirror that allowed him to drive without a riding mechanic. Indianapolis Motor Speedway

Warner Horograph had been developed to keep track of the standings, but the perilously complicated mechanical contraption failed early and often. It didn't help that the 40 entries made hundreds of pit stops and that the race was marred by several serious accidents, one of them fatal. The situation was so confusing that the results weren't finalized until a day and a half after Harroun took the checkered flag. Then, when Harroun and his Marmon—a local product built by one of the city's most influential entrepreneurs—had been declared the winner, track owner Carl Fisher inexplicably ordered that the official scoring records be destroyed. All of which has led modern conspiracy theorists to speculate that the fix was in.

Then again, maybe this says more about twenty-first century cynicism than it does about the first Indy 500. Back in 1911, nobody harbored any doubts about who won the race. Even before the closed-door review of the scoring, Harroun had been declared the winner by the dozens of journalists who covered the race in person, and despite some grousing by the Lozier team, no independent observer challenged this finding. Mulford himself didn't publicly claim to have won the race until long after the fact. And outside of family, friends, and members of the Lozier team, he had no supporters until 1969, when Russ Catlin wrote an article in *Automobile Quarterly* bearing the provocative title, "Who really won the first Indy 500?"

Catlin was a longtime journalist and public relations maven who was best known for his biography of circle-track legend Ted Horn and his

Lozier team driver Ralph Mulford was one of the preeminent figures of the Brass Era—a two-time national champion and winner of the 1911 Vanderbilt Cup. Should he also have been credited with winning the first Indy 500?
Indianapolis Motor Speedway

controversial role in retroactively awarding national championships for AAA racing during the Brass Era. His story in *AQ* ran as a companion piece to a detailed racing memoir ostensibly written by Mulford, but more likely shaped by Catlin. A close reading of Catlin's article about the 1911 Indy 500 suggests that Mulford was one of his principal sources. In his account of the race, Catlin devoted several paragraphs to an accident on the front straight about halfway through the event. Catlin claimed that the scorers were so discombobulated by the mayhem unfolding in front of them that they failed to credit Mulford with one of the laps he completed. This, he implied, was the reason Harroun was incorrectly declared the race winner.

At the same time, and in contrast to volumes of eyewitness testimony, Catlin also argued that Mulford crossed the finish line before Harroun. According to Catlin, Mulford was leading when he took the green flag, which was shown in those days to signify the start of the final lap. One lap later, Catlin wrote, Mulford received the checkered flag. His team told him to run a few "safety" laps, as they were known back then, to make sure he'd gone the full race distance. "Due to the importance of this race," Catlin wrote, "the Lozier was ordered to take three extra laps in all and when it finally stopped, Harroun and the Marmon were receiving the winner's laurels." Catlin didn't cite a source for this incredible claim, nor did he explain the obvious inconsistency: Why would Harroun have been anointed the victor if Mulford had been flagged as the winner only a few minutes earlier? Purely because he made it to Victory Lane before Mulford arrived? To Catlin, at least, the fact that the official records had been destroyed was proof that Mulford had been the victim of "a thinly veiled cover-up."

Whether because *AQ* was so obscure or because the allegations were so implausible, Catlin's article didn't prompt a groundswell of support for Mulford, and the issue remained dormant for another generation. Then, in 1997, Internet motorsports historian Russell Jaslow resurrected Catlin's claims in an article he posted online. In it, drawing on an article published in *Scientific American* in 1910, he provided fascinating details about how the Warner Horograph worked—or didn't work, as the case may be. When the wheels of a car hit a fragile timing wire stretched across the start-finish line, an electromagnet tripped a hammer and recorded the time on four wheels that rotated like an odometer. There were also 12 scoring stands and four Burroughs adding machines tracking the results, and two Dictaphones were used to record car numbers as they crossed the start-finish line.

The weak point in the system—literally—was the timing wire, which broke (and was repaired) before the start and a second time during the race. Like Catlin, Jaslow is convinced that Harroun and Marmon benefited from hometown scoring. "Facts, rumors, and claims point to Ralph Mulford as the true winner of the first Indy 500," he wrote. Regarding the race itself, Jaslow relied primarily on Catlin's account, and he repeated the unsubstantiated claim that Mulford actually beat Harroun to the finish line. In retrospect, Jaslow says, he should have been more skeptical of Catlin. "He sometimes stretched the truth," he acknowledged. These days, Jaslow takes a more circumspect view of the results. "It's a mystery," he says. "I believe we'll never know who really won that race."

For better or worse, Jaslow's article—titled, like Catlin's story, "Who really won the first Indy 500?"—still survives on the Internet, without any qualifications. Whereas *AQ* has always enjoyed the loyal support of a hardcore but tiny circle of old-car enthusiasts, Jaslow's piece found an exponentially wider universe of less discriminating readers. Over the years, the legend that Mulford had crossed the finish line first and then was robbed of victory became a favorite Internet meme. It's now enshrined in the Wikipedia, with Jaslow cited as the source. A few years ago, Donald Davidson, the official historian of the Indianapolis Motor Speedway, remembers (with vast exasperation) being pulled aside by a four-star general who asked him, in an undertone, "So who really won the first Indy 500?"

Davidson is generally considered to be the most knowledgeable man alive about the Indy 500, and his book, *Autocourse Official History of the*

Indianapolis 500, is the definitive work on the subject. In print, Davidson discussed and dismissed several arguments in favor of Mulford and declared Harroun the winner while admitting that his victory was "somewhat clouded in controversy." In conversation, Davidson is more forthright and definitive about what he considers to be the unsubstantiated myth that Mulford was robbed. "Officially, Ray Harroun won the race, and I haven't seen any evidence to prove that he didn't," he insists. "Personally, I'm convinced Harroun was the winner, probably by a greater margin than the official results show."

Among serious fans of the Indy 500, Davidson's words carry the weight of pronouncements from on high, and his version of what happened stands as the quasi-official account of the race. But more casual fans of a contrarian bent found a champion in the person of author Charles Leerhsen. A major league writer/editor who'd done stints at *Newsweek*, *Sports Illustrated*, *People*, and *Us Weekly*, Leerhsen knew next to nothing about racing when he turned his attention to the first Indy 500. He spent two years crisscrossing the country in search of material before finishing *Blood and Smoke*, published in 2011 by Simon & Schuster. In it, he conducted a "thorough journalistic look-see" to "discover what is possible to know about the first 500-mile race." His book represents the most detailed examination of the event ever written.

Leerhsen's principal subject was the milieu of automobile racing in the pioneering years before World War I, and most of his book dealt with the events leading up to and the major players involved in the first Indy 500. The race itself got surprisingly short shrift beyond considerable attention paid to the crashes and scoring debacle. Although Leerhsen seemed to promise some sort of resolution to the controversy surrounding the finish, he ended up tap dancing around the issue of who he thought won the race. In a subsequent interview with *Popular Mechanics*, he explained, "I try to give enough good information so that the reader can make his or her own decision." But despite a veneer of journalistic objectivity and commonsense analysis, Leerhsen missed no opportunity to belittle Harroun's claim to victory, and he did his best to characterize Mulford in the most favorable light possible. According to Leerhsen, the race was such a shambles that nobody really knew who'd actually won. So a pragmatic decision was made. "The public wanted a winner [and] Fisher wanted a winner from Indiana, ideally driving a Marmon," he wrote. "And so it came down to the Wasp and Ray Harroun, the combination of which made the most people happy."

Leerhsen characterized the race as a fiasco. "A weird mashup of cars, money, and misdirection," he called it, and "far beyond a stumble, or even

And they're off! Engine tolerances were awfully crude back in 1911, and cars were expected to burn oil by the quart. Between the smoke and the dust, there were times that the first Indy 500 looked more like a sandstorm than a race. Indianapolis Motor Speedway

a face-planting pratfall." He even invoked Churchill's memorable description of Russia: "A riddle wrapped in a mystery inside an enigma." To be sure, the event unfolded in a time and place so alien to twenty-first century America that it might as well have been a foreign country. And it was a comically messy affair in comparison with the fastidiously choreographed Indy 500 we've come to expect, with the schedule calculated down to the minute (driver introductions at 12:32 p.m., the invocation at 12:59 p.m., Jim Nabors singing "Back Home Again in Indiana" at 1:02 p.m., and so on). But, of course, those who attended the race in 1911 had no other Indy 500 to measure it against, and most accounts radiate a sense of awe about the spectacle that the correspondents had just witnessed.

"Superlatives almost fail when one attempts to describe the race itself," the magazine *Automobile Topics* wrote in its next-day coverage of the 500. "It was a contest of the Homeric kind—in which giants of the wheel matched skill against skill, brain against brain and daring and courage against like precious qualities. For nearly seven hours they circled the brick paved speedway, measuring exactly 2½ miles, to the cheers of 85,000 people who lined the immense oval, filling stand after stand, and parking spaces by the score, and overflowing into the field by thousands, a goodly number of whom flocked to the danger spots—the steeply banked turns leading into the straights."

The flowery language calls to mind a distant age. But, in fact, the race was run as the era of mass media was dawning. On YouTube, you can find

RACING

Cars were numbered and gridded based on when their entries were filed rather than qualifying speeds. The car on pole was a Stoddard-Dayton driven by track owner Carl Fisher as a pace car for the rolling start. Indianapolis Motor Speedway

nearly five minutes of newsreel coverage showing the start, the finish, cars drifting through the turns, tires being changed in the pits and plenty of other fascinating action. (Davidson says nearly 12 minutes of footage has survived.) Numerous newspapers and wire services assigned reporters to cover the race. Their stories tended to be uneven, uninformed, and full of clichés about the "hoodoo" lap (unlucky number 13) and other nonsense you'd expect from writers who'd rarely, if ever, attended another automobile race. But by 1911, the car—and car racing—industries were surprisingly robust, and several special-interest magazines had sprung up to chronicle them. *The Horseless Age*, *Motor Age*, *Automobile Topics*, and *The Automobile* were essentially the *Car and Driver*, *Motor Trend*, *Road & Track* and *Automobile Magazine* of the day. Among the four of them, they devoted more than 50 pages—in really tiny type—to raceday and follow-up coverage and analysis of the 500.

At the same time, the very existence of the Indianapolis Motor Speedway was one of the best signs of the health and promise of the racing community. The huge complex had been built in 1909 by a consortium led by Carl Fisher and James Allison, local entrepreneurs who'd started the Prest-O-Lite headlight company. (Allison also founded Allison Engine Company, and Fisher later spearheaded the development of Miami Beach.) The first races, staged on an inappropriate surface of tar and crushed rock, were catastrophic: one driver, two riding mechanics, and two spectators were killed. This prompted Fisher to have the track repaved with bricks—3.2 million of them, most from the Wabash Clay Company in nearby Veedersburg, Indiana. Numerous races were held the next year, and Harroun won several of them in a Marmon Wasp. But for 1911, Fisher came up with the formula that would make the Indy 500 the most important event on the international calendar: he decided to race at Indianapolis only once a year, on Memorial Day weekend, and as a carrot, he dangled the most lucrative purse in motorsports.

The inaugural race was officially known as the 500-mile International Sweepstakes. The total payout in 1911 was $27,550, which is close to $650,000 in current dollars. The stellar field included the cream of the prewar American racing scene—Bob Burman, Ralph DePalma, David Bruce-Brown, "Terrible" Teddy Tetzlaff, Howdy Wilcox, Eddie Hearne, Johnny Aitken, Joe Dawson, Spencer Wishart, and of course, Mulford and Harroun. The 40 entries ranged from factory teams representing several American automakers to Grand Prix cars from Fiat, Mercedes, and Benz (which were then separate entities). Ironically, the European manufacturers are the only companies to survive to this day. All of the American car companies—National, Simplex, Mercer, Case, Amplex, Apperson, Pope, Knox, etc.—have long since gone out of business and faded from memory.

To modern eyes, the cars were behemoths, most of them powered by foor-cylinder engines displacing as many as 597 cubic inches, which is just a bit short of 10 liters. (Think for a moment about the size of those cylinders and the pistons chugging up and down inside of them.) It took Harroun nearly seven hours to finish the race, averaging 74.602 mph over 500 miles. This sounds like a sedate pace on a racetrack where cars have since lapped at nearly 240 mph. But the racers of 1911 were just as committed to running at the limit as their modern counterparts. Remember, they were driving over a choppy brick surface in gargantuan cars built around willowy buckboard-style chassis that flexed with every bump. Handling vices were endemic and stopping power, via drums at the rear, was virtually nonexistent. Engines of the day consumed—and spewed out—oil by the quart, drenching the track with so much fluid that sand was dumped periodically over the surface to soak up the moisture. (At times, there was so much smoke in the air and sand on the track that it looked like a beach race in the fog.) Although sand provided more traction than oil, neither one was ideal; film footage from the race shows cars skating through the mildly banked turns at the limit of adhesion.

These brief snippets of live action leave viewers yearning for a more complete understanding of what exactly happened during the race. Unfortunately, none of the participants left detailed accounts of their own, and the scoring records were destroyed by official fiat. There were dozens of contemporary reports about the race, but none of them agrees on all particulars. Depending on the reporter, events occurred on different laps, sometimes involving different drivers. The discrepancies—about who was leading after 350 miles, for example—seem to support Leerhsen's contention that the confusion in the press box and grandstands was so pervasive that nobody really knew what was going on.

But a careful reading supports a contradictory conclusion. Yes, the accounts differ when it comes to details. But what's more telling is where they agree: according to every contemporary report, without exception, Harroun and his Marmon Wasp dominated the second half of the race and convincingly beat Mulford to the checkered flag. This scenario was laid out with particular clarity in the four big car magazines, whose coverage suggested that Harroun was "rating" the competition, modulating his speed to maintain a safe margin to the finish. Again, for the record, these accounts weren't written by overmatched newspapermen who were more accustomed to covering baseball games and political rallies. They were automotive journalists who infused their stories with plenty of racing savvy.

"It was largely a tire race," *The Horseless Age* reported in a fine bit of analysis. "The grind was infernally hard on tubes and casings." And therein lay the secret of Harroun's success. Presumably basing his strategy on his experience winning races at the Brickyard the previous year, Harroun was determined to limit his lap speed to roughly 75 mph to preserve his Firestone rubber. As a result, he changed his right rear only three or four times during the race, and all of his other tires went the entire distance. His major rivals, all running on Michelins, pitted far more often, in some cases more than a dozen times.

And these weren't Formula 1 style pit stops where rigorously trained crews swarmed over the cars as soon as they stopped and swapped tires in a few seconds. Back in 1911, simply jacking up the cars took lots of time, effort, and ingenuity. (This is commented on at length in *The Horseless Age*.) Also, most cars of the day were equipped with demountable rims, meaning that they remained attached to the axle while the clincher-style tires were levered off and on. In an advertisement that ran in *Motor* magazine after the race, the Dorian Remountable Rim Company crowed that Harroun's tire changes averaged 30 seconds, which suggests that most tire changes took considerably longer. And this was a best-case scenario. If a tire failed on the track, which happened again and again during the race, the rim had to be hammered into some semblance of roundness before a new tire could be manhandled back on. In addition to tires, teams had to add fuel, oil, and water at periodic intervals, not to mention keep the engine in tune. (One team adjusted the valves during the race.) Drivers

Start of The First 500 Mile Race = 1911 =

The engines have been started, and now the field of 40 drivers waits for Fisher to lead them around on the pace lap. When the race began, Johnny Aitken took the lead from the outside of the front row in his National (Car #4).
Indianapolis Motor Speedway

also lost precious time coming into the pits, since stopping their cars took so long, and even more time was wasted getting back up to speed after leaving the pits with their low-revving engines and marginal gearboxes. At a minimum, it's hard to imagine a driver losing less than a full lap during a pit stop, and considerably more than that seems likely.

The early part of the race, before tire wear became the determining factor, was dominated by Bruce-Brown's exotic Fiat. But Harroun moved up to second by one-third distance before handing over to relief driver Cyrus Patschke. (Ironically, Patschke's biggest win to date had been scored as a co-driver with Mulford in another Lozier in a 24-hour enduro.) Contemporary reports say that Patschke steered the Wasp into the lead, while the revised results cobbled together after the race say he didn't. It's impossible to reconcile the differences between these conflicting versions of events. But everybody agrees that Patschke pushed the pace after Harroun ordered him to "go get Bruce-Brown." As he was leaving the pits, Patschke shouted back to Harroun, "I'll give it back to you in first place!"

This after-the-fact account comes from longtime Indy car historian L. Spencer Riggs, who based it upon his conversations with the Wasp's chief mechanic, Harry "Billy" Goetz. As Goetz remembered it, Patschke lapped at better than 80 mph as he sped past several cars—including Mulford's

After Bobby Unser took the checkered flag the previous day, an overnight protest gave the 1981 Indy 500 victory to Mario Andretti. Therefore, Andretti was featured in the traditional day-after photo with the Borg-Warner Trophy, but an appeal later restored the original results. Indianapolis Motor Speedway

Lozier—that had passed the Marmon during the driver change. "Ray may have told Cy to go after the Fiat, but he never thought he'd go that far beyond the agreed pace of 75," Goetz told Riggs. "Ray paced around the pit area muttering to himself, watching every move the Wasp made." Riggs, at least, is convinced that, without Patschke's burst of speed, Harroun never would have won the race.

One way or another, the yellow Wasp was in the lead about halfway through the race. Contemporary reports say Harroun led every lap thereafter, while the revised results have Mulford leading briefly on two occasions—Laps 138 to 142 and Laps 177 to 181. Again, there's no way to reconcile these accounts. But it's clear that Harroun's rivals suffered a variety of problems as they picked up the pace near the end of the race in a last-ditch effort to catch him. DePalma pitted with a blown tire. Bruce-Brown's ignition soured. As for Mulford, *Motor Age* wrote: "All the way through Mulford had been fighting the puncture demon, having no fewer than fourteen tire changes charged against him, and on the one hundred and ninety-third lap, with only seven more to go, a flat tire developed which made him run on the rim to the pits for quite a distance. It required 2 minutes 30 seconds to make the change and straighten the rim, and in the meantime, Harroun was steadily pulling away."

The car magazines, as well as the contemporary newspaper reports, agreed that Harroun took the green flag as the leader and then the checkered flag as the winner. In fact, there are several photographs, and even some newsreel footage, of the Marmon Wasp crossing the finish line first. There are no accounts (much less photos or movies) of Mulford taking the checkered flag. Catlin didn't cite a source for his fanciful version of the finish. Curiously, Leerhsen also chose to finish his recap of the race with Mulford finishing first, though he at least met his journalistic obligation to attribute it to a source, however biased—"several members of the Lozier camp." There's no record of anybody outside "the Lozier camp" publicly challenging Harroun's claim to victory, though published reports note that some observers believed Bruce-Brown had beaten Mulford for second.

After the race, Mulford heartily congratulated Harroun, which doesn't sound like the reaction of a man who's just been cheated out of the most lucrative purse in the history of motorsports. Several days later, he drove his Lozier back to Detroit, where he was interviewed by the *Detroit Free Press*. "He expressed himself as more than satisfied with the outcome of the race and gives full credit to Ray Harroun and Cyrus Patschke for their great victory," the newspaper reported. Catlin, Jaslow, and Leerhsen argue unpersuasively that Mulford was too much of a gentleman to complain about the miscarriage of justice. But it's worth noting that, four months later, Mulford successfully filed a protest to win his class in the Philadelphia road race in Fairmont Park. And as late as 1919, in a wire service advance for the upcoming Indy 500, Mulford still seemed to accept the official results. As the reporter wrote, "Ralph always figured that last tire change beat him."

There's no question that the scoring of the 1911 race was royally screwed up. Conspiracy theorists suggest that the timing snafu was underplayed in contemporary accounts because reporters had been bought off or were somehow beholden to Carl Fisher. In fact, it was mentioned explicitly in numerous newspaper and magazine articles about the race. The failure of the timing system was the subject of a widely circulated Associated Press dispatch that includes a complaint by the Lozier team not that Mulford won the race but that it ordered Mulford to slow down because the scoreboard allegedly showed him leading at one point. It's true that subsequent accounts of the race in 1911 rarely mention the scoring controversy. But not, it seems, because the writers were "protest deniers" (Leerhsen's odd phrase), but because nobody's ever produced a shred of proof that the official results were rigged.

Race officials spent nearly two days after the race trying to make sense of the scoring records. This must've been a thankless task, and it seems safe to

"Not to the Swift"

It's not surprising, considering how the first race ended, that the Indy 500 has been no stranger to controversial finishes.

In 1947, rookie Bill Holland was beaten squarely, but not quite fairly, when his pit crew gave him the E-Z signal late in the race, prompting him to let teammate Mauri Rose speed past for the win. In 1963, Parnelli Jones outraced Jim Clark to the checkered flag despite leaking copious amounts of oil because car owner J. C. Agajanian successfully lobbied race officials not to throw a black flag. Three years later, Clark was victimized again, this time losing to Graham Hill after what the Lotus team claimed was a scoring error.

Scott Goodyear was the goat in 1995, when he was black-flagged for passing the pace car while leading Jacques Villeneuve 10 laps before the end of the race. In 2002, victory was snatched from Paul Tracy when Indy Racing League officials ruled that the racetrack had gone yellow on Lap 199, thus freezing drivers in position, due to a crash milliseconds before Tracy passed Helio Castroneves for the lead.

The 2002 race is probably the most controversial in Indy history. But the most contentious finish came in 1981. On Lap 149, when he exited the pits during a yellow-flag stop, race leader Bobby Unser passed 14 cars on the track apron before merging into traffic. He went on to beat Mario Andretti (who passed 2 cars himself) to the checkered flag by 5.18 seconds and enjoyed the traditional post-race bottle of milk.

Andretti's car owner, Pat Patrick, filed a protest. The next morning, USAC penalized Unser one lap for passing under caution, thereby handing victory to Andretti. Unser's car owner, Roger Penske, immediately appealed the results. Hearings were held, and in October, a USAC appeals board voted 2-1 to rescind the penalty. Although it was an imperfect solution, the decision was generally approved since it reflected not only what had happened on the track but also the fact that Unser had been the class of the field.

So Bobby Unser won his third and final Indy 500. And victory in "The Greatest Spectacle in Racing" has eluded the Andretti clan—Mario, sons Michael and Jeff, grandson Marco, and nephew John—ever since.

assume that Fisher ordered the documents destroyed because they made no sense and would, therefore, have been the source of further embarrassment. In the end, the official times and the final standings were revised, but the top three finishers remained the same—Harroun, Mulford, and Bruce-Brown, in that order. But even before race officials sequestered themselves to study the timing records, they'd announced that Harroun was indisputably the winner. Catlin, Jaslow, and Leerhsen see this as yet another sign that the fix was in. On the contrary, it's perfectly understandable that everybody would know who won the race even if they were confused about the also-rans. The lead car is the one most people watch most closely. All sources agree that Harroun was the car to beat during the second half of the race. It would have been easy to follow his progress vis-à-vis the cars chasing him, and everybody clearly would have seen him being passed. Race scoring isn't rocket science. Remember, until the advent of electronic transponders in the 1980s, all races were scored by hand. Maintaining a lap chart doesn't require a Warner Horograph—or even a stopwatch. All you need is pencil and paper and the ability to make a mark every time the car you're scoring crosses the finish line.

Harroun retired immediately after the race, but Mulford went on to become one of the most successful drivers of the Brass Era. Despite coming up short at Indy, he (retroactively) won the national championship in 1911, and earned a second retroactive crown in 1918. But he's probably best known, ironically, for a less impressive record—posting the slowest finishing time in Indy history, taking nearly nine hours to complete 500 miles in 1912 at an average lap speed of 56.285 mph. And therein lies a quirky story.

Although Mulford had been the second-fastest qualifier, he was slowed by various mechanical woes during the race, and he was a distant 10th when Joe Dawson was flagged off as the winner. At the time, the rules required that a driver complete all 500 miles to earn prize money, so even though Mulford was the last car still running, officials compelled him to continue pounding around the racetrack. Naturally, he wasn't too pleased by this display of bureaucratic pettiness. So instead of racing around to the finish, he took his sweet time. Contrary to legend, he didn't pit to order hot dogs from a concession stand. But he stopped to soften the damping of his shock absorbers, and he then puttered around the track slowly enough to snack on fried chicken and sandwiches from a hamper in his lap. Riggs says that, as darkness approached, racetrack officials decided that enough was enough. Mulford would get his prize money even if he didn't finish the race. But Mulford insisted that they keep scoring him until he completed all 500 miles. "And this time," he said, at least according to legend, "I want to make sure you count all my laps."

VERDICT: False.
The race was a mess, and certain mysteries will never be unraveled, but there's no question that Ray Harroun won the first Indianapolis 500. –*Preston Lerner*

TAKING A FALL: DID VARZI AND NUVOLARI RIG THE RACE?

LEGEND: Achille Varzi and Tazio Nuvolari conspired to fix the results of the Tripoli Grand Prix in 1933.

If a sport attracts gambling, then you can bet your bottom dollar that it's been the subject of fixing at one time or another.

The most notorious example was the Black Sox scandal, which resulted in eight baseball players being banned for throwing the 1919 World Series, produced a memorable catchphrase ("Say it ain't so, Joe"), and even merited a breathless mention in *The Great Gatsby*. Boxing has been the subject of so much corruption that it sometimes seems that the brawling inside the ring is the most wholesome part of the sport. Point-shaving scandals have rocked college basketball on numerous occasions since the 1950s. Mystery writer Dick Francis sold more than 60 million books largely on the basis of cheating in the horse racing industry. Fixing scandals have long been a part of professional soccer. And sumo wrestling. And even cricket, whose very name is supposed to be synonymous with fair play.

But when people talk about corruption in sports, automobile racing rarely comes up. Oh, there's plenty of cheating, but most of it is limited to the garage, where car builders and crew chiefs do their best to circumvent the rulebook in an unofficially sanctioned effort to come up with an unfair advantage. And the action on the track doesn't always conform to the ethical standards prescribed by good sportsmanship. (We're looking at you, Ayrton Senna and Michael Schumacher.) Meanwhile, cynical stock car haters are convinced that NASCAR officials throw caution flags simply to bunch fields back together, and the tinfoil-hat crowd claims that the fix was in when Dale Earnhardt Jr. won the Pepsi 400 in July 2001, the first race at Daytona after his father had been killed there the previous February. Still, when it comes down to allegations that drivers themselves conspired to rig the results of a race, pretty much the only major event that comes up is the Tripoli Grand Prix of 1933.

There's no dispute about most of the facts. Millions of lire were riding on the race because it was the subject of state-sponsored lottery, hence

Tazio Nuvolari, the Flying Mantuan, is flanked by his protégé, Baconin Borzacchini, right, and Alfa Romeo test driver Eugenio Siena. Borzacchini died at Monza later in 1933, while Siena was killed at Tripoli in 1938. SSPL via Getty Images

its name, *Corsa dei Milioni*, or "Race of Millions." Winners of the lottery were paired with drivers in the race, with lottery prizes being paid to the ticket holders associated with top three finishers. The lottery winners represented by the two drivers most likely to win the race—Tazio Nuvolari and Achille Varzi—got together beforehand and pooled their resources. During the race, Varzi and Nuvolari swapped the lead back and forth, twice on the last lap alone. They came down the finishing straight side by side, and Varzi's Bugatti beat Nuvolari's Alfa Romeo to the flag by a mere one-fifth of a second. It was a thrilling, hard-fought battle that had fans standing on their feet in the massive grandstands. Or was it a sham orchestrated by Varzi and Nuvolari, coconspirators in the greatest fraud in Grand Prix history?

Alfred Neubauer, the huge German who famously micromanaged the pre- and postwar Mercedes-Benz racing teams, was convinced that the fix was in. "Nuvolari entered on the last lap thirty seconds ahead of Varzi," he wrote in his memoir, *Speed Was My Life*. "With a mile and a half to go, the crowd noticed that Nuvolari was also throwing anxious glances over his shoulder. They cheered him on wildly. When his Alfa appeared at the beginning of the home straight, they went mad with excitement. But the shouting quickly died away when they saw the red Alfa slow down and stop only a few hundred yards from the finish. Nuvolari climbed out of the car and stood in the middle of the track, wringing his hands.

"'No petrol,' he howled. 'No petrol!'"

The beret worn by Achille Varzi, Nuvolari's greatest Italian rival, seems appropriate since he's leaning against the cockpit of a French-built Bugatti. He would drive a Type 51 to victory over Nuvolari at Tripoli. SSPL via Getty Images

According to Neubauer, mechanics rushed out of the pits with gas cans and dumped fuel into the tank of the Alfa. Meanwhile, Nuvolari watched apprehensively for Varzi, who'd been slowed by engine trouble. Finally, the Bugatti crawled around the last corner. Nuvolari dutifully pulled in behind it, "joining in what appeared to be a funeral possession," in the words of British motorsports journalist Richard Garrett. The farcical finish prompted Eoin Young, the New Zealander who's been covering racing for half a century, to dismiss the race as "an obvious fiddle."

Over the years, Neubauer's lively account has become the basis of most modern versions of the race. These days, in fact, the belief that the race was fixed is probably the default position of most postwar historians. In a 1965 issue of *Car and Driver* and, more recently, in his controversial biography of Enzo Ferrari, Brock Yates promoted an even-more-fantastic version of the race, which he characterized as a "comic-opera scandal." According to Yates, *all* of the drivers were in on the fix, and one of them later had to be bribed into dropping a lawsuit he threatened to file after he didn't get his share of the loot.

Neither Neubauer nor Yates actually attended the race at Tripoli, and their many critics have pointed out that both of them had what might charitably be called a less-than-scrupulous attachment to the facts. But plenty of eyewitnesses and participants also detected the sour scent of impropriety.

"This was the Tripoli G.P. which turned Varzi, Nuvolari and Borzacchini into millionaires and caused a great deal of bad feeling among other drivers," Piero Taruffi, who finished fifth, wrote later in his autobiography. And in a race report published a week after the event, the dispatch in *L'Auto Italiana* read: "Nuvolari was duly beaten in this race by Varzi but many people, without knowing the reason, did not really believe in this defeat."

So what really happened at Tripoli in 1933? It's hard to make a definitive case one way or the other. Not, mind you, because so much has been obscured by the mists of time. On the contrary, the problem here is TMI—too *much* information. Accounts of the race are studded with marvelous vignettes and seemingly telling details. Unfortunately, a lot of them conflict, and there's no way to perfectly reconcile them. So picking one scenario over another isn't simply a matter of evaluating the evidence. We've also got to look into the hearts and minds of the major players in the controversy.

It's been half a century since Bugattis, Maseratis, and Alfa Romeos faced off in a major race, and it's impossible to imagine Bernie Ecclestone leading Formula 1 back to shores of North Africa any time in the foreseeable future. But during the decades before World War I, Tripoli was the crown jewel of Italy's modest colonial empire, and the exotic locale and concentration of local wealth made it an obvious choice for a race venue. The first event was held on a makeshift 44-mile circuit in 1925, and it remained a minor-league affair for the next two years. But in 1928, it was grandiloquently dubbed the Grand Prix of Tripoli and granted a prestigious slot on the Italian national calendar. Many of the top Italian aces showed up, with Nuvolari winning in his Bugatti and Varzi finishing third. Two years later, Baconin Borzacchini—a third major player in the 1933 scandal—claimed victory. Then, nothing for three years as the Great Depression discouraged continental race teams from making the expensive trip to Africa.

Enter Giovanni Canestrini, an Italian journalist whose name—and influence—runs through every aspect of the tainted Grand Prix in 1933. Cunning and ambitious, Canestrini was the racing editor of *La Gazzetta dello Sport*, a popular daily newspaper that focused on sports (and still does today). He believed that it would be possible to revive the Grand Prix of Tripoli through a lottery based on the example of the Irish Sweepstakes. Although the sweepstakes involved horse racing, Canestrini reasoned that the concept could be applied to motorsports. Bettors bought lottery tickets tied randomly to individual horses—or, in the case of the Race of Millions, individual drivers. After sales ceased, tickets were drawn, with one winner being selected for each horse (or driver). Ticket holders were then rewarded depending on how their entries performed in the race, with prize money being taken out of the revenue generated by the original ticket sales.

In 1932, Canestrini sold his idea to the president of the Automobile Club of Tripoli. The concept quickly percolated up through the hierarchy of the National Fascist Party, and before long, Benito Mussolini himself signed off on the plan. Based on the history of the Irish Sweepstakes, the lottery had the potential to generate vast sums of revenue, and some of it, no doubt, seemed likely to find its way into the pockets of party officials. On August 13, King Victor Emmanuel III signed a royal decree creating an annual lottery to support a North African grand prix. The *pioggia dei milioni*, or "rain of millions," was about to start falling on the arid shores of Tripoli.

Tickets went on sale for 12 lire apiece. By April 1933, more than 1 million tickets had been sold. Hard numbers are difficult to come by. The most comprehensive figures come from Canestrini—not the most trustworthy source, admittedly, but better than nothing. In his memoirs, he calculated the total take at 15 million lire. Different sources cite different breakdowns of the payout. But for big-picture purposes, the person holding the ticket for the first-place driver was entitled to something in the neighborhood of 3 million lire, with 2 million going to second and 1 million to third. Slightly more than 1 million went to the organizers, and about 550,000 was earmarked as prize money for the drivers. (For the record, that left roughly half the money unaccounted for.) The numbers were staggering, especially during the Depression, and the lottery received plenty of coverage in both the sporting press and the general-interest media. Since currency fluctuated so wildly in that era, it's difficult to make an accurate apples-to-apples comparison of 1933 lire to 2011 Yankee greenbacks. But we're clearly talking about millions of dollars in modern American currency—remarkable for the time, and pretty impressive even today.

Then as now, the inevitable result of the influx of serious amounts of money was the transformation of sport into business. As Valerio Moretti wrote in *Grand Prix Tripoli 1925–1940*, the definitive book on the subject: "Millions for everyone, then, and it was quite natural that the fact did not just stimulate the drivers' competitive spirit. Taking advantage of a bizarre article in the race regulations, something very much like a fraud was set up between the drivers and holders of the tickets to which they were linked. An audacious bargain, to say the least, to which, and it pains me to say this, the most important names in Italian motor racing, including Giovanni Canestrini, were party."

Eight days before the race, the lottery winners were selected and paired with drivers, 1 for each of the 30 entries. As a practical matter, only

Nuvolari was tiny by the standard of pre-war race car drivers, and he seems dwarfed by the heft of his Alfa Romeo monoposto. Note the prancing horse shield on the hood, connoting that the car was campaigned under the auspices of Scuderia Ferrari. Collection of Matt Stone.

a handful of drivers had a legitimate shot at winning the race. Varzi and Nuvolari were the prohibitive favorites. (Of the others, only Giuseppe Campari, Luigi Fagioli, and Tim Birkin were remotely in their class.) But even the holders of what seemed to be winning tickets couldn't be assured of a windfall. First of all, lottery money was paid out only for win, place, and show. Also, cars of this era were far more fragile than their contemporary counterparts, and the Mellaha Circuit—newly configured to be the fastest on the schedule—promised to be a car-breaker. (As it happened, fewer than half the cars would make it to the finish.) With so much money at stake, it made sense for the holders of what seemed likely to be winning tickets to hedge their bets.

Five days before the race in Tripoli, Varzi, Nuvolari, and Nuvolari's protégé, Borzacchini, met with their respective ticket holders (and their lawyers and a notary public) in the Massimo D'Azeglio hotel in Rome. History doesn't record who arranged this meeting, though Canestrini—who served as the moderator—seems like an obvious suspect. The drivers and their ticket holders, subsequently known as "The Six," agreed to pool their resources and equally share their winnings no matter who won. So the finishing order wasn't arranged, per se, but there was no reason for these drivers to fight amongst themselves. A contract laying out the terms of the agreement was written up, witnessed, and filed at the local branch of the Banca Nazionale del Lavoro.

Although this arrangement hardly seemed ethical, it was strictly legal, and the identities of The Six were reported in several Italian newspapers. (One glaring exception was *La Gazzetta dello Sport*, where Canestrini presumably had suppressed the story.) By the time practice began in Tripoli, the understanding was common knowledge. The other drivers were understandably miffed by this scenario, which promised to turn them into high-speed spear carriers. In response, they pushed their cars harder during practice and made overtures about forming alliances of their own. Enzo Ferrari, who was independently running the Alfa Romeo team at the time, angrily demanded that Nuvolari write a declaration that he—Ferrari—wasn't party to the arrangement. Although Nuvolari seemed chastened by the complaints, the aristocratic Varzi ignored them. "Do whatever you like," he told his critics, "I drive my own race."

For his part, Canestrini was less concerned about anybody beating Nuvolari and Varzi than he was about Varzi and Nuvolari beating each other. They were the Prost and Senna of their era, the preeminent drivers of the day but temperamental opposites—the yin and yang of prewar Italian motorsports. Nuvolari was passionate and flamboyant, a diminutive figure with the expressive face of an operatic clown. Varzi was elegant and impassive, a ruthless tactician who relied on methodical calculation rather than the grand gesture. Their historic clash in the long-distance Mille Miglia in 1930, when Nuvolari supposedly ran down and passed Varzi by running through the night with his headlights off, had already entered the realm of racing legend. And just two weeks before the race at Tripoli, Varzi had outlasted Nuvolari on the serpentine streets of Monaco after a titanic battle that prompted one modern writer to call it "the greatest Grand Prix of them all."

According to Canestrini, Varzi came to him the morning before the race and confided that he was worried about Nuvolari. He believed, Canestrini said later, that despite their agreement, Nuvolari intended to drive with his customary brio, possibly breaking not only his car but also causing Varzi's to fail as well as he chased his rival. So Varzi and Canestrini confronted Nuvolari in his hotel room. There, the two drivers agreed to toss a coin to choose a winner. (It was assumed that Borzacchini would go along with Nuvolari.) Varzi won the toss. So the fix was in. Or so Canestrini said.

The problem with this story is that it's not confirmed by any other sources. For his biography of Nuvolari, Aldo Santini interviewed Varzi about the 1933 Tripoli Grand Prix, and Varzi never mentioned the coin flip. Neither does the anecdote appear in another Nuvolari biography written by Count Giovanni Lurani, who was himself a major player in the world of Italian motorsports. Many years later, Lurani wrote a letter to the editor of *Motor Sport* in response to a Bill Boddy article questioning Alfred Neubauer's version of events. In it, Lurani provided details that, he said, had been confirmed by Canestrini himself. "There was *no arrangement whatsoever* for a 'fix' of the results of the race itself," Lurani wrote. "Obviously, it was in the three drivers' interest to finish the race and possibly to win it. The order was of no importance."

Was Canestrini telling the truth in his memoirs or when he spoke with Lurani? It's impossible to say. All we can do is look for clues in the race itself.

At precisely 3 p.m. on the first Sunday in May, the race began with all the pomp and ceremony that a fascist Italian regime could muster, which is to say considerable. Birkin led the first four laps in his 3.0-liter Maserati while Borzacchini retired early with a broken gearbox (and wasn't unhappy about it since he still was a full partner in the deal with Varzi and Nuvolari). Varzi languished in the middle of the pack because the sump of his supercharged straight-8 had been overfilled with oil, causing his engine to stutter. Meanwhile, Campari swept past Birkin and dominated the race in his works Maserati 8C. But he ran into trouble when he pitted halfway through the race, and he soon retired with a deranged oil tank. This left Nuvolari in the lead in his Monza, with Varzi chasing him as the excess oil burned off and he got his Bugatti Type 51 up to speed.

According to Brock Yates—an iconoclast who loved to challenge conventional wisdom—all of this action had been as well-orchestrated as a Pirandello farce. Drawing on the research of racing journalist Hans Tanner, Yates claimed that all of the drivers other than Birkin met before the race to arrange the results. "A brief discussion of ethics versus opportunity reached a predictable conclusion," he wrote in *Car and Driver*, "and it was agreed that Achille Varzi and his Type 51 Bugatti would win." Thus, Yates wrote, Birkin was saddled with an inept mechanic who sabotaged his pit stop. (Whether or not this was part of a nefarious plot, it proved to have catastrophic consequences as a burn suffered during his pit stop turned septic and Birkin died six weeks later.) Borzacchini crashed on purpose into an oil drum. As for Campari, his long pit stop—nudge, nudge, wink, wink—was a sham, and there was nothing wrong with his oil cooler. And why was Varzi going so slowly? Dawdling because he knew the fix was in, obviously.

In retrospect, Yates' account seems to be an early indication of his preference for what he later dubbed "faction"—a fanciful mix of fact and fiction. It's riddled with errors large and small: Italo Balbo, described as playing a major role in the Corsa dei Milioni thanks to his position as the governor of Libya, wasn't appointed to that post until months after the race. Nuvolari drove an 8C, not a P3. Louis Chiron, characterized as a coconspirator, wasn't even in the race. Also, several of Yates' claims are contradicted by contemporary race reports. For example, Borzacchini DNFed with a bum gearbox, not after hitting an oil drum, and the crowed was cheering, not jeering, at the photo finish.

For a man who'd allegedly been guaranteed first place, Varzi was pushing awfully hard, clocking the fastest lap of the race—better than 109 mph—while dicing with Nuvolari. At nearly three-quarters distance, Nuvolari pitted for a splash of fuel while Varzi, who'd cleverly fitted his Bugatti with an auxiliary tank to run nonstop, was able to stay out. Driving furiously, Nuvolari made up the 20 seconds he'd spent in the pits, plus time lost during his In and Out laps. Against all odds, he ran down Varzi and, despite the coin toss in his room only a few hours earlier, took the lead as they swept past the grandstand to begin the last lap.

At least, that's the standard account, based on contemporary race reports. But, as usual, Canestrini has a different version of events. He claims that Nuvolari was able to catch up after his pit stop only because Varzi had trouble switching from his main gas tank to the auxiliary. By the time Varzi had gotten back up to speed, Canestrini claimed that the two men were shouting and gesticulating at each other as they raced side by side, presumably arguing over who was supposed to win. Canestrini, who'd positioned himself about two miles from the finish, frantically signaled for them to slow down. But neither driver paid any attention to him. According to Canestrini, Varzi later told him: "On the finishing straight, I was level with Nuvolari, and I knew that our cars were equally fast. Therefore, I stayed in his slipstream until I could see the finish, then swept to the left and I could just overtake him." Varzi's margin of victory was one car length—a mere two-tenths of a second.

So, if Canestrini is to be believed, the fix *was* in, but it fell apart, and the finish turned out to be completely, if accidentally, aboveboard. Moretti, on the other hand, saw it differently. Without citing a source, he insists in his history of the Tripoli Grand Prix that Nuvolari suffered a "crisis of conscience" on the finishing straight. "He lifted his foot from the accelerator pedal imperceptibly, just enough to allow the Bugatti to shoot ahead and Varzi to cross the finish line a few meters ahead of him," he wrote.

But Betty Sheldon, co-author of the authoritative history, *A Record of Grand Prix and Voiturette Racing*, rejects this scenario. As she wrote, "Contemporary reports describe that race as a superb event with no evidence of 'letting someone win' and indeed the actual finish as enthralling, with the crowd on their feet!" After examining eyewitness accounts, it's impossible to imagine where Neubauer got his farcical version of events, with its last-lap pit stop and unseemly crawl to the finish. "I am inclined to think this legend is the product of sensational post-war journalism," wrote Bill Boddy, the legendary *Motor Sport* editor who spent eight decades covering the sport. "I cannot see, unless contemporary reports were written by half-blind lunatics, how the story put out by Alfred Neubauer . . . can be substantiated."

To be sure, Neubauer's story sounds more like summer-stock musical comedy than Grand Prix motor racing. But just because this particular account isn't true doesn't necessarily mean the race in Tripoli wasn't a scam. Even seen in the most favorable light, the well-documented machinations of The Six look awfully sordid. And it doesn't require a leap of faith to conclude that men who would agree to split their earnings would just as easily agree to finish in predetermined positions. After all, a 1-2 finish was the perfect result, and it was most easily and safely achieved if Varzi and Nuvolari didn't fight over it. As for contemporary reports that they appeared to be dicing right up to the checkered flag, let's face it: for drivers with that much talent, faking a fight to the finish would have been a piece of cake.

Then again, when they're blinded by the red mist of competition, drivers aren't always what economists call "rational actors." Once Campari was out of the race, and with Birkin too far behind to threaten them, Varzi and Nuvolari could have done whatever they pleased. Under the circumstances, why would either man *want* to finish second, especially if it meant handing victory to his bitterest rival? Nuvolari was leading as they sped toward the finish line. What possible motive would have inspired him to pull back when the 1-2 finish was already assured? A crisis of conscience over honoring a dishonorable agreement? Hard to imagine. It seems far more likely that he would have been thinking about the Monaco Grand Prix that he'd lost to Varzi the previous month. He came up short again in Tripoli, but not, it appears, for lack of trying.

VERDICT: False.
The 1933 Tripoli Grand Prix was the subject of a sordid conspiracy. But the race results weren't rigged by the drivers. *–Preston Lerner*

THE ROCKET CAR THAT BROKE—OR DIDN'T BREAK—THE SOUND BARRIER

LEGEND: The *Budweiser Rocket* broke the sound barrier at Edwards Air Force Base in 1979, long before the ThrustSSC, which is widely credited with the feat.

Shortly after sunrise on Monday, December 17, 1979, with his breath clearly visible against the sky brightening over the Mojave Desert, Stan Barrett crunched along the cracked surface of Rogers Dry Lake at Edwards Air Force Base. This was the repository of the Right Stuff, hallowed home of the Air Force Flight Test Center, the sanctified soil over which Chuck Yeager had broken the sound barrier in 1947 and Pete Knight set the all-time aviation speed record of Mach 6.72 in 1967. Today, the thrills were going to be provided by a vehicle that would never leave the ground—a bright-red, needle-nosed dart with outrigger rear wheels and a tall dorsal fin. Barrett wriggled into the tight-fitting cockpit of the so-called *Budweiser Rocket* and flexed his gloveless hands around the dragster-style butterfly steering wheel. When he firewalled the throttle, he would unleash 24,000 pounds of thrust from the hydrogen peroxide hybrid motor. A button on the steering wheel gave him access to an additional 4,000 pounds of thrust from the Sidewinder missile mounted a few inches behind his head. Barrett was a premier Hollywood stuntman by trade, fearless by definition, and as precise as a high-wire trapeze artist. Four months ago, the fastest he'd ever driven was 150 mph. Today, he hoped to become the first man to drive through the sound barrier.

Contrary to popular belief, you can't put a number, or at least one and only one number, on the speed of sound. That is to say, the speed fluctuates depending on the density of the air through which the sound wave is propagating, and density is affected by temperature and humidity. Generally speaking, at a temperature of 59 degrees, the speed of sound is 761.519 mph, but when Yeager broke the sound barrier at 45,000 feet, he was flying closer to 700 mph. At Edwards, it was 20 degrees this Monday morning, which meant the speed of sound stood at a tick less than 732

Burt Reynolds is flanked by film director Hal Needham, who owned the Budweiser Rocket, and stuntman Stan Barrett, who drove it (and, later, Needham's Winston Cup cars). The three of them worked together on *Hooper* and *Smokey and the Bandit*.

mph. Barrett had pushed the *Budweiser Rocket* to an unofficial 714 mph the previous Friday, igniting his Sidewinder 3 seconds into his run. But today, in an effort to break the sound barrier, he wasn't going to fire the solid-fuel missile motor until 12 seconds after he began his pass, and nobody, least of all him, knew exactly what would happen when he lit the fuse.

"Stan, would you pray for us, please?" car builder Bill Fredrick said over the radio.

Although Barrett was a newcomer to land-speed record racing—incredibly, this was only his 18th run in a land-speed record (LSR) car—Fredrick was a veteran of the speed game. A one-time butcher and self-taught engineer, Fredrick crafted exquisite LSR and drag racing cars of his own design out of his shop in Chatsworth, a northern suburb of Los Angeles. Fredrick was among the earliest adopters of jet technology and, later, rocket propulsion. In fact, his rocket-powered *SMI Motivator* had set an unofficial women's record when Hollywood stuntwoman Kitty O'Neil exceeded 500 mph in 1977.

Fredrick's day job was creating devices used to propel cars and stuntmen across movie sets, usually at great velocity and often to improbable heights. Through his film work, he'd met Hal Needham, a legendary stuntman who'd graduated to directing action hits such as *Hooper* and *Smokey and the Bandit*. Besides breaking the land speed-record, Needham also wanted to pierce the sound barrier. So he replaced Kitty O'Neil, and

December 17, 1979–Stan Barrett begins his final run at Edwards Air Force Base. A few seconds later, he would fire the Sidewinder motor–the small nozzle is visible just above the main one–and break the sound barrier in his Budweiser Rocket. ISC Archives via Getty Images

he and Fredrick took the *Motivator* to Mud Lake in Tonopah, Nevada. Needham quickly got the car up to 620 mph. That was the good news. The bad news was that none of his three parachutes opened after he ran out of fuel. He was still doing 350 mph when he ran out of dry lake. Then he embarked on the world's fastest off-road excursion.

Although neither he nor the *Motivator* was badly damaged, the experience prompted Needham to cede the cockpit to another driver—but not to abandon the project. If anything, he was more determined than ever to break the sound barrier. Although he considered several drivers, he kept coming back to Barrett. Needham was the guy who'd brought Barrett—a 36-year-old black belt in two forms of karate, a former Gold–Gloves boxing champion, and a devout Christian—into the stunt business in the first place, and he'd served as his mentor. Skeptics said he was crazy to entrust the car to a neophyte who'd never raced before, and they urged him to hire somebody else. "Nope," he told them, "there's only one guy who can do the job, and that's Stan Barrett." When Needham formally offered him the drive, Barrett had only one question: "When do we start?"

The effort was dubbed Project SOS, for sound of speed. Needham put more than $1 million of his own money into the program. Fredrick built a new chassis—a slightly larger version of the *SMI Motivator*—and upgraded the monopropellant motor to a bipropellant hybrid. Through Barrett's close friend Paul Newman, the team hooked up with Budweiser and negotiated a potentially lucrative sponsorship deal. The contract called for Project SOS to receive $250,000 for its part in a one-hour TV special on the car and another $250,000 for setting a new land-speed record mark. Breaking the sound barrier would pay a $500,000 bounty. The team realized that eclipsing the land-speed record—which had been set at 630.388

mph by Gary Gabelich in *The Blue Flame* in 1970—would be a stretch because of the strict and esoteric protocols of LSR racing. But from the start, Needham's overarching goal was going supersonic, and everything he did was designed to achieve that end.

Over the radio at Edwards, Frederick ordered Barrett to crank up the pressure in his fuel tank to levels the team had never tried before. The creaking of the expanding metal spooked the normally unflappable Barrett. *Oh, man*, he thought. *I hope this thing doesn't blow up.* All things considered, though, that seemed no worse than crashing during a run. "They won't find any of you if something goes wrong," the base's chief medical officer, Col. Grant McNaughton, had told him. "At that speed, you're going to be liquefied."

Fredrick began the countdown. "10, 9, 8, 7, 6, 5, 4, 3, 2, 1, ignition!"

Barrett mashed the throttle. A thick, awe-inspiring flame spurted out the back of the main motor, and the *Budweiser Rocket* knifed across the dry lake with a giant plume of white smoke trailing behind it. Barrett felt the force of 2.5 Gs pressing against him as the car accelerated from 0 to 250 mph in about four seconds. Inside the cockpit, the noise and vibration were fierce almost beyond belief, and while Barrett was prepared for it, he never got used to it. On his first run in the car, the ride had been so rough that he honestly thought he'd broken the land-speed record. When the crew informed him that he'd gone "just" 350 mph, he thought to himself, *Ain't no way.*

The car picked up speed. Three-hundred miles per hour. Four hundred. Five hundred. Barrett was busy watching gauges and keeping the car centered on the 50-foot-wide track. The single front wheel could be turned only 1.5 degrees in either direction, which resulted in a gargantuan turning circle measuring half a mile. But at these speeds, it was critical to stay ahead of the car, so Barrett was constantly making minute steering corrections. Mostly, though, he was looking ahead. *Way* ahead. At about three-quarter distance down the track were red flags marking the spot where he was supposed to punch the Sidewinder, and there was literally no room for error.

The *Budweiser Rocket* had maxed out at 677 mph with the hydrogen peroxide motor. To get the car up to and beyond Mach 1, Needham bought half a dozen AIM-9 Sidewinder air-to-air missiles—without warheads, naturally—and Fredrick jury-rigged a mount in the vertical tail, directly above the main motor. Fredrick and chief aerodynamicist Ray Van Aken had calculated exactly where the Sidewinder had to be ignited to propel the car to supersonic speed. The timing was so precise that they wanted a computer to start the burn automatically. "No, I'll fire it," Barrett told them. "I want my destiny in my own hands." Fredrick and Van Aken complained to Needham, but he backed his one-time protégé. "My car, my money, his life," Needham said. "If he says he can hit it, he can hit it."

Twelve seconds into the run, precisely as he passed the red flags, Barrett ignited the Sidewinder, and his head snapped back with the force of an additional G. A long, wicked flame erupted from the tail, momentarily seeming to engulf the car. Barrett rocketed past 700 mph. Inside the cockpit, he felt the car buffeting sharply. Then the ride magically smoothed out, and he knew instantaneously that he'd finally punched through the sound barrier. He felt the rear wheels leave the ground, and when the last of the fuel was burned, the car slowed so abruptly that it seemed as though he'd hit a wall. From start to the sound barrier had taken a mere 16.8 seconds.

Afterward, a beaming Needham yanked Barrett out of the car. "Here's what we've got so far," Fredrick shouted. "We ran out of fuel between 200 and 400 feet before the timing lights. But we got 734 on radar and 739 on air speed." Then, to wild cheering from the crew, he added: "We probably broke the speed of sound!"

Probably broke the speed of sound?

The run marked the end of Needham's two-year quest to make history. Now, he embarked on an even tougher battle, one that continues to be waged to this day—proving that his car broke the sound barrier.

Although Needham had decided not to chase after an official Fédération Internationale de Motocyclisme record, he'd hired longtime FIM steward Earl Flanders to time the runs at Edwards. Unfortunately, the team miscalculated the fuel consumption, so Barrett ran out of thrust about 1,000 feet before hitting the timing lights. As a result, the car was slowing rapidly when Flanders caught it at 666.234 mph. So Project SOS was forced to rely on radar tracking provided by Air Force personnel at the Flight Test Center (AFFTC). The system had worked perfectly in previous runs, and with radar operator Bud Chatterley manning the controls, there was no reason to suspect that anything would go wrong today.

"Did you get that?" Capt. David Hamilton, one of the engineers assigned by the Air Force to the project, radioed Chatterley after the run was over.

"Not really," Chatterley said glumly. "The radar lost the range track."

During the previous runs, the lake bed had been virtually empty. But with Barrett gunning for the record this morning, Edwards was full of spectators, media types, and extra vehicles. Unfortunately, during this pass, the radar ranging data—that is, the exact distance to the car—got lost in all the clutter along the track. Also, because the *Budweiser Rocket* was moving so quickly, Chatterley wasn't able to keep his fast-moving target firmly fixed in the crosshairs of his manually operated radar at all times. So there was some "noise" in the data. But AFFTC engineers believed

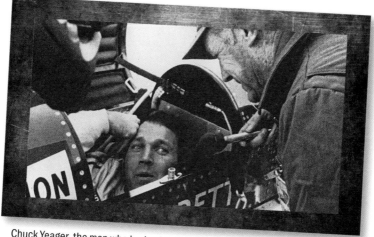

Chuck Yeager, the man who broke the sound barrier in the air, leans over the man who pierced it on the ground at Edwards Air Force Base. It's clear that somebody larger than Stan Barrett would have had a hard time squeezing into the ultra-tight cockpit. Popperfoto/Getty Images

they'd collected enough solid numbers to accurately extrapolate the car's peak speed. This required time-consuming number crunching and cross-correlation, and the Project SOS team and the rest of the onlookers waited impatiently while the calculations were made.

Nearly 11 hours after Barrett climbed out of the *Budweiser Rocket*, the team announced that the car had maxed out at 739.666 mph—almost 8 mph faster than the speed of sound. "Radar Confirms Supersonic Run," declared a banner headline on the front page of the local newspaper, the *Antelope Valley Press*. "The best engineering practices and judgment were used to reduce the data," an Air Force spokesman said. At the same time, Air Force officials realized that if Barrett had broken the sound barrier, he'd done it by the skin of his teeth, and they didn't want to be drawn into the awkward position of playing umpire in a nasty game of did-he-or-didn't-he? So the spokesman added two caveats: First, the radar was "not calibrated or certi-fied." Second, "In our judgment this data would not be certified."

Needham ignored the qualifications and accentuated the positive. "If [Air Force engineers and technicians] are accurate enough to tell the speed of an airplane at 10,000 feet 20 miles away, I'll take their word on the car's speed down here," he crowed to the *Press*. "If they won't believe the Air Force, who will they believe?" Needham's friend Chuck Yeager, who'd been instrumental in bringing the project to Edwards, also weighed in. "It's obvious that the car broke the sound barrier," he told the *Press*.

This claim was taken at face value by the general public, and the *Budweiser Rocket* graced the cover of the next edition of the *Guinness Book of World Records*. But there was considerable skepticism among hard-core

RACING

The original Budweiser Rocket was donated to the Smithsonian Institution, but a modified version with a narrower rear track is housed at the International Motorsports Hall of Fame's museum near Talladega Superspeedway. Robert W. Ginn/Alamy

enthusiasts. Henry N. Manney III's arch feature story in *Road & Track*—which ran under the ironic headline "SOS—Hooray For Hollywood"—ended on a satirical note: "Back to you, P.T." And the reviews were even more contemptuous within the LSR community, whose most ardent members derided the project as a sideshow attraction offering plenty of sound and fury but signifying nothing.

"They made some absurd claims, but the whole thing was a farce," says Dick Keller, who was one of the principal architects of *The Blue Flame*, which held the land-speed record from 1970 to 1983. Craig Breedlove, the Southern California hot-rodder who'd set a land-speed records on five earlier occasions, shared Keller's disdain for the supersonic claim. "Frankly, it just didn't happen," he says. "It was a marvelous car, and it was a tremendous effort, but it didn't go supersonic. That claim, in my opinion, was fraudulent."

The land-speed record is one of the most esteemed marks in the automotive world. It made an international hero out of Belgian Camille Jenatzy, a.k.a. The Red Devil, way back in 1899, and it helped put Henry Ford on the map in 1904. (The experience was so terrifying that he immediately retired from racing.) The first record-setting cars were powered by electric motors, then steam. But by the teens, LSR cars tended to be purpose-built behemoths housing gargantuan internal-combustion engines originally developed for airplanes. Speeds ratcheted up slowly but inexorably until the arrival of jet technology in the 1960s. Between 1963 and 1965, during a magnificent series of daredevil runs at the Bonneville Salt Flats known collectively as The Jet Wars, Breedlove and the Arfon brothers, Art and Walt, pushed the land-speed record from 407.447 to 600.601 mph. The next logical step was rocket power. A team led by Dick Keller built *The Blue Flame*—which looked like the older brother of the *Budweiser Rocket*—and Gary Gabelich claimed the land-speed record in 1970.

By this time, standardized protocols for record attempts had long since been established by the Fédération Internationale de L'Automobiles (FIA; for four-wheel vehicles) and the FIM (for three-wheelers). The rules stated that records were calculated on the basis of the average speed through a measured mile or kilometer. Moreover, a record run had to be followed, or "backed up," by a second run over the same course, but in the opposite direction, no more than an hour after the first run. The record speed was then calculated by averaging the average speeds over the measured mile/kilometer in the two runs. Thus, Gabelich averaged 629.412 mph on his first pass and 631.367 on his second, for an official mark of 630.388 mph. But he briefly—and unofficially—hit a peak, or transient, speed of nearly 660 mph.

When Bill Fredrick started working on what would ultimately become the *Budweiser Rocket*, a hydrogen peroxide motor made a lot of sense. It was powerful and relatively simple, and it had already been proven in drag racing. The principal downside, other than volatility, was that the fuel burned very quickly. This wasn't an issue in quarter-mile runs, but it meant that maintaining anything close to peak velocity for a measured mile was going to be impossible. (Refueling the car in an hour would have been another challenge.) Hal Needham asked the FIM to waive the requirement for back-to-back runs with speeds based on the measured mile/kilometer. While awaiting a ruling on this special dispensation, the team's top priority remained the sound barrier. If Stan Barrett could breach it even for a millisecond, that would be enough for the team to claim a piece of history. And why not? After all, Chuck Yeager had never been credited with setting an official speed record, yet everybody knew him as the stud who broke the sound barrier. Needham also couldn't see the point of the FIA/FIM requirement for two runs in two directions in less than an hour. It wasn't as if track and field officials had told Roger Bannister that he had to run a second sub-four-minute-mile backward right after finishing the first one if he wanted to get credit for setting a record.

Members of the LSR community weren't impressed with Needham's reasoning. Setting a land-speed record is unfathomably difficult and insanely dangerous, and the FIA/FIM regulations make the task even more exacting. Critics felt, not without justification, that Needham was trying to make an end run around the rules that the rest of the LSR competitors had been playing by for the past half-century. The LSR world is small but fiercely territorial, and there was a sense that Project SOS hadn't paid its dues. Fredrick was best known for his drag-racing exploits, crew chief Kirk Swanson was just 19 years old, and Needham and Barrett seemed to be a pair of Hollywood interlopers who planned to swoop in, grab some glory, and get out while the getting was good.

The Project SOS team had its share of teething problems after it descended on the Bonneville Salt Flats in September 1979 to mount its assault on the sound barrier. Barrett's ninth run—when his forged-aluminum rear wheels dug deeply into the salt and sent him bicycling down the course at 638.637 mph—was a showstopper. Although Barrett miraculously managed to avoid crashing, the episode made it clear that the speed of sound couldn't be achieved on the salt flats.

Shortly after this disastrous run, Gen. Phil Conley, commander of the Flight Test Center at Edwards Air Force Base, received a call from Yeager. To his astonishment, Yeager pitched the idea of letting Project SOS continue its program at Edwards. "Chuck," Conley said with some exasperation, "I've got enough problems here without worrying about some guy trying to kill himself in a car."

Eventually, though, Conley's curiosity was piqued enough that he ordered a formal review of Project SOS. He put together a team that evaluated the dangers associated with the car's aerodynamics, rocket motor, mechanical systems, driver, and parachutes. When his commanding officer asked him whether he wanted to proceed, Conley told him, "It's high risk, and there might be a fatality. But this is a program we're prepared to do and we're capable of doing." So the Air Force gave Needham and company its blessing to come to Edwards.

Project SOS made its first run at the base on November 22. Although there were a few hiccups that required some on-the-fly redesigns along the way, Barrett reached the threshold of the sound barrier on only his ninth pass at Edwards. But did he break through into supersonic territory? Officials at Edwards were convinced that he did, and he was honored "in recognition of his pioneer achievement in breaking the sound barrier on land" with a certificate signed by Hans Mark, secretary of the Air Force, and Air Force Chief of Staff Gen. Lew Allen. Adds Conley, an engineer by training: "I looked at the raw data. There was scatter in it. But it looked to me like he did it."

A lot of people in the LSR community disagreed. Dick Keller was infuriated by claims that the *Budweiser Rocket* had broken the top speed mark set by his *Blue Flame*. In fact, Barrett didn't make back-to-back runs or sustain his speed through the measured mile, as required by the FIM, so the only record he set was awarded by the International Hot Rod Association, which is sort of like getting a People's Choice Award instead of an Oscar. Keller also doubted that the car exceeded Mach 1. After his

The superlative craftsmanship embodied in the Budweiser Rocket is clearly visible in this hero shot of Stan Barrett with the car at Bonneville. After the wheels dug into the salt, the team moved its assault on the sound barrier to Edwards Air Force Base. Tony Korody/Sygma/Corbis

request for information was stonewalled by Project SOS and the Air Force, he enlisted the aid of U.S. Senator William Proxmire, who was influential enough to compel an official response. "The Air Force never intended to give official sanction to test results, nor to give the appearance of expressing an official view as to the speed attained by the test vehicle," Lt. Col. Michael Alba wrote.

Digging deeper, Keller found more apparent discrepancies. Through correspondence with Lt. Col. Guy E. Brown II, he learned how the digital instrumented radar at Edwards worked—or didn't work, as the case may be. Brown explained that because the range data was lost during Barrett's run, it had to be reconstructed after the fact by radar-tracking a heavily instrumented truck driven along the path the *Budweiser Rocket* had taken. (For the record, this was child's play since the car barely deviated from the centerline during the pass.) Also, since radar operator Bud Chatterley was tracking the car manually, the azimuth—or angle to the object being tracked—wasn't perfect. This resulted in disturbingly large fluctuations in speed that were later "smoothed" by data reduction.

Keller was convinced he'd found a smoking gun. "Using azimuth data obtained by manually panning a TV camera and distance data from the reconstructed path of the *Budweiser Rocket* results in a saw-tooth plot of the calculated speed," he wrote in his own persuasive analysis of the run. "Typical calculated speeds alternately increased and decreased continuously by as much as 100 mph 20 times per second during the 1.4 seconds of released data!" By creating his own graph of the speeds recorded by radar,

Fearless Hollywood stuntman Stan Barrett was car owner Hal Needham's first and only choice to drive the Budweiser Rocket. After breaking the sound barrier, Barrett also drove several Winston Cup races in Needham's stock cars. Getty Images

he clearly demonstrates what a mess they were. "The obvious lack of precision suggests the calculated speed cannot be known at the 1 percent level," he says. "Not even close! So a claim of Mach 1.01 is even more ridiculous than the claim the car was 'timed' by radar."

Another prominent nonbeliever was Craig Breedlove. "It was unofficial, uncalibrated, and unsanctioned," he told the *Los Angeles Times*. "The rocket car represents an achievement in design and driving skill, but it was a non-event, a travesty to people who work toward the goal of setting records legitimately." Needless to say, this didn't go over very well with the Project SOS team. "Needham had an attorney threaten to sue me," Breedlove recalls with obvious relish, "and I said, 'You go ahead. I can substantiate my opinion, and you don't want to drag me into a courtroom.'"

But the biggest thorn in the side of the Project SOS crew turned out to be a machinist, race car fabricator, and LSR devotee by the name of Don Baumea. A one-time member of Breedlove's team, Baumea decided to investigate Yeager's claim, published in 1980, that the fact that the rear wheels left the ground proved that the car went supersonic. In a long and powerfully reasoned piece posted on the Roadsters.com website in 1996, Baumea offered several credible reasons for this phenomenon that don't entail exceeding Mach 1. He also questioned the absence of a visible shock wave—commonly associated with breaking the sound barrier—and challenged the accuracy of the analysis of the spotty data from the run.

"So fragile is their proof that after many years of research, the author is unable to find any evidence whatsoever that can establish the validity of the Project SOS claim," he wrote.

Thanks to the reach of the Internet, the article has become the single most destructive attack in the campaign against the *Budweiser Rocket*. Yet Baumea himself now wishes he'd never posted it. "I keep trying to have it retracted," he says. The article generated threats of lawsuits, and he still receives ugly hate mail. But what really bothers Baumea is that he's developed great admiration for Barrett over the intervening years, and he's no longer dogmatic about his belief that the *Budweiser Rocket* didn't go supersonic. "I think the car went really, really fast," he says. "I don't know that it went Mach 1. I don't think anybody knows. But whatever happened, Stan earned his paycheck."

So what *did* happen on Rogers Dry Lake on December 17, 1979? Is it possible to make a definitive determination after all this time? Certain facts have been lost forever in the mists of time. Other points are fated to remain perpetually disputed. Take the sonic boom, for example. Numerous reports insist that there was no sonic boom—proof, critics say, that the sound barrier wasn't breached. Yet the in-depth *AutoWeek* feature story about the run tells a different story: "Eight photographers near the timing zone and a bunch of Air Force people testify that they heard the sonic boom and saw the shock waves in the air around the rocket."

That sounds definitive. But in an Air Force history report written two years later, Captain Hamilton offered a completely different version of events: "No audible sonic boom was heard by anybody except the possibility of one of the photographers near the speed trap, and this was probably the sound of the Sidewinder as it ignited. However, a sonic boom would not be expected at speeds slightly in excess of Mach 1." Then again, Mary Shafer, an aeronautical engineer at the Dryden Flight Research Center, which is based at Edwards, reported that she heard a boom. "It was loud enough and strong enough for me to have little doubt that the vehicle was above Mach 1," she wrote in 1989. "My husband, who is Dryden's Chief Scientist, was right there, too, and he says the same thing."

In retrospect, the Project SOS team has to shoulder most of the blame for the cloud of skepticism surrounding the run because it failed to come up with a foolproof method of accurately measuring velocity. Both the pitot tube in the nose and sensors mounted to the wheels proved to be worthless at high speed. The timing lights worked perfectly. But since peak speed could be maintained for only a short distance and each run was faster than the last, it turned out to be impossible to set the lights in precisely the right spot. Although the car was equipped with an accelerometer—a godsend,

In 1970, Gary Gabelich set a one-kilometer land-speed record of better than 630 mph at the Bonneville Salt Flats in *The Blue Flame*. The rocket-powered streamliner, built by a team led by Dick Keller, served as the template for the *Budweiser Rocket*. Hulton Archive/ Getty Images

as it happened—it was used primarily to evaluate rocket performance, not measure velocity. So after Barrett's potentially historic run, the team found itself relying on Air Force radar that hadn't been designed—or optimized—to perform this task.

Although this hadn't been the original plan, it wasn't necessarily a disaster. As Hamilton wrote: "The initial analysis of the raw radar data was in fact very simple from a mathematical point of view." Determining the speed was based on the principle of triangulation. The elevation and range were both known quantities, so the critical variable was the change in azimuth as the car made its run. Because the *Budweiser Rocket* had such a small radar signature, the auto-tracking feature couldn't be used. This meant that Chatterley had to track the car manually, doing his best to keep it centered in the crosshairs of a display monitor fed by a high-powered camera with a 40-inch lens mounted on the radar. This sounds like a challenge, and it was. But Chatterley was an experienced radar operator, and he'd tracked all eight of the *Rocket's* previous runs. Videotape of his performance showed that he lagged behind at the start of the run and ran ahead when the car began slowing. But during the highest-speed portion of the pass, he appeared to be spot-on. "Therefore," an unnamed AFFTC officer (probably Hamilton) was quoted in Lieutenant Colonel Brown's letter to Keller, "Any error introduced to the absolute ground speed was insignificant."

Chatterley rightfully gets annoyed by the complaints about the radar. Contrary to official Air Force comments, he says he calibrated the radar himself. As for it not being certified, certified for what? The radar was considered trustworthy enough to regularly track military aircraft worth exponentially more than the *Budweiser Rocket*, so the certification issue seems to be a red herring. On the other hand, there was no denying the essential truth of Keller's complaint—that, technically, the speed was based not on how fast the car was moving but on how fast Chatterley was moving the radar. "I could ride my bicycle and get the same number," Keller scoffs, meaning that operator error could translate into an implausible speed.

At the same time, the radar data was indisputably compromised by statistical noise. "It looked like what you'd expect—ugly and kind of primitive," says David Audley, then a captain, who worked on the data reduction. After a lot of laborious calculations and mathematical acrobatics, Audley and his cohorts came up with three data points in a flat area of the speed curve where the car appeared to have exceeded the speed of sound. The Air Force then handed the data off to Project SOS and basically stepped away from the table. (It's important to understand that the program didn't have the imprimatur of the Air Force; Project SOS was essentially renting space and services at the base.) Van Aken and his team averaged the three data points, which yielded a speed of 739.666 mph, or Mach 1.0106.

Needham declared victory and ended the program even though Barrett wanted to take one more blast in the car. But before formally committing itself to supporting the supersonic claim, the Air Force wanted more proof. Fortunately, the accelerometer contained data that could be used to confirm—or deny—Project SOS's claim. As its name implies, an accelerometer measures and records acceleration, and using it to calculate velocity had long been standard practice in aviation. So the day after Barrett's final run, the accelerometer was removed from the car and taken to the instrumentation calibration laboratory of Northrop Corp. By comparing acceleration with two known speeds and distance points—0 at the start and 666.234 mph at the timing trap—the device was accurately calibrated. Then, it was a straightforward matter of using calculus to translate acceleration into velocity.

A few days later, after manually reading and integrating the accelerometer data, AFFTC engineers recalculated the speed and reconfirmed that the *Budweiser Rocket* had gone supersonic. Only then did the Air Force allow Pete Knight to officially congratulate the Project SOS team and set into motion the commendation that Barrett would later receive from the highest echelons in Washington, DC. Six months later, AFFTC engineers re-examined the radar data more thoroughly and again demonstrated to their satisfaction that the car had exceeded Mach 1.0. And 18 months after that, with the blessing of Gen. Conley, engineers gave the accelerometer data a more rigorous look-see. This prompted them to adjust the peak speed to 736.4 mph, or Mach 1.006.

Still, some doubts lingered in Audley's mind. "I thought they broke the sound barrier, but there was a lot of noise in the data, and I knew that the level of our analysis wasn't great," he says. By this point, he was teaching at the Air Force Institute of Technology and serving as an advisor to a student—Capt. David Reinholz—who was looking for a thesis for his master's degree. So Audley decided to kill two birds with one stone by suggesting that Reinholz analyze the data from Barrett's final run at Edwards.

In December 1983, Reinholz presented a thesis titled "Stochastic Estimation Applied to the Land Speed of Sound Record Attempt by a Rocket Car." According to the abstract, "A forward-backward estimation method is used which employs a seven state forward-running extended Kalman filter and a Meditch-form backward recursive 'fixed interval' smoothing algorithm." What followed were 183 pages filled largely with impenetrable formulas, opaque charts, and even a few hundred lines of computer code that Reinholz wrote himself. The basic idea, though, is easy to understand. Essentially, Reinholz plugged the accelerometer and radar data into well-established mathematical models designed to minimize the errors. According to the Kalman filter, he determined the peak speed to be 740.94 mph, or Mach 1.0123. Using the "smoother" technique, the speed came out to be 737.75 mph, or Mach 1.008. He calculated the mathematical certainty that the car exceeded the speed of sound at 99.99999999999965653422 percent.

"You have to believe my assumptions and my models, and you have to believe the data," he says. "But I've got a very high level of confidence that the car was barely—*barely*—over the speed of sound. We had really, really good accelerometer data. Without that, the USAF never would have claimed anything. So I can happily ignore the radar data controversy and stand by the data from the accelerometer." The same goes for his one-time advisor David Audley, who's now a professor of applied mathematics and statistics at Johns Hopkins University. "There are always plausible arguments against something," he says. "But I don't have any skin in this game, and I'm convinced they did it."

But Eric Ahlstrom raises one last red flag. He's an aeronautical engineer who designed the modified wingtips found on the jets that have dominated the Reno Air Races in recent years. He was brought into the LSR world by the late Steve Fossett to work on his stillborn project to exceed 800 mph. As part of his research, Ahlstrom analyzed the data from the

"Bonneville Jet Wars"

If the 1970s was the era of rocket power in land-speed racing, then the previous decade had been the Jet Age.

In 1962, three streamliners showed up at the Bonneville Salt Flats built around J47s, the General Electric jet turbines used most famously in F-86 Sabres. One crashed fatally at close to 400 mph. The second spun at 331 mph. The third made nothing but noise. But its driver, Craig Breedlove, returned the next year and claimed the land-speed record at 407 mph with his car, dubbed the *Spirit of America*.

Before rocket cars attacked the land-speed record, first came the jet cars of the Arfons brothers, Art and Walt, and Los Angeles hot rodder Craig Breedlove, shown here with his original record-breaking *Spirit of America* three-wheeler. ISC Archives via Getty Images

In 1964, Breedlove faced stiff competition in the form of the Arfons brothers. Do-it-yourselfers touched by genius, Walt and Art worked out of adjacent junk-strewn lots on Pickle Road in Akron, Ohio, separated by nine years and decades of estrangement. Independently, they built two jet cars, each designed around a different military engine.

Walt opted for a Westinghouse J46, used most notably in the F7U Cutlass. On October 2, driver Tom Green screamed across the salt at 413 mph to claim the record. Three days later, while the newly crowned speed kings were driving home, they heard the news that their record had just been broken—by *Art Arfons*, whose *Green Monster* was powered by a General Electric J79, best known as the engine of the Mach 2 F-104 Starfighter and B-58 Hustler.

One week after Art snatched the record from his brother, Breedlove took it away from Arfons. But while trying to go even faster, Breedlove veered out of control at 500-plus mph, flew over a dike, and nosed into the water. "And now for my next act, I'm going to set myself on fire," he joked. Still, Art Arfons got the last laugh: after tweaking his engine back in Akron, he returned to the salt and squeezed out a 536-mph run to one-up Breedlove.

In 1965, Breedlove shoehorned a J79 in a brand-new *Spirit of America* dubbed Sonic I and tripped the timing lights at 555 mph to become the Fastest Man on Wheels. Less than a week later, Art Arfons made a heroic pass curtailed by a tire that shredded at top speed, emerging from the broken cockpit of his smoking car with another record—576 mph. Fast, but not fast enough. A week later, Breedlove went 600.601 mph and was immortalized in a Beach Boys ditty as "a daring young man [who] played a dangerous game."

Budweiser Rocket. "Did it go supersonic?" he says. "There's no evidence that it did, and there's a lot of evidence that it didn't." Ahlstrom concluded that the car topped out in the mid-730s, which would have been supersonic if the temperature had been 20 degrees. But he suspects that it was a few degrees warmer than reported, which would have raised the target speed. (At 25 degrees, for example, the speed of sound is about 737 mph.) Still, as he says, "It could *barely* have touched Mach 1.0000."

Keller remains unconvinced by Reinholz's thesis. He continues to maintain that the radar data was worthless, and like Ahlstrom, he's not satisfied that the measurements taken at Edwards to determine the speed of sound—which is based not only on temperature but also on barometric pressure, relative humidity, and wind speed—were sufficiently accurate. "Nobody knows how fast the *Budweiser Rocket* went, nor what the target ground speed was for Mach 1.0," he says. "I would suggest a hung jury at best regarding the sound barrier. If you can't prove it—don't claim it!"

The Air Force officers who worked on the program insist that their data—including the temperature—was accurate and that their analysis was correct. Nevertheless, all of the arcane arguments about what happened on December 17, 1979, were overshadowed on October 15, 1997. During the previous month, on the playa of Black Rock Desert in Nevada, a high-speed, high-stakes duel had been waged by Craig Breedlove and Royal Air Force fighter pilot Andy Green. On October 15, Green indisputably broke the sound barrier in a blunt-force object known as the ThrustSSC. He then made the requisite pair of runs in opposite directions to become the first man to set a supersonic land-speed record. His official mark was 763.035 mph, but because of the temperature, this translates to only Mach 1.016.

In the years since then, the achievements of Project SOS have been marginalized, and the *Budweiser Rocket* car has been reduced to a footnote in most accounts of land-speed racing. But Stan Barrett insists that he's not bitter about being written out of the history books. "I know what I did, and the prayer I prayed was that God would get the glory, not me," he says. Then his blue eyes twinkle, and he adds, "I welcomed Mr. Green to the club. But he was not the first member."

VERDICT:
Sort of. The *Budweiser Rocket* didn't set a land-speed record—or any official record of note. But it was the first land-based vehicle to break the sound barrier.
– *Preston Lerner*

SMOKEY YUNICK'S THREE-QUARTER-SCALE CHEVELLE AND OTHER CHEATS

LEGEND: After Smokey Yunick's notorious Chevelle was banned from the Daytona 500 in 1968, he drove it back to his shop—without a gas tank.

What's the most famous NASCAR race car of all time? The tailfin Oldsmobile that Lee Petty drove to victory in a photo finish in the inaugural Daytona 500? Junior Johnson's Mystery Motor Impala? The David Pearson/Wood Brothers Mercury Cyclone that dominated superspeedway racing? Richard Petty's high-wing Superbird? Dollar Bill Elliott's awesome Thunderbird? The Intimidator's Aerocoupe? Wonder Boy's DuPont Chevrolet?

Bench racers could spend several off-seasons and consume millions of six-packs talking this over without ever coming close to agreement on the subject. But picking the most *infamous* car in the 60-plus-year history of NASCAR? Well, that's a no-brainer: There's no car in the same class as Smokey Yunick's last Chevrolet Chevelle, a car so ingenious that it was turned away during tech inspection before the Daytona 500 in 1968 and never permitted to run a single lap in NASCAR competition.

Yunick called it "the little car that could . . . but didn't." After being rejected by the tech inspectors, he angrily drove the car crosstown to his nearby race shop, roaring through stoplights while its unmuffled exhaust blasted through the city streets. There it sat, a black-and-gold beauty regally holding court at the Daytona Beach landmark known as the Best Damn Garage in Town. Banished from the racetrack but not from memory, the car was unofficially enshrined as the apotheosis of the cheater's art, and it became the subject of some of NASCAR's most memorable lore. People said it wasn't a Chevelle at all, but a 7/8th-scale model (or 15/16th, depending on who was telling the story). It was powered, supposedly, by a destroked big-block V-8 pumped up with nitrous oxide. And then there was the legend of the missing gas tank, which is everybody's favorite anecdote about crafty race car cheats.

The story goes like this: To run farther than the competition on the racetrack, Smokey allegedly fabricated a network of oversized gas lines and hid them inside the frame rails. The tech inspectors didn't find them, of course. But they objected to several other, er, irregularities, and they even

Smokey Yunick was an American original—a self-trained engineer who became one of the legends of motorsports thanks to his technical ingenuity, disdain for convention, and creativity in stretching the rules.
Trish Yunick

went to the trouble of pulling the fuel cell out of the car. When the inspection was finished, they handed Smokey a list of 10 infractions that had to be addressed before the Chevelle would be approved for competition. Smokey was enraged. "Make it 11!" he said after knocking one of the inspectors to the ground. Then he jumped into the cockpit and drove off in a haze of tire smoke, leaving the fuel cell—theoretically containing the gasoline the engine needed to run—on the ground in the garage behind him.

True? Well, some stories are so good that it seems like a shame to let the facts—whatever they are—get in the way. And Yunick himself told the story in different ways on different occasions. And why not? With his signature oil-stained Stetson and cigar (later, a meerschaum pipe), Smokey was a larger-than-life character and a uniquely American success story. He was born into crushing rural poverty, and his formal education ended when he was in 10th grade, but his self-taught genius, personal charm, and natural hardheadedness enabled him to enjoy a career more fantastic than even the most creative Hollywood screenwriter could have imagined. He was, in turn, a World War II combat aviator, one of the earliest heroes of NASCAR, a race-winning Indy 500 crew chief, an inventor with dozens of patents to his credit, an oilman in the jungles of South America, and, when he'd retired from racing, a prolific journalist who wrote for *Popular Science*, *Hot Rod*, and *Circle Track* magazines.

His professional training taught him the benefits of secrecy. Why, after all, let his competitors in on his tricks? And what NASCAR officials didn't know couldn't hurt him. At the same time, he was unusually articulate for a mechanic, and he had no use for public relations or what we now call political correctness, so he was a darling of the media and a popular interview. Later, of course, he did plenty of writing of his own. Shortly before he died in 2001, he finished writing his memoir, aptly titled *Best Damn Garage in Town*. This is, without question, the funniest and most brutally honest book ever written about racing. Still, it's very much history as seen through the eyes of Smokey Yunick. Finding the truth about the man, like the last of his Chevelles, takes a little digging.

Henry Yunick was born dirt-poor on a farm in Pennsylvania. He came by his mechanical aptitude naturally: When he was 14, he transformed a $10 Dodge into a crude tractor. By the time he was 16, he was turning wrenches professionally. A short stint racing motorcycles earned him his nickname (because his bike smoked so badly). Next came a job with a company that built autogiros, and this experience fired his ambition to become a fighter pilot. With World War II on the horizon, he volunteered for the Army Air Corps, managing to qualify as an officer candidate even though he hadn't graduated from high school, much less college. To his chagrin, he didn't get fighters. Instead, he was to assigned to B-17 Flying Fortresses and dispatched to bomb the Axis into submission. He was 19 years old.

Yunick saw plenty of combat piloting B-17s out of Italy, then flew B-25s over the Hump and served with the Flying Tigers. In his spare time,

Curtis Turner qualified on the pole at Atlanta in the second of Yunick's Chevrolet Chevelles and led the Dixie 400 before the engine soured. "Pops" was always fast in Smokey's Chevelles, but he never managed to put one in victory lane. Trish Yunick

Turner loiters next to his Chevelle in the primitive pits when the Chevelle saga began. Like Yunick, Turner was one of the pioneering superstars of NASCAR. But both of them were on the downside of their careers of the 1960s. Trish Yunick

he checked out in B-29s, various fighters, and even a PBY Catalina flying boat. (If his account is to be believed, he also slept with half the able-bodied women on three continents.) After the war, he moved to Daytona Beach and landed a job as a copilot on an Eastern Airlines DC-3. But peacetime flying didn't appeal to him, and his only other marketable skill was working on cars. So in 1947, he found a piece of property that backed up against the Halifax River, and he opened what would eventually become famous as Smokey's: Best Damn Garage in Town.

It wasn't Yunick's original intention to go racing. But Daytona Beach had a proud motorsports heritage, with land-speed record attempts on the sand dating back to the turn of the century. The city was also the home of an ambitious promoter by the name of Bill France, around whom a bunch of talented stock car racers had coalesced. Yunick wasn't a member of the cult of Big Bill. Yunick characterized France as mean and dictatorial, a liar and a cheat, and Smokey was even harder on his successor, Bill France Jr. As far as Yunick was concerned, and in contrast to conventional wisdom, NASCAR succeeded in spite of the Frances, not because of them. But there's no question that Bill France put stock car racing on the national map. And Yunick was part of the action virtually from day one.

In racing, the ex-bomber pilot bored by civilian life found the perfect avocation. It challenged his engineering talents, and it fed his fierce need for competition. "Racing is a Missouri sport—'Show me,'" he wrote with obvious approval. "For a curious-minded person addicted to speed, I was there at exactly the right time. Stock car racing was a format whereby everyone started even, next to no education and no money. A racer was a social outcast, no chance for credit, no insurance, not wanted in hotels, social status just a little better than an ex-con or a 'mon-backer.' In spite of all the drawbacks, to me it was still a thrill on race day morning to walk into the pits, pull up my pants, look around and say, 'All right, you sons of bitches. . . . Let's have a race.'"

Yunick started working with a pair of Daytona Beach neighbors who happened to be pretty fair race car drivers: Fireball Roberts and Marshall Teague, two of NASCAR's earliest stars. It didn't take long for the cognoscenti to recognize Yunick's singular mechanical wizardry. In 1951, he landed the first of what turned out to be several factory deals, this one running so-called Fabulous Hudson Hornets for Teague and one-time tobacco farmer Herb Thomas. Despite the modest power of the straight-6 engines, the step-down Hornets were the cars to beat in the early '50s, with Thomas earning championships in 1951 and 1953 and just missing out in 1952 and 1954. Altogether, the fabulous Hudsons won 39 races in four years.

The principal secret of Yunick's success was his ability to coax power out of engines. Well, that and an unparalleled ability to bend the rules in creative ways. Cheating? Uh, not exactly, at least not according to Smokey's idiosyncratic but scrupulous definition of the term. "He stretched the rules about as far as they could be stretched," says Cotton Owens, a car-building legend who bent plenty of rules himself. Or as Yunick put it himself: "NASCAR could have gotten me to 'behave' by writing rules without ambiguities because I refused to cheat. There was no craft or fun in that."

Yunick's code of ethics didn't allow him to do anything blatantly obvious or outright illegal. No supersized engines, for example. No jumbo gas tanks. No ultra-expensive materials to save weight. When nitrous oxide was banned, he stopped using it. Ditto for chilled fuels (which squeezed more gas into the tank) and hydraulic pads (to lower the suspension). On the other hand, the rules didn't prohibit angling the nose down (to increase downforce) or using taller tires (only the width of the wheels was specified). "Smokey believed that if the rulebook didn't say you couldn't do it, then you *could* do it," says NASCAR historian John Craft. "He would spend a week trying to get away with something. It was a mano a mano thing between him and the NASCAR tech guys. He believed that he was smarter than those 'comic book-reading sons of bitches.'"

This is a good time to point out that, strictly speaking, the notion of racing genuine stock cars was a sham from the moment NASCAR was founded. Consider the modern car. Consider the ramifications of running it flat-out on a racetrack for three or four hours. The car probably wouldn't last, and even if it did, it wouldn't make for much of a spectacle. The cars of the 1940s were several orders of magnitude slower and more shoddily built than the cars of today (much less the Car of Tomorrow). And back then, races weren't run on impeccably paved asphalt speedways. They were held on dirt-track bullrings that developed ruts deep enough to surf down. How many legitimately "stock" cars do you think would have survived 175 laps around Occoneechee Speedway or 100 miles at the Monroe County Fairgrounds, especially with all the beating and banging that was par for the course back then?

At this time, the entire NASCAR rulebook—everything from business regulations to technical specifications—was less than a dozen pages. It was up to the car builders to fill in the blank spaces, and nobody did it more inventively than Yunick. "I really just read the rule book carefully," he explained. "If a nut, bolt, or part wasn't specifically mentioned, or a measurement wasn't given, I assumed those items were 'fair game.' Even when they said 'stock,' what the hell did that mean? They needed to say 'stock as of a certain day.' Hell, stock can change a lot depending on when and where a part was made. As a result of my reading of the rules, I think that by 1970, one half of the technical rule section of a NASCAR rule book was dedicated to me—quite an honor, actually."

By the mid-'50s, Yunick had gotten crossways with Bill France on so many occasions that he was at the top of the tech inspectors' hit list. But if you were a manufacturer, he was the guy you wanted massaging your motors. So in 1955, Yunick was tapped by Ed Cole, the father of the small-block Chevy, to shepherd his seminal engine's introduction into NASCAR. This led to a long association with General Motors, most notably in the person of Bunkie Knudsen, who'd just been named the general manager of Pontiac. Knudsen and his Number Two, the young John DeLorean, wanted to remake Pontiac as a performance brand, and Yunick was hired to win races. That he did, mostly with Paul Goldsmith and Fireball Roberts at the wheel. But around this time, Yunick was seduced by the siren call of Indianapolis Motor Speedway, which he described as the "real racer's proving ground." And as the '60s progressed, he tended to limit his NASCAR work to one-offs and special projects.

The Chevelle story began in the winter of 1965, when Knudsen—now running Chevrolet—brought Yunick to the Milford Proving Grounds in Michigan to test the prototype of the company's latest muscle car. Smokey wasn't especially impressed with the new Chevelle, but Knudsen wanted to race it at Daytona. That left Yunick less than two months to build a race car. The only available chassis was the prototype, so that's exactly what he used to build it. Because Yunick didn't have time to go wild on the car,

Turner sits on pit road at Daytona International Speedway. In 1967, he effortlessly stuck Smokey's second Chevelle on the pole before breaking in the race. The next year, Yunick returned to Daytona with his third and last Chevelle. Trish Yunick

he decided to bring in a ringer to drive it—a young charger he'd seen in Indy cars and sprinters. His name was Mario Andretti, and he'd just won the national title during his first full season on the Championship Trail.

Andretti's only NASCAR experience had come on the road course at Riverside. But he'd just raced a Ferrari prototype in the 24 Hours of Daytona, so he was familiar with the banking, and he knew that fellow Indy car driver Johnny Rutherford had set fast time qualifying at Daytona in another of Yunick's creations, so he was eager to sample the Chevelle. Still, he was aware of Smokey's reputation for, ah, eccentric behavior. "It was the most bizarre thing I've ever been involved in in racing," he recalls with a laugh. "I called him when I got to Daytona and asked him for directions to his shop. He told me, 'You don't need to come over here.' I said, 'Smokey, don't I need to get fitted up?' And he said, 'No, you'll be fine.' He didn't want me coming over to the garage so I could see what he was doing there. Even when he was working on the engine, the hood opened only five or six inches, and the mechanic would burn his nose on the valve cover."

The engine was plenty stout, but suspension geometry of the Chevelle was badly flawed, and Yunick's unconventional chassis tuning made matters even worse. "He was a real artist. Every detail of the car was perfect," Andretti says. "But it was just diabolical to drive. There's loose

RACING

Wearing his signature Stetson and a shirt bearing the logo of his shop in Daytona Beach, Yunick watches his Chevelle circulate around Atlanta. A few months later, Turner would destroy the car here in a spectacular wreck near the entrance to pit road. Smyle Media

and there's *loose.* I remember telling Donnie Allison, 'Jesus Christ, my car's loose all over the banking. Is that what yours is like?' 'Hell, no!' he goes. When I got alongside another car, I could turn the steering wheel from lock to lock and it would just go straight. I'm telling Smokey what's wrong, and he's not paying any attention to me. My words are just bouncing off his forehead."

Andretti was as brave as they came, but he wasn't stupid. Although he managed to lead a lap in the qualifying race, he finished three laps behind the leader. He started the 500 in 39th and wrecked early. "I've never been so happy to crash in my life," he says. "That was the worst car I ever drove. It scared the shit out of me." Yunick agreed with Andretti's assessment. "Car had power to spare," he declared, "but the chassis was so fucked up God couldn't have drove it."

When Daytona was over, Yunick sold the Chevelle to a local racer and got a new one from Knudsen. This time, the chassis was tweaked by Frank Winchell and Jim Musser, two of the unsung heroes of Chevy R&D (and major players in Jim Hall's Chaparral program). To drive the car for an abbreviated schedule, Yunick brought in Curtis Turner, his boon companion from way back. Although Turner had been one of NASCAR's first superstars, he was an old 42 and near the end of an illustrious career that had begun when most races were run on dirt tracks that didn't demand much engineering know-how.

"The only thing Curtis could tell you about a race car was, 'It's a little bit hairy' or 'It's beautiful,'" says mechanic T. A. Toomes, who helped Yunick build the car. "He tested for three days at Daytona in the Chevelle, and he couldn't go more than 178. We had Marvin Panch, too, and he ran 178. Then Paul Goldsmith got in the car, and on the second lap, he went 181 damn miles per hour! Curtis was holding it flat around the track, never cracking the throttle, and went 178. Paul lifted in Turn 1 and Turn 3 and went 181 because the car wasn't binding up."

The Chevelle's final race was the Daytona 500 in 1967. Yunick was so confident that he didn't bother rolling out the car until the end of qualifying. Then, Turner stuck it on the pole so effortlessly that Yunick parked it rather than risk running it in the qualifying race. "The car came back in, Smokey put the car cover on it and left," says Craft. "No working on the engine. No reading spark plugs. He and Turner went out and got a drink. People just freaked. This was when the manufacturers were spending money at a Homeric clip, and here's this privateer blowing their asses away."

Unfortunately, the engine let go on race day while Turner was running near the lead. (Mario Andretti became the Daytona 500's unlikeliest winner.) The next time out in the Chevelle, during practice at Atlanta Motor Speedway, Turner lost control of the car between Turns 3 and 4 and went end over end about 14 times. While the car was pirouetting in midair, Yunick said to Toomes, "Adios, one good race car." The Chevelle landed on the pit entrance guardrail right in front of them, which was convenient, since they had to drag Turner out of the burning car. Yunick later took the wreckage to a junkyard and had it squashed into a four-foot-square cube.

Yunick parted ways with Turner after that. But he was still sold on the Chevelle. So he got car Number 3 from Knudsen and fashioned his most renowned masterpiece. He spent four months working flat-out on the project, which was designed specifically and solely to win the Daytona 500. "Smokey put everything he'd learned about NASCAR into that car," Craft says. There's hardly a single body panel, structural element, or component that Yunick didn't tweak in some way. Wearing Smokey's usual black-and-gold livery and carrying his customary Number 13, it just might be the most perfectly proportioned stock car ever built.

The most noteworthy aspect of the Chevelle was that it was designed around a scratch-built chassis, standard practice now but never done before in NASCAR. This allowed Yunick not only to save 80 pounds but also to create a more rigid frame. He further reduced chassis flex by making the engine a structural member. Speaking of the motor, Smokey wanted to shift it to the left to increase the left-side weight bias, thereby helping the car get around the turns. According to the rules, the motor had to be located in the centerline of the chassis. But there was no rule saying that the frame itself had to be centered. So Yunick moved *everything* to the left, including the driver.

The suspension was state of the art and then some, with a Watts linkage and control arms fitted with turnbuckles so that the geometry could be adjusted during pit stops. The lower arms at the rear were tear-drop shaped to improve airflow, a trick Yunick had picked up from his Indy car experience. In fact, the entire bottom of the car was streamlined to an extent never before seen in NASCAR. Strictly speaking, a belly pan was illegal. So Smokey sidestepped this prohibition by lowering the floor-boards until they were flush with the frame rails and fairing in the rear suspension and gas tank.

But when it came to aerodynamics, the body was the *piece de resistance*. The door handles were shaved, the grill was filled, and the bumper was sectioned so it could be lowered one inch and widened two. Fenders and wheel wells were reprofiled to improve airflow. The chrome supporting the windshield and back glass were made flush. The center of the roof was flattened, and the rear edge was subtly recontoured to create what Yunick called a "vortex generator," the idea being that it would enhance the performance of the rear spoiler. The car was not—repeat, was not—shrunk to 7/8 (or 15/16) of the stock dimensions. On the contrary, Yunick made damn sure that it fit the NASCAR template. It just looked completely different than a stock Chevelle.

Naturally, Smokey also slicked up the engine. He was especially proud of the exhaust system, which he fabricated with sliding inner ventricles that were designed to melt at operating temperature and improve engine breathing. Yunick didn't believe in running oversize motors. In fact, the Chevelle was fitted with a big-block destroked to 416 cubic inches even though 427s were perfectly legal. He figured the shorter stroke would allow him to turn more rpm, which would translate into more power. Sounds crazy. But at Daytona the previous year, Turner had put the second-gen Chevelle on the pole with an engine that displaced only *404* cubic inches.

After an epic thrash, Yunick made it to Daytona in time for tech inspection before the 500 in February 1968. He expected to be given a hard time—he was NASCAR's poster child for cheating—but he figured he'd eventually be approved. To begin with, he believed that he'd already gotten the unofficial blessing of Bill France, who'd visited Yunick's shop and seen the car when it was under construction. Also, Toomes insists that the Chevelle was strictly legal. "The only thing wrong with that car was that it was too damn fast for what NASCAR wanted," he snaps.

In light of all the modifications Smokey had made, Toomes' statement seems like an incredible claim. After all, Yunick had built the chassis from

Yunick reacquired the last and most magnificent of his Chevelles and thoroughly restored it, using many of the spare parts he'd fabricated back in 1968, with the help of Bill Ellis. It was displayed for many years at Floyd Garrett's Muscle Car Museum. Bruce Canepa

Now owned by vintage racers Mark and Linda Mountanos, the Chevelle just might be the most beautiful stock car ever built. Note the workmanship that went into the metal shaping around the rear window and the gas filler. Bruce Canepa

Contrary to legend, the Chevelle isn't 7/8th or 15/16th the size of a "real" car. But there was virtually no piece of sheet metal that Yunick didn't subtly reshape, from the front bumper to the rear spoiler. Bruce Canepa

RACING

"No Joke"

If Smokey Yunick's never-raced Chevelle has a serious rival for the title of NASCAR's most notorious car, it was the one-and-done cheater created by Junior Johnson for driver Fred Lorenzen.

The year was 1966. Bill France was having one of his periodic dust-ups with the Big Three over the eligibility of exotic

Known as the Yellow Banana or Junior's Joke, this was the cheated-up Ford Galaxie that Junior Johnson built for the Dixie 400. Here, Fred Lorenzen sweeps past the outclassed Oldsmobile of Buck Baker on the banking at Atlanta. Smyle Media

engines, and disgruntled fans weren't feeling that old-time religion. So NASCAR inspectors turned a blind eye when Johnson showed up at Atlanta with a strange-looking Ford Galaxie dubbed both the Yellow Banana (because of sponsor Holly Farms' paint scheme and the sloping shape) and, more appropriately, Junior's Joke.

The nose of the car had been visibly angled down, the top had been chopped like a '51 Merc, and the rear end had been raised to produce downforce. Not only did the car look blatantly illegal, but it also featured extra-long truck trailing arms and a Watts linkage. Yet even as the tech inspectors tossed out a trio of other cars—including the Dodge prepared by Cotton Owens for David Pearson—for cheating, Johnson's Joke got a free pass.

So, too, ironically, did Curtis Turner in the second iteration of Smokey Yunick's Chevelle, the immediate predecessor to the car that would be banned during tech inspection before the Daytona 500 in 1968. "I realize that Lorenzen and Turner are valuable drawing cards," Owens griped. "But that doesn't make what's happening right."

Curtis claimed the pole for the Dixie 400, while Lorenzen qualified third. The two of them dominated the race until the Chevelle's engine soured and the Galaxie plowed into a wall after blowing a tire. Afterward, NASCAR officials quietly told Johnson to take his Yellow Banana home—and keep it there.

Still, it obviously got Yunick to thinking. And after Turner returned to Atlanta the next year and barrel-rolled the Chevelle into oblivion, Smokey started working on a third Chevelle that would make Junior's Joke seem like the mildest of gags.

scratch, which seems antithetical to the whole notion of stock car racing. But, in fact, NASCAR had a long history of permitting deviations, often radical, usually to entice manufacturers to compete in Grand National racing when their "stock" car wouldn't otherwise be competitive. At the time, for instance, Ford teams commonly grafted front clips from full-size Galaxies onto the frames of intermediate-size sedans, and tech inspectors never made a peep about it. This was also the era when Junior Johnson was allowed to run a car for driver Fred Lorenzen so blatantly illegal that it was dubbed The Yellow Banana. Yunick himself figured he might have trouble getting his widened front bumper through Tech, so he brought a stock piece with him to replace it just in case he got busted.

Sure enough, the tech inspectors crawled over and under the Chevelle for several hours. It's hard to say exactly what happened at Daytona because accounts—including those provided by Yunick—differ over the details. But eventually, NASCAR chief inspector Bill Gazaway handed Yunick a list of 10 items that needed to be fixed. Or maybe it was 11 items. Or 12 items. Or 15. However long the list really was, the first item was an immediate showstopper: "Remove pan from under car and box frame are to resemble GM frame at standard frame locations. Frame not standard. Must appear standard." In other words, Smokey had to replace his scratch-built chassis—with the track about to close in 90 minutes.

This is when Yunick knocked down a NASCAR official, jumped into the Chevelle, and rumbled out the track tunnel and along Volusia Avenue. Or maybe he just loaded it on a trailer and sedately towed it back to his shop. At this point, it's impossible to say for sure. Either way, Smokey insisted that the story about him taking off without any fuel in the gas tank was completely bogus. "As if anybody in his right mind would go to the trouble of creating a secret fuel tank, then give it away like that," he said. "There was a time when just hearing that story would get me teed off at NASCAR all over again. Now, I don't give a damn if people believe it or not."

Then again, Smokey couldn't resist adding that he *could* have taken off without the gas tank since, he said, he had enough fuel in his fuel line—which was 2 inches wide and 11 feet long—to drive the 90 miles north to Jacksonville if he'd wanted to. (NASCAR didn't establish a maximum diameter for the fuel line until after this incident.) He was convinced that the gas tank legend had been invented and leaked to the press by none other than Bill France in an effort to justify the rejection of the Chevelle and to embarrass Yunick. If so, then Smokey got the last laugh. The Chevelle became a thousand times more famous for being banned than it ever would have been for racing at Daytona.

Ironically, many of the innovations that kept the Chevelle off the track in 1968 are now standard equipment on the modern Car of Tomorrow, so you could say that Smokey's greatest sin was being too far ahead of his time. But after NASCAR made it clear that the Chevelle would never be allowed to enter a Grand National event, Yunick gave it to a short-track racer who ran it in some Saturday night shows. In the late 1980s, Yunick repossessed the car with the intention of restoring it.

The years hadn't been kind to the Chevelle. Bill Ellis, who helped restore it, describes the car as "rough." The interior had been gutted, and many of Smokey's trick parts were gone. The one-of-a-kind front bumper, for example, had been replaced with a cow-catcher grille for dirt-track racing. Fortunately, Yunick had fabricated plenty of spares back in 1968, so he was able to restore the car to its original mechanical form. Meanwhile, he hired a body man to redo the bodywork. After the restoration, the Chevelle was bought at auction by Floyd Garrett, who displayed it for many years in his Muscle Car Museum in Tennessee before selling it to stalwart vintage Trans-Am racers Mark and Linda Mountanos in Northern California. Today, the car looks both gorgeous and purposeful. With some fuel dumped in the infamous fuel tank, it's not hard to imagine it rumbling around the high banks of Daytona at 180 mph and change.

Over the years, tens of thousands of people have seen the car in person, either in vintage races or on static display. Gordon Johncock, who was supposed to race it in the Daytona 500, isn't one of them. Back in 1968, he was—like Mario Andretti—an Indy 500 winner-to-be, and Yunick figured he was the perfect hot shoe for the Chevelle. "He didn't give me no warning or nothing," Johncock recalls. "In February, I got a phone call from Smokey. He said, 'I've got a new car. Why don't you come to Daytona and drive it?' He knew how to make a stock car run. So I said yes. But when I got to the track, he'd already driven the car away. I never sat in it. I never even saw it. I don't think I saw Smokey, as a matter of fact." Johncock chuckles: "I just got back on another plane and went home."

VERDICT: False.
But in the case of Smokey's final Chevelle, the truth is stranger than fiction. –Preston Lerner

JOCKO FLOCKO, NASCAR'S ONLY RACE-WINNING MONKEY

LEGEND: A monkey named Jocko Flocko won as many NASCAR Grand National races as Mario Andretti, Buddy Shuman, and Mark Donohue.

Contemporary stock car racing is the world's most regimented form of motorsports. NASCAR has rules covering everything from the placement of signage to how pit crews are supposed to stand for the national anthem. All of the race cars are designed to meet the same template, and drivers are fined for fighting, complaining, or simply failing to toe the company line. It sometimes seems that the only unscripted portion of a NASCAR weekend is the race itself, and some conspiracy theorists—citing yellow flags for phantom pieces of debris and seemingly arbitrary penalties for pit-lane speed limit violations—even wonder about that.

Stock car racing inhabited a completely different world back in 1948 when a group led by Big Bill France formed NASCAR. At the time, the sport was a largely Southern phenomenon that hardly registered in a nation fixated on open-wheel racing at the Indianapolis Motor Speedway. The cars were glorified jalopies rather than thoroughbred racers, and aside from the celebrated Daytona Beach Road Course, most of the tracks were dirt-track bullrings. The drivers were a motley crew of daredevils, mechanics eager to make a few extra bucks, and moonshine runners looking to put their high-speed driving skills to lawful use. Prize money was measured by the hundreds, not the millions, and as an entertainment venue, the races had more in common with Barnum & Bailey than the World Series.

Into this sideshow landscape came the fabulous Flock Brothers—Bob, Fonty, and Tim. (Their sister, Ethel, also ran more than a hundred races of her own). Bob and Fonty had learned their trade "whiskey trippin"—that is, running moonshine in hot-rodded coupes and sedans—for their uncle, Peachtree Williams, an Atlanta corn liquor tycoon. Bob, the eldest, was a modified ace before and during NASCAR's formative years. Fonty, the most flamboyant of the three, won the last of the pre-NASCAR stock car

In 1955 Tim Flock scored 18 wins—and earned 19 poles—in 45 races driving Carl Kiekhaefer's powerful Chrysler 300s. A lot of those victories were posted on dirt tracks like this one at Asheville-Weaverville Speedway. Smyle Media

championships and finished second in the 1951 Grand National title hunt. But Tim, the baby of the family, proved to be the most successful driver of them all.

Tim won a pair of Grand National championships, the early-day equivalent of the modern Sprint Cup title. He's the only driver to win in every class on the Daytona Beach Road Course, and driving a mighty Chrysler 300 for car owner Karl Kiekhaefer, he earned 19 poles and won 18 races in a single season. His career ended prematurely when he and fellow legend Curtis Turner were blackballed by Bill France for trying to start a drivers union. But Flock won 40 of 189 races, setting a record for winning percentage that remains unmatched to this day. Shortly before dying in 1998 at the age of 74, he was named one of NASCAR's Greatest 50 Drivers.

Flock grew up poor, and he had no affinity for—or interest in— turning wrenches as a mechanic. So from day one, he depended on car owners who were willing to give him rides. Early on, he befriended a race-loving Atlanta car dealer by the name of Ted Chester. In 1951, Chester bought an Olds 88 that Flock campaigned as the *Black Phantom* to go along with Bob's car, known as the *Gray Ghost*. Tim won seven races and finished third in the championship. (Fonty was second.) The following year, Chester traded the Oldsmobile for a Hudson Hornet. This time around, Tim won eight races and his first Grand National title.

Flock was the only driver to win races in every NASCAR division at Daytona Beach—when they actually raced on the sand rather then the superspeedway. But he didn't have much luck there in this Hudson Hornet.
Frances Flock

But the youngest of the Flock brothers struggled at the beginning of 1953, and Chester was looking for ways to change the team's luck. While browsing through an Atlanta pet store, he saw a Rhesus monkey for sale. According to the sign on his cage, the monkey's name was Jocko. "Jocko," Chester mused. "Jocko . . . Jocko . . . Jocko. . . ." And then, he was struck with a bolt of inspiration:

"Jocko Flocko!"

Chester bought the monkey and hustled over to Blackburn Auto Service, where mechanic B. B. Blackburn was prepping Flock's race car. Chester sidled up to Flock and said, "Now, don't holler when you hear this. But I've got an idea: I thought maybe we could put this little monkey in your race car."

"You're crazy!" Flock said. "You must've been hitting the jug!"

But Chester wouldn't drop it, and it didn't take him long to persuade Flock. After all, promotion was in Flock's blood. One of his older sisters had been an air show wing-walker and stunt parachutist, and Fonty—a debonair raconteur who sometimes raced in shorts—was the greatest showman of his era. So Tim shrugged and told Chester, "You're the boss."

Of course, NASCAR promised to be a tougher sell. Flock and France had already gotten crossways over several issues in the past, and putting a monkey in a race car wasn't going to encourage people to take stock car racing more seriously. So for Jocko's debut, at Charlotte Speedway, the team decided that it would be easier to seek forgiveness than ask

Tim Flock, left, and his showman brother, Fonty, fool around with Jocko Flocko in front of the Ted Chester-owned Hudson Hornet in which the monkey became the only nonhuman to win a NASCAR race. Smyle Media

permission. Nobody said anything about the monkey, and just before the race was scheduled to begin, Flock smuggled him into the car.

Flock later claimed that Blackburn built a special seat for Jocko, who would wave at fans—and drivers—during races. Several others remember it being more of a perch attached to the big bench seat of the Hudson. But Junior Johnson, who raced against the monkey at Hickory, recalls the monkey being confined to a small cage mounted on the right side of the cockpit. "Seemed like he went round and round in that cage like he was scared to death," he says. Then again, Jocko wasn't the only competitor who was freaked out. As Flock told his biographer, the late Larry Fielden: "Other drivers would look over at my car as I passed them on the straightaways and almost run into the guardrail when they saw Jocko looking back at them."

Considering that Flock had qualified on the pole and led 87 laps, his fourth-place finish wasn't cause for celebration. But Jocko was an unqualified hit with the fans, and Chester wasted no time capitalizing on his popularity. He hired a seamstress to sew a custom driving suit with the car number—91—embroidered on the back and a hole in the seat for the monkey's tail. The name "Jocko Flocko" was also painted on the roof of the Hornet just over the passenger door. During the spring of 1953, the monkey became one of NASCAR's biggest draws. After races were over,

With Tim Flock's blessing, Jack Petty and his son Jim re-created the step-down Hudson Hornet Flock drove to the NASCAR championship in 1952. The street-legal coupe has a 308-cubic-inch flathead-6 and a 3-on-the-tree transmission. Jim Petty

Flock led Jocko over to the grandstand and let kids feed him peanuts. Between races, the monkey lived in a cage in the backyard of Flock's house in Atlanta, where his children walked him on a leash and joined him on the swing set. "That monkey got took care of real good—got fed the best bananas and everything," Flock told Kim Chapin, author of *Fast as White Lightning*, an engaging history of NASCAR's early days.

With Jocko riding shotgun, Flock's fortunes improved. He was sixth at Central City Speedway, a scruffy half-mile dirt track in Macon, Georgia. Then the team headed north to Pennsylvania and the daunting D-shaped oval at Langhorne, a.k.a. The Big Left Turn, where Flock started on the pole and led 67 laps before finishing fifth. A week later, he was back in South Carolina and an encouraging second at Columbia Speedway. Then, on May 15, 1953, Flock and Jocko made NASCAR history during the first Grand National race at Hickory Speedway. There, on the red clay of the North Carolina Piedmont, a monkey made it to Victory Lane. The feat earned Flock $1,000 and Jocko Flocko a unique place in racing legend.

Unfortunately, after the win at Hickory, there was nowhere to go but downhill, and Jocko's star plummeted as quickly as it had risen. DNFs followed at Martinsville and Columbia. Then came disaster in North Carolina. Shaped like a mile-long paper clip, with mildly banked corners at either end, Raleigh Speedway was one of only two paved tracks on the

RACING

Grand National circuit in 1953. (Darlington was the other.) More than 15,000 fans turned out for the races over the Memorial Day weekend. The headline event was scheduled for 300 miles, which took more than four hours back in those days. That gave Jocko plenty of time to get loose, and that's exactly what he did while Tim was chasing Fonty for the lead.

Tim had cut a trap door in the floorboard so that he could check how badly the right front tire was wearing between pit stops. During the previous seven races, Jocko had seen Flock pull periodically on the chain to open the flap. Naturally, now that he was free, he aped his owner and yanked the chain. When the door swung open, a rock flew through the floorboard and whacked him right between the eyes. Stunned by the blow, the monkey went berserk, shrieking at the top of his little lungs and scampering around the cockpit. Flock was maxing out close to 100 mph on the straights, and he nearly lost control when Jocko attacked him.

"Tim wanted to kill that monkey," says West Coast stock car ace Hershel McGriff, who was making a rare Grand National appearance at Raleigh. "It was running around the bench seat of that Hudson and climbing all over the steering wheel." Dick Passwater, who'd won the race at Charlotte where Jocko had made his debut, got an even closer look at the shenanigans. "I was behind Tim when old Jocko got loose, and I could see the monkey running around like crazy. That monkey was wild! At one point, he jumped on Tim's back, and it looked like old Jocko was going to choke him."

Like most racers, Flock was used to performing with grace under pressure. But this was more than he'd bargained for. "Listen, it was hard enough to drive those heavy old cars back then under normal circumstances," Flock said later, "but with a crazed monkey clawing you at the same time, it becomes nearly impossible! So I reached up with my left hand—kept my eyes on the race—and got him by the neck and slowed down coming through the fourth turn and went down pit road and held him out and gave him to the mechanic. It was the only time I know of in NASCAR that an official pit stop was for a monkey being put out of the car. That pit stop cost me 2nd place and a $600 difference in my paycheck. Jocko was retired immediately. I had to get that monkey off my back!"

This was not only Jocko's last race but also his final public appearance. In later years, fans never tired of asking Flock about his co-driver. Flock had a stock answer, delivered with a mischievous grin: "I couldn't teach him to sign his autograph, so I had to fire him!" According to Flock, Jocko retired to a life of leisure with the rest of the Flock family.

This, as it turns out, is the only part of the Jocko Flock legend that wasn't true. Flock's vivacious widow, Frances, explains that the monkey must've suffered some sort of brain damage from being clobbered in the head. "He was never the same after that," she recalls. "He was listless, and he wouldn't eat. They took him to a veterinary hospital, and the vet advised them to put him down." Which is exactly what happened.

So add Jocko Flocko to the long list of drivers who died as a result of injuries suffered while racing. But not before he secured a little piece of immortality while winning at Hickory in 1953.

VERDICT: Absolutely true. *–Preston Lerner*

MODERN CYCLE

Vol. 1, No. 5   Oct.

A 75c

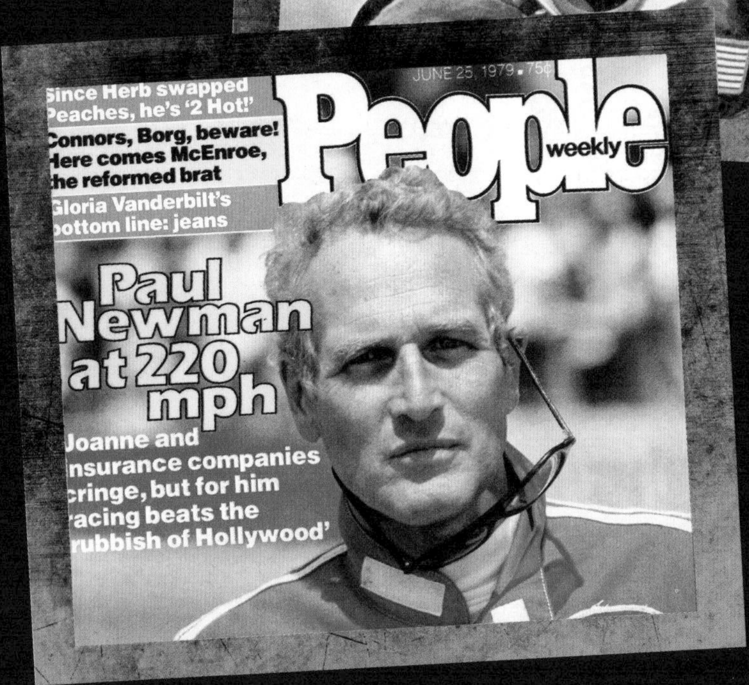

JUNE 25, 1979 · 75¢

People weekly

Since Herb swapped
Peaches, he's '2 Hot!'
Connors, Borg, beware!
Here comes McEnroe,
the reformed brat
Gloria Vanderbilt's
bottom line: jeans

Paul
Newman
at 220
mph

Joanne and
insurance companies
cringe, but for him
'racing beats the
rubbish of Hollywood'

4
HOLLYWOOD

YOU DRIVE LIKE
STEVE MCQUEEN

LEGEND: Steve McQueen drove all of his own stunts in the 1968 film *Bullitt*

In the eyes of many film fans, the chase scene from the 1968 movie *Bullitt* was, is, and remains the best ever filmed. There have been some valiant challengers: the late John Frankenheimer's heart-pounding work through the streets of Paris in *Ronin*; making Minis fly in *The Italian Job* (the original and remake); and the *Seven-Ups*, which involved some of the same folks who worked on *Bullitt*. And let's not forget some great action driving sequences several of the Jason Bourne movies.

But when the lists are made and the bets are laid down, *Bullitt* comes out on top. Every time. In spite of a few charming continuity goofs and cameras occasionally visible in the back seat of Lieutenant Frank Bullitt's tire-smoking Mustang fastback, the scene was lauded for its authenticity and realism at the time. So much so that is garnered an Oscar win for film editing. See it on a big screen today, and the views out the windshield as the Mustang and bad guys' Dodge Charger careen down San Francisco's Taylor Street will still make your stomach roll.

McQueen plays Frank Bullitt, a grizzled veteran investigator with the San Francisco P.D. His girlfriend is a young, nubile Jacqueline Bisset, and the reptilian politico villain is played by Robert Vaughn at his handsome and snarky best. I visited San Francisco, and drove most of the chase scene route, in preparation for an article for *Motor Trend Classic* magazine.

From its earliest iterations, the script called for an "automotive action scene"; this was likely one of the reasons McQueen and his Solar Productions were involved in the first place. This actor/producer insisted on absolute realism, with no camera speedups, and of course this was long before the notion of computer-generated animation. The rest of the plot is inconsequential to this exercise.

Ford was the official car provider for the movie, the main four-wheeled characters being two 1968 Mustang GT 390s, painted that now famous shade of Highland Green Metallic. The cars carried back-to-back serial numbers, and although rumors persist that one was really a 302-powered car and one had an automatic trans, hard-core Bullitteers have vetted the build codes and confirm both were 325-horse, big-block, four-speed models.

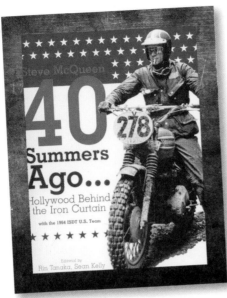

McQueen was on the team that represented the United States at the 1964 International Six Day Trials off-road motorcycle enduro in Europe. He was a more-than-accomplished rider and racer, preferring off-road and desert racing to road-racing on two wheels. A freak crash damaged his bike beyond repair, taking him out of the competition. Collection of Matt Stone

Dave Kunz's credible Bullitt Mustang tribute faces the wrong way on San Francisco's Larkin Street; in the film's famous chase scene, the cars head down this curvy street with its unobstructed view of Alcatraz. Matt Stone

It's all downhill from here. Dave Kunz's handsome Bullitt Mustang tribute 1968 GT 390 fastback, taking the same path used in the movie's iconic chase scene. Note Kunz's replicated license plate, which matches that of Bullitt's car in the movie. Matt Stone

Ford's publicity shot of Kunz's Mustang replicates the nose-up attitude of Bullitt's car as he chased the bad guys' black Dodge Charger up and down the streets of San Francisco.
This photo was taken and used in the launch of the 2001 Ford Bullitt Edition Mustang. Ford publicity photo

One of the most engaging scenes in Bullitt is when McQueen enters the little liquor store/market across from Bullitt's apartment and buys a handful of frozen TV dinners, then steals a newspaper. The market is still in business, and proudly displays photos of McQueen on the wall. The proprietor says that many fans visit and fondly remember McQueen and the scene. Matt Stone

Race car driver and constructor legend Max Balchowsky (of *Old Yeller* fame) was called upon to modify the cars for heavier-than-routine duty. Suspensions were beefed up, as were their pickup points. Koni adjustable shocks were installed, along with numerous camera mounts. The stock exhaust systems retained their small glasspack mufflers but lost the rear-mounted transverse muffler in favor of straight pipes out the back, all the better to hear the thumping 390s. Stories vary as to the level of engine mods. The Mustangs had manual steering and no air-conditioning.

Equally important is what's not there. All the badging was removed, and various chrome pieces were painted black or body color. All the chrome pieces from the grille were binned. The stock wheels were

McQueen's other automotive magnum opus in addition to *Bullitt* is his epic motorsport drama, 1971's *Le Mans*. With his steely glare intact, and his blondish locks looking just a bit shaggy in proper 1970s style, McQueen never looked better. In this film, he insisted on the same realistic cinematography that he did in *Bullitt*. McQueen drove all of his own action photography in this film—no stand-ins need apply—and was ably coached by several professional drivers. Collection of Matt Stone

swapped for 15-inch American Racing Torq-Thrust D mags. McQueen had the stock, none-too-pretty steering wheel replaced with a 1967 Shelby piece, which Tony Nancy wrapped in leather for him. The radio antenna was moved to make room for camera mounts. The look was menacing to say the least.

The villains' famously black 1968 Dodge Charger, as manhandled about by actor/stunt driver Bill Hickman, is an equally integral plot element. Two matching Chargers R/Ts were employed, equipped with 375-horsepower, single four-barrel 440-cubic-inch Magnum V-8s and four-speed transmissions (it's possible one may have had an automatic). Although they were R/T models, the movie Chargers ran more conservative hubcap and whitewall rolling-stock combos. That's an important point because, if they'd had Magnum 500 or alloy wheels, they wouldn't have been able to toss away all those hubcaps (at least five) during the chase scene. There's no question the Charger's large, flat body panels, hideaway headlights, and black grille and paint job helped further the ominous bad-guy look.

The 10-minute-or-so chase sequence was filmed during May 1968. The crew for any given scene numbered 50 to 60, including the actors, stuntmen, and drivers, plus camera, sound, and communications people. Because of some clever editing, the scene flows seamlessly from location to location. Contrary to popular belief, however, the various locales are disjointed, and the chase route cannot be driven as it takes place in the film.

Steve shows off his terrific physique and two-wheeled riding skills on one of his many dirt bikes.
Collection of Matt Stone

There's always been a bit of speculation as to how much of the wheel work McQueen performed. "Steve originally intended to do all his own stunt driving," recalled the late Bud Ekins, McQueen's longtime friend, motorcycle muse, racing teammate, and stunt double. This is the same Ekins that, six years earlier, worked with McQueen on the motorcycle scenes and stunts in *The Great Escape*. "A friend of mine named Cary Loftin was the stunt coordinator on *Bullitt*. He wanted me to come up to San Francisco and be one of the stunt men."

"Steve started the chase scene [in the Mustang] behind Bill Hickman [in the Charger]" Ekins continued. "Hickman was a real dingbat, but man could he drive. Steve tried to follow him, and the second turn he went around, he lost it and spun out, and damn near hit a camera. Cary said 'get him out of the car' and said to me 'Ekins, get in the clothes.' Next thing I know, I'm at the top of this big hill, following Hickman, jumping down the hills, flying through the air. Any time Hickman was in front of me, I could see the entire undercarriage of his car. If he lost it, I'd have had him. It would have been a bad wreck. But it all worked out. Steve never had any problem with being taken out of the car."

"He also said, 'You've done it to me again. Everybody thought I did that jump in *The Great Escape*,' and on one of those nighttime talk shows he had to admit that I [Ekins] did it. 'And now,' he said, 'whenever someone thinks I was jumping that Mustang down the streets of San Francisco,

Steve was featured on the cover of *Modern Cycle* magazine, wearing his ISDT racing suit. Note the American flag; each team represented its country.
Collection of Matt Stone

McQueen, a blue turtleneck, a tweed blazer, and a Highland Green '68 Mustang GT fastback: it could only be Bullitt. All that's missing from this shot are his Persol shades. McQueen was at his icy cool best during this era and considered by many to be the world's most popular actor.
Collection of Matt Stone

and the next talk show I go on, I'm going to have to say, "Well, no I didn't do all of it."' Steve didn't do the most difficult stunt driving in the movie, although he drove it a lot of the time. Any time that you can't see his face very plainly, it's me. They'd cut back and forth between him at the wheel and me; you see a lot of the back of my head."

The Mustang in these photographs isn't, unfortunately, one of the original cars used in the filming. The genuine, remaining Bullitt Mustang is an automotive Holy Grail, equaled in significance only by the modified Aston Martin DB5s used by James Bond in *Goldfinger*. One of the

Mustangs was so badly damaged during filming it was judged unrepairable and scrapped. The second, chassis 8R02S12559, was sold to a Warner Brothers employee after filming was completed. He elected to sell it a few years later and advertised it in 1974 in *Road & Track* magazine. There may have been another owner or two in between, but its current owner has remained anonymous since then, and the rumor is that the car lives in a dog- and shotgun- guarded shed or barn, somewhere in the deep South.

Over time, other film producers, countless Mustang fans and car collectors, and even McQueen tried to purchase it—all so far unsuccessfully. When last seen, it showed about 66,000 miles on the odometer and had suffered minor front end accident damage. The paint was faded and chalked, but the welded-in camera mounts were intact, and numerous holes that were drilled to accommodate other filming and lighting equipment are confirmed present.

As the original was not to be had, a suitable facsimile stood in during my trip to San Francisco. Dave Kunz is a consummate car enthusiast and Mustang lover. He bought his Highland Green 1968 Mustang GT 390 in November 1992. "It was bone stock, in clean condition, and even though it was the same model and color as the *Bullitt* movie cars, I had no initial intention of building a replica. A few things in my garage tumbled onto it during the 1994 Northridge earthquake, gouging the paint. My insurance company paid to have it stripped and redone. I visited the paint shop

Cinema Retro magazine celebrated cult movies and TV of the 1960s and 1970s. This street scene from the filming of *Bullitt* was a perfect fit and shows off the elevation of some of the San Francisco streets used to such good effect in the filming of *Bullitt*'s famous car chase scene. Collection of Matt Stone

before the white C-stripes and some of the chrome trim was reinstalled. Something clicked, and before I knew it, I was looking at *Bullitt* movie photos trying to figure out the rest of the details."

Kunz's Mustang is a faithful, but not exact, replica. Kunz doesn't go out of his way to market or promote the car as any kind of "official" replica, but he's friendly with Ford, which has used the car a number of times in that capacity. It appeared in a TV commercial filmed for the launch of the Ford Puma and also in Sheryl Crow's music video for her song "Steve McQueen." Ford used the car during its launch of the 2001 Bullitt Mustang, and it's been autographed by Sheryl Crow and Chad McQueen.

There was no Transamerica building on the San Francisco skyline when *Bullitt* was filmed in 1968. The hotel where Frank Bullitt attempts to protect a witness was destroyed in the Loma Prieta earthquake in 1989. What's called the Thunderbolt Motel in the film is a Clarion today. But an amazing number of the iconic locations in the movie appear much as they did then, even after nearly 40 years.

In a 1968 *Motor Trend* interview, McQueen said, "I always felt a motor racing sequence in the street, a chase in the street, could be very exciting because you have the reality objects to work with, like bouncing off a parked car. An audience digs sitting there watching somebody do something that I'm sure almost all of them would like to do."

Ekins acknowledged that McQueen was absolutely capable of great stunt driving, and he proved it by doing all the wheel work for the action scenes in the original *Thomas Crown Affair*, which he filmed the same year as *Bullitt*. Ekins recalled that "Steve was very good physically. He moved well, was very competitive, and had a good internal gyro. Remember he was a black-belt martial artist, and was really good on his feet. In one movie, he did all his own work in the filming of an aggressive knife fight; it looked almost like ballet, he was so swift and smooth. And remember by this time, Steve had driven in a number of motor races, and ridden with great success in several important motorcycle races. If you want to see how good he was on a bike, watch *On Any Sunday*." McQueen oversaw the construction of the Corvair-powered dune buggy seen terrorizing the beach (and costar Faye Dunaway) and drove all the stunts for that film. Dunaway hung on for dear life, her high heels digging into the buggy's fiberglass floor, and McQueen acknowledged her as being a "real good sport through all of it."

VERDICT: False.
Though McQueen gave it a shot. –*Matt Stone*

PAUL NEWMAN WAS JUST A POSEUR ON THE RACETRACK

LEGEND: Paul Newman's prowess in a race car was a fairy tale spun by inventive press agents.

Hype wasn't invented by Hollywood. But few industries boast a more effective myth-making machine than the motion picture business. That's why so many "news" stories about movie stars are as accurate as movies that are supposedly based on true stories. Who honestly believes the uplifting profile of the troubled actor who's left rehab behind for good or the perky feature about the oft-married actress who's taking "until death do us part" seriously this time around? So it's easy to understand why a lot of racing fans rolled their eyes when they heard repeated media reports that Paul Newman was a top-tier racing driver who could have been a world-class professional if he hadn't, you know, been a world-famous movie star. Yeah, right. At the time, the guy was already pushing 60, and he hadn't been a spring chicken when he got started in the sport.

To be sure, there were plenty of things about Newman that were hard to believe, starting with the unnaturally blue eyes that captivated filmgoers for half a century. He was improbably handsome, yet rather than skating on his looks, he honed his craft until he was one of the finest actors of his generation. In a culture where serial divorce was the norm, he enjoyed a notably robust marriage to an actress—Joanne Woodward—who was every bit as talented and attractive as he was. In addition to winning countless awards for acting, he was one of the country's most committed philanthropists, creating a camp (The Hole in the Wall Gang Camp) for terminally ill children and founding a multimillion-dollar food-service company (Newman's Own) to fund charitable and environmental causes. All this, and he could also race wheel-to-wheel with give-no-quarter pros such as Willy T. Ribbs, Wally Dallenbach Jr., and Dorsey Schroeder? Give me a break.

Although Paul Leonard Newman, a.k.a. PLN, didn't run his first real race until he was 47, he was a car guy as a kid growing up in suburban Cleveland. His first car was a 1929 Model A Ford. His second was a 1937 Packard. After moving to New York City to chase the acting dream, he bought a Volkswagen Beetle that was progressively modified—first with a

Newman on the grid in his trusty Bob Sharp–built, –prepped, and –maintained Datsun 510. Newman won many races in this fast, reliable Japanese compact before stepping up into bigger cars in higher level series.
Joe Cali

In his day, the always-photogenic Paul Newman was as popular on magazine covers as Brad Pitt is today. Newman raced in spite of the occasional objections of his wife and the incessant objections of his agents and producers. It was something he felt good doing and was most capable at, so he proceeded undaunted.
Collection of Matt Stone

Newman and Sharp wanted to step up to the top prototype IMSA classes, but they were committed to Nissan, which didn't compete in those classes, so they built this wide-bodied, twin turbo V-8-powered GTX racer. The car was wicked fast, but proved unreliable and never won a race in 1981. Collection of Matt Stone

stock Porsche engine and then a Super 90 with a hot cam—as his career blossomed. Even after becoming a box-office sensation, he preferred sleepers to flamboyant Ferraris or extravagant Rolls-Royces. One of his favorite cars was a Bug retrofitted with a 351-cubic-inch Ford V-8 and a Hewland five-speed transaxle. "That Volks was really wacky," he said approvingly. Later, he owned a series of sedate-looking Volvo station wagons customized with a turbocharged V-6 out of a Buick Grand National, a supercharged Ford V-8, and fastest of all, a 6.0-liter LS2 from a 2005 Corvette. This was the car, in fact, that gave him his last ride around his "home" racetrack, Lime Rock Park, six weeks before his death in 2008 at the age of 83.

Like most car guys, Newman had a need for speed. In 1965, he got his baptism by fire at Willow Springs International Raceway, a crude but challenging club track about 90 miles north of Los Angeles. He did some laps in his hot-rodded VW and tested in an Elva Formula Junior before the suspension collapsed after a spin in the diabolical Turn 9. Three years later, Newman was driving a McKee Can-Am car, a NASCAR Grand National racer, and even an Eagle Indy car. But this was just acting rather than racing, part of the filming for the movie *Winning*. Still, Newman had to learn how to drive the cars at a reasonable pace, so he and costar Robert Wagner became the fourth and fifth students in the race driving school that had just been opened by Bob Bondurant. Newman was better than Wagner, and Bondurant described his driving as "very smooth." But he didn't light the world on fire. And the experience didn't light a fire under him.

Fast-forward to 1971. Newman took his son, Scott, to nearby Lime Rock Park, a natural-terrain road course in a lovely pastoral setting not far from their home in Westport, Connecticut. There, they got thrill rides from a local hot-shoe, Bob Sharp. Besides owning a nearby Datsun dealership, Sharp was the pre-eminent Datsun road racer on the East Coast in Sports Car Club of America club racing—that is, amateur—competition. Sharp was about to start building new Datsuns for SCCA B Sedan and C Production races. After talking things over, Sharp agreed to build a Datsun 510 for Newman to run in SCCA regionals.

Newman could have used his money or influence to leverage a ride in a much faster car in a much sexier series than club races attended almost solely by family and very accommodating friends. But despite all the time he spent in the public eye, Newman preferred to learn his race-craft in relative obscurity, where he could be just one of the guys rather than the perpetual center of attention. In baseball terms, regional racing was a quantum leap up from beer-and-pretzel softball leagues. But it was very much the low minors of the road racing world. SCCA national races, which culminated in the year-end championships known as the Runoffs, were the high minors. And the major leagues, of course, was professional

CHAPTER 4

152

By the end of the 1979 sports car racing season, Newman had pretty much been there and won that, so sponsor Budweiser dedicated this advertisement to his accomplishments. By this time he'd competed at Le Mans, won numerous sports car racing titles, and was well on his way to becoming a successful Indy car team owner. Collection of Matt Stone

Folgers was also an associate sponsor of Newman's racing efforts; they photographed this advertisement at the Nelson Ledges Race Course in 1980. Collection of Matt Stone

Newman drove this Datsun 300ZX Turbo in the SCCA TransAm race at Riverside International Raceway in 1984. He started 6th and finished 20th on this October day. He ended his TransAm racing career with two wins and three poles. Matt Stone photo

PAUL NEWMAN -- NEWMAN-SHARP RACING NISSAN 300ZX TURBO

Newman also enjoyed considerable success in IMSA's GTO category, running this 300ZX Turbo in 1984.
Nissan publicity photo

By the mid 2000s, Newman's face carried the deepset lines of age and experience, but he was still a formidable competitor. Here he suits up and prepares to hop in the cockpit at the 2005 running of the Rolex 24 Hours of Daytona. Ford publicity photo

racing, though even here there was a hierarchy topped by series such as Formula 1 and Indy cars, which were light years away from the racing Newman would be doing.

From the start, Newman was competent on the track, but he didn't show much speed. "He was so slow that I thought he'd never make it," says Sam Posey, who saw him practicing at Lime Rock. "I thought he'd do it for a few more days, and that would be it." To use the internal parlance of the Skip Barber Racing School, which was based at Lime Rock, Newman looked like typical OSB material—meaning "other sports beckoned." But Newman didn't quit, and he made a believer out of Posey. "He proved me completely wrong," Posey says. "Exactly how he did it is a big mystery. One way to look at it is that he *acted* his way into being a racing driver. He used his powers of concentration and his image of himself succeeding, and he played it like a role."

Having Sharp's top-shelf organization behind him obviously helped, but there's no question that Newman raised his game as he got more seat

Newman's mount for the 2005 Rolex 24 was this Ford-powered Daytona prototype racer; he was teamed with his Indy car team drivers Cristiano da Matta and Sebastien Bourdais. Ford publicity photo

time. He finally won his first regional race in 1973 and finished midpack in the Runoffs. In 1975, running under the banner of PLN Racing, he won a regional title and was fifth in the Runoffs. The next year, he won the SCCA D Production national championship in a Triumph TR6 after his friend Jim Fitzgerald's car broke while leading. Being a perfectionist, Newman wasn't thrilled by the victory. "I inherited the win there," he said. Three years later, reunited with Sharp and rededicated to racing, he went flag to flag and set fast lap en route to winning the C Production title. At 54, Paul Newman, the racer, had come of age.

"I don't know anybody who had his ability to concentrate, and I think the acting contributed to that," Sharp says. "His first year was a struggle. He wasn't naturally fast. But he had a sensitive touch and was very easy on equipment. Even in the beginning, when he wasn't the fastest guy out there, he was always clean and disciplined. He improved very logically, systematically, and as he got more and more races under his belt, he got better and better and better, like a fine wine. It was unbelievable. He became a very, very good professional driver."

In 1979, Newman made his only foray racing overseas, but it was a good one. With team owner Dick Barbour and German ace Rolf Stommelen, he finished a fighting second overall, and first in class, at Le

Even though the twin Turbo ZX prototype built for Newman's 1981 IMSA season wasn't successful, he could have asked for no finer support group than team owner Bob Sharp (Kneeling, speaking with Newman) and seasoned veteran Sam Posey. Nissan publicity photo

Newman's own PLN Racing team won it all at the 1976 SCCA Runoffs, giving Newman his first national title as a driver and team owner. His compact yet fast Triumph TR-6 barely carries the weight of his entire team. Wife Joanne Woodward is next to him in the cockpit, wearing glasses, and you can just see her waving out of the car. It was the first of Newman's four SCCA National level championships. Bill Warner

Mans. Driving a hairy-chested Porsche 935 in the rain whetted his appetite for more high-horsepower cars. He spent much of the early and mid-1980s campaigning twin-turbo Datsun (soon to be Nissan) ZXs, not only in club races but also in IMSA competition and, later, Trans-Am.

This was a major step up for Newman. Trans-Am was SCCA's premier professional series, with a storied history dating back to the fierce pony car wars of the mid-'60s. His first serious outing was at Brainerd International Raceway in Minnesota in 1982. He qualified a mediocre seventh. But on a slick track, he rocketed immediately into the lead and never looked back. He led every lap and beat future Trans-Am champion Tom Gloy to the flag by 4.5 seconds. When he arrived at the pressroom with a bottle of champagne, he was crestfallen to find it virtually deserted. "Where is everybody?" he asked. "I guess I'll have to win something a little bigger than this to get any attention."

If nothing else, he got the attention of his fellow pros. "He was fast," says 1982 Trans-Am champ Elliott Forbes-Robinson. "He didn't make very many mistakes. He was a guy you could run close to. He raced hard, but he was always predictable, and he was always fair. He was a guy you had to beat. He wasn't a club racer who was out of his element. He was a good, fast, competent professional driver." Adds 1983 Trans-Am champ David Hobbs, "I'd thought he was just a gentleman driver. [But] by the 1980s, he was unbelievably quick, and he was damn near 60! I'm convinced that he if had started racing when he was 18, he would have been right up there with the best of them."

During the mid-'80s, he earned back-to-back GT-1 championships with majestic drives at the Runoffs—pole, fast lap, flag-to-flag victories. In Trans-Am, he racked up several poles but precious few podiums until

CHAPTER 4

the 1986 race at Lime Rock. Early leader Wally Dallenbach Jr. broke. Then midrace leaders Pete Halsmer and Jim Miller crashed. At two-thirds distance, Newman forced his way past Forbes-Robinson and held him off for the final 20 laps to win by three-tenths of a second. Also finishing behind him were the Jack Roush Mercurys of Scott Pruett and Chris Kneifel, who were no slouches. From a driving standpoint, this was the pinnacle of Newman's career in motorsports. As he put it himself in his characteristically modest fashion: "I was never a great driver—I started racing when I was 47 years old—but I got to be pretty good. I was a pretty good driver for about five years."

PLN's last hurrah on a big stage came in 1995, when he, Tommy Kendall, Mark Martin, and Newman's friend Michael Brockman finished first in class—and a remarkable third overall—in a Roush Mustang at the Rolex 24 at Daytona. By then, he was 70. "It ain't bad for an elderly gentleman," Newman said at the victory celebration. When somebody asked him if he was pleased with his performance, he quipped, "I'm just pleased to have a pulse."

In many respects, Newman cast a much smaller shadow over the racing world as a driver than he did as a team owner. He had a race-winning Can-Am team for five years. Then, in 1983, he joined forces with Lola importer Carl Haas to form Newman/Haas Racing, which won 107 Indy car races and 8 Indy car champions with Mario and Michael Andretti, Nigel Mansell, Cristiano da Matta, and Sebastien Bourdais. But even after his own driving skills started to decline, Newman continued to race—not for the glory, and certainly not for the money, but because he loved the camaraderie in the paddock and he never lost his passion for driving on the limit. "I'm not a very graceful person," he once explained. "I was a sloppy skier, a sloppy tennis player, a sloppy football player, and a sloppy dancer with anyone other than Joanne. The only thing I found grace in was racing a car."

Newman ran his last club race in a GT-1 car at his beloved Lime Rock in 2007, almost exactly a year before his death. He started second, bulled his way to the lead in the esses, and beat his old bud Michael Brockman by less than a car-length. A whole lot of bogus stories have come out of Hollywood over the years. But as the old racing adage goes, when the green flag drops, the bullshit stops, and Paul Newman was proof positive.

VERDICT: Indisputably false.
Paul Newman really was Cool Hand Luke behind the wheel of a race car. –Preston Lerner

JAMES BOND'S HIGH-FLYING HORNET

LEGEND: A humble AMC hatchback played the starring role in one of the most daring and dazzling stunts ever to appear in a James Bond film.

When one thinks of James Bond and cars, it's usually an Aston Martin, Bentley, or BMW that comes to mind. Not so in 1974's *The Man with the Golden Gun*, which starred Roger Moore as Agent 007, Christopher Lee, Britt Ekland, and Maud Adams—and a mildly customized '73 AMC Hornet hatchback. Unlike the Aston Martin DB5 that Bond drove in *Goldfinger* and *Thunderball* the Hornet's modifications were strictly cosmetic—with not a machine gun or ejector seat in sight. The classic muscle car era was pretty much over by 1973, yet the Hornet was a relatively light car and even running its stock 360-cubic inch, two-barrel-carburetor-equipped V-8, it was a mildly spirited performer.

American Motors was the vehicle provider for *Gun*, which featured not only the red Crager SS wheel–equipped Hornet, but a larger and more luxurious Matador coupe for bad guy Scaramanga. In more typical Bond style, the Matador could be equipped with detachable wings and an airplane engine and propeller, turning into Scaramanga's flying getaway car.

The plotline was that Bond needs to chase Scaramanga while gallivanting through Bangkok and runs into an AMC showroom, making off with the bright red/orange Hornet. As a humorous nod to *Live and Let Die*, the previous year's Bond flick, J. W. Pepper (a hapless bungling Southern Sherriff, beautifully played by character actor Clifton James) was sitting inside the car when Bond made off with it via a glorious, glass-shattering exit through the dealership's large plate glass windows. This oddly matched crime-fighting duo takes off in pursuit of Scaramanga, and, find themselves running parallel to a river. They and Scaramanga are running in the same direction, the only problem being that they are on opposite sides of a river. Bond misses the bridge to cross the river, but later sees the remains of a long, washed-out, now sunken bridge. Bond aims the car at the remains of the bridge, which launches the car into the air at an angle, heading toward the opposite side. The car performs a perfect, 360-degree barrel roll in midair, landing safely on its wheels on the other side and continuing to give chase.

How did they do it? In a studio, against a green screen? With a gutted, unmanned car on the Pinewood Studios back lot? By computer-generated animation? No, none of the above.

Without movie magic, most American Motors products of the early 1970s tended to remain earth bound, although the elevation achieved by this display Hornet seems to impress the young onlooker. AFP/Getty Images

Stunt coordinator W. J. Mulligan worked with the producers to come up with something even more fabulous than when Bond drove a Mustang down an alleyway in *Diamonds are Forever*. Mulligan named this amazing barrel roll stunt the Astro Spiral Jump, which describes it perfectly. There was no computer-generated imagery involved, but the stunt team did spend a considerable amount of time modeling the stunt on Cornell University computers (remember, there were no home "personal" computers in the early 1970s). Only the government and higher learning institutions had computers powerful enough to process all the data required for this type of undertaking.

Even though the Hornet appeared stock from the outside, it was in fact specially built for the job. Nonessential equipment was stripped out of the car to reduce overall vehicle weight, and the driver's seat, steering column, and other essential controls were moved to the middle of the car to give it equal side-to-side balance.

Veteran stuntman Loren "Bumps" Willard was identified as the man who would take the wheel for this most unlikely of jump stunts. Willard was somewhat used to this type of work, being an original member of a troop of car stunt specialists called "helldrivers." The computer analysis told Willard how fast he needed to be traveling as he hit the launch ramp, and in June 1974, Bumps pointed the modified Hornet toward the twisted, angled launch pad, accelerated to a speed of approximately 40 mph, and nailed the looping spiral jump in one take with absolute perfection. Naturally, medical personnel, divers, and a crane were on hand in case Willard missed the mark, but none of those measures were needed. The cameras caught the action, and the champagne flowed.

"Oh, James...."

VERDICT:
True. Considering the relatively undeveloped state of computer analysis in those days—and all that could go wrong—it is somewhat amazing that this stunt was pulled off on the first try with no misses or mishaps. It was a historic combination of knowledge, instinct, technology, planning—and very good luck. –Matt Stone

HOLLYWOOD

THE GREATER
LOS ANGELES
SAFETY COUNCIL
Presents
JAMES DEAN'S
LAST
SPORTS CAR.

THIS ACCIDENT COULD
HAVE BEEN AVOIDED...

⑤ DEATH

DEATH COMES FOR THE BISHOP

LEGEND: Mike Hawthorn caused the wreck at the 24 Hours of Le Mans in 1955 that killed more than 80 people in the worst racing catastrophe in history.

Death has always been racing's bedfellow. In the sport's formative years, the ability to defy death—most of the time—was part of racing's essential appeal. Nowadays, thanks to a century of safety improvements, death is the exception rather than the rule. But just when we complacently convinced ourselves that all of the danger has been legislated out of racing, reigning Indy 500 champion Dan Wheldon died in a fiery multicar wreck at Las Vegas, and we remembered the line attributed (mistakenly) to Hemingway: Automobile racing, bull fighting, and mountain climbing are the only real sports. All the rest are just games.

Thousands of drivers have been killed since the first automobile race—from Paris to Bordeaux and back to Paris again in 1895—and each one of these incidents has been a tragedy. But drivers understand the risks when they climb into their cockpits, so our tears are tempered by the realization that they died knowing the dangers they faced. Not so the fans who attend races. When even one of them is killed, it's not merely a tragedy; it's a catastrophe whose effects linger long after the checkered flag flies. Think of the carnage during the calamitous Paris-Madrid race of 1903, where two spectators died (along with three drivers and three riding mechanics) and more than a dozen were injured, causing such an outcry that organizers started creating purpose-built tracks to get racing off public roads. Or Fon de Portago's crash near the Italian village of Cavriana in 1957, killing himself, his co-driver, and nine onlookers, and just as surely killing off the Mille Miglia at the same time. Or the ghastly funny car wreck at Yellow River Dragstrip in Georgia in 1969, where the death of 12 spectators led to the end of big-time drag racing on unsanctioned tracks without guardrails or insurance. There are numerous unwritten rules in racing. But one of the most important, certainly, is "Don't kill the paying customers."

The worst accident in racing history, by several orders of magnitude, occurred on June 11, 1955, during the 24 Hours of Le Mans. Then as now, the race was—along with the Indy 500 and Monaco Grand Prix—one of the crown jewels of motorsports. In 1955, it was contested by factory teams from Mercedes-Benz, Jaguar, Ferrari, Maserati, Aston Martin, and

Known as "The Bishop," Pierre Levegh was 49 when he was tabbed by Mercedes-Benz to drive its new 300SLR at Le Mans in 1955. Three years earlier, he'd nearly beaten the then new 300SLs after a heroic but ill-starred single-handed drive. *Mercedes-Benz Classic*

numerous smaller manufacturers, and 300,000 spectators thronged to the circuit. As always, the race produced a carnival atmosphere. There was, in fact, an amusement park inside the track, and fair-weather fans could occupy themselves gazing at freak show attractions and swilling cheap wine without ever so much as glimpsing a race car. But most people's attention was riveted on the drama unfolding on the track. There, on the 8.4-mile circuit created by linking together two-lane highways around the ancient French town of Le Mans, a titanic battle was unfolding between Grand Prix stars Juan Manuel Fangio and Mike Hawthorn.

For more than two hours, Hawthorn's D-type Jaguar and Fangio's Mercedes-Benz 300SLR had swapped the lead at speeds exceeding 180 mph. Their pace was unprecedented—some said foolhardy; they'd already lowered the lap record by 10 seconds, and there were still more than 21 hours to go. During an era when cars were much more fragile than they are today, drivers customarily kept something in reserve at Le Mans. But both Fangio and Hawthorn had been flat-out from the start. Onlookers couldn't help but be reminded of their titanic dice in the French Grand Prix at nearby Reims two years earlier, when the 24-year-old Hawthorn had nipped Fangio at the checkered flag to become the first British driver to win a Formula 1 World Championship event. On an eerier level, the battle between the British thoroughbred and the Teutonic brute reprised the war that had been waged so disastrously on this very ground less than a generation ago.

In mid-June, it doesn't get completely dark at Le Mans until nearly 11 p.m., but the heat had dissipated and the wind had dropped to create a glorious summer evening. At about 6:24 p.m., Eugenio Castellotti, running a distant third in his Ferrari, eased into the pits. On the track, Hawthorn led

Fangio by a few hundred yards as they exited Tertre Rouge and pounded down the Mulsanne Straight for the 35th time. Hawthorn applied the Jaguar's disc brakes—the finest in racing—while Fangio deployed the Mercedes' imaginative air brake to bleed off speed for the Mulsanne Hairpin. On the high-speed run to Arnage, Hawthorn blew past a second Mercedes-Benz driven by Karl Kling, who was struggling with throttle problems. At Maison Blanche, the last corner on the circuit, Hawthorn slipped past the third SLR, this one driven by Pierre Levegh. At this point, Hawthorn had lapped everybody except for Fangio. But now it was time for him to stop in the pits to refuel and hand over to co-driver Ivor Bueb.

At the kink leading onto the front straight, Hawthorn motored past the Austin-Healey 100S of British playboy Lance Macklin. Although Macklin was a gifted and experienced driver, his car was much, much slower than the Jag; at the moment, he was being lapped for the fifth time. Hawthorn drifted to the right edge of the road, directly in front of the Austin-Healey, and braked as he approached the pits. Macklin, evidently surprised by Hawthorn's move, locked up his brakes in a desperate effort to slow down. When he realized he couldn't avoid rear-ending the Jaguar, he swerved to the left and nearly spun. As he struggled to regain control, the Austin-Healey slid across the dotted line marking the center of what was normally a two-lane highway. This put Macklin's car directly in the path of Levegh's Mercedes, which was hurtling toward the Austin-Healey at 155 mph.

It was 6:27 p.m., and there was nothing anybody could do to turn back the clock.

The Mercedes ran up the left rear quarter of the Austin-Healey. The sloping rear deck of the 100S proved to be a calamitously well-designed launching pad. The SLR soared into the air like a jet fighter being catapulted off an aircraft carrier. It flew up about 20 feet, nearly going vertical as it vaulted over an earthen embankment. As it came down in the spectator enclosure, it decapitated 14 people before crashing into the concrete wall of the tunnel leading under the track. Besides hurling Levegh to his death, the ferocity of the impact caused the Mercedes to disintegrate. The engine, exhaust manifold, and front axle, with the wheels still attached, scythed through the tightly massed crowd like three implacable and insatiable angels of death. There was an explosion as the gas tank erupted, and the lightweight magnesium body of the Mercedes burned with hideous intensity directly in front of the main grandstands while the rescue efforts continued.

As the Mercedes careened through the crowd, Macklin's Austin-Healey spun through the pits. Back then, this wasn't a discrete area separated by a wall but simply an unprotected section of track on the far right side of the road. His car clipped a policeman and a marshal as it slammed

Levegh looks relaxed as he bends his Mercedes into the Arnage corner on the Circuit de la Sarthe at Le Mans. Although the 300SLR lacked the aerodynamic efficiency and disc brakes of the D-type Jaguar, it was a robust marvel of exotic Teutonic engineering. Mercedes-Benz Classic

against the pit counter. Macklin was unhurt but distraught. So was Hawthorn, who overshot the Jaguar pit as he watched the tragedy unfold to his left. Unnerved, he climbed out of his car, unwilling to continue. But Jaguar team manager Lofty England sternly ordered him back in the cockpit, and Hawthorn reluctantly complied. Fangio had miraculously managed to slip through the wreckage and into the lead. He attributed his escape to a hand signal that he—and he alone—said Levegh had flashed just before the accident. If so, this was the last act performed by Levegh before he died.

The death toll—which is disputed even to this day—was 82 or 83 (or 79, 80, or 84), and more than 100 people were injured. At the time, most of the participants had no conception of the enormity of the disaster. (Amazingly, the first official acknowledgment over the PA system wasn't made until six hours after the accident.) Early on, Clerk of the Course Charles Faroux made the controversial decision to let the race continue because, he claimed, stopping it would cause panic and traffic that would hinder emergency efforts. After the accident, Fangio and Hawthorn pitted for driver changes, with Le Mans rookie Ivor Bueb climbing into the Jaguar and the estimable Stirling Moss taking over the Mercedes. Moss drove away from Bueb at a staggering pace. By Sunday morning, the SLR was two laps ahead of the D-type, and Mercedes seemed to be on pace for an easy 1-2 victory.

But nobody was celebrating back in Stuttgart. Daimler-Benz executives were sensitive to the understandable French resentment that lingered from the war years. Back at the track, Levegh's would-be co-driver, American sports car ace John Fitch, was thinking along the same lines. Fitch had flown against the Luftwaffe—in fact, he shot down an Me 262 jet and later landed in a Nazi prison camp—so to him, like many Frenchmen, the war was by no means ancient history. As soon as he realized that dozens

DEATH

A Panhard is cautiously driven through the wreckage at Le Mans shortly after Levegh's horrifying plunge into the crowd massed along the front straight. Lance Macklin has already hustled out of the wrecked Austin-Healey 100S in the foreground. Mercedes-Benz Classic

of spectators had been killed, he began urging Mercedes officials to withdraw from the race. "If Mercedes won, I felt it would be a public relations disaster," he says. "I told them what people would say: 'Ruthless Germans win Le Mans over the dead bodies of I don't know how many Frenchman.' Withdrawing was the only thing to do."

After much discussion, the Daimler board of directors agreed. At about 1:45 a.m., to the eternal disgust of Stirling Moss, team manager Alfred Neubauer ordered both remaining Mercedes to retire. "It is finished," he said. "There are too many dead." Rain started pouring later that morning, almost like tears of the racing gods. With no serious competition, Hawthorn and Bueb slogged through appalling conditions to win by five laps. The victory celebration was understandably muted. Levegh was eulogized in Paris three days later. But disputes about the race have persisted long after the other participants in the crash were buried.

The irony, of course, is that the accident was witnessed by thousands of observers, the vast majority of them racing fans and many of them motorsports professionals. Dozens of photos were shot. Numerous experts, including some participants, issued exhaustive postmortems. Inevitably, they differed in some details—relative speeds, precise positions, possible motives, and so on. But about the essential contours of the wreck, there's widespread consensus. So there's no real question about what happened, where it happened, when it happened, or how it happened. But exactly *why* it happened—that is, who exactly was to blame—has been the source of acrimonious debate for the past half-century.

A tragedy of such unthinkable proportions demanded a scapegoat. Levegh, predictably, was generally given a free pass by the French media. He was dead, after all, and couldn't speak for himself. Plus, he was French, and while he wasn't a top-ranked driver, he'd enjoyed a solid career, coming within an hour of winning Le Mans in 1952—and defeating Mercedes-Benz—while single-handedly driving a home-grown Talbot.

Macklin had preemptively laid out his own defense—blaming Hawthorn for swerving in front of him and then braking unexpectedly—in interviews shortly after the race. So the French media promptly anointed Hawthorn as their villain. Unlike Levegh, Hawthorn was an alien character. Tall and blond-haired, with his jaunty air and customary bow tie, he epitomized the public school Englishman, and his eat-drink-and-be-merry-for-tomorrow-we-die Byronic flair didn't play well in postwar France. After the race, he celebrated with what the French considered to be excessive glee. For many of them, the image that lingered like the aftertaste of acidic wine was a photo of Hawthorn drinking from the winner's traditional bottle of champagne. To this photo, the magazine *L'Auto-Journal* appended a caustic caption, "À votre santé, Monsieur Hawthorn!" (To your health, Mr. Hawthorn!)

In Great Britain, on the other hand, Hawthorn was a national hero and widely considered to be Stirling Moss' foremost rival. Lofty England defended him aggressively, lobbing a few bombshells at the hated Boche at Mercedes. Meanwhile, the chauvinistic British media closed ranks around their favorite son, and Hawthorn's supporters wasted no time trying to shift blame away from him. At first glance, Macklin would have seemed like the obvious choice. It was his car, after all, that sent Levegh into the crowd. But like Hawthorn, Macklin was a Brit—an Etonian, as a matter of fact, and something of a war hero, not to mention the son of a wealthy and influential industrialist. In any event, there was no reason to censure Macklin because in Pierre Levegh, the British media found a made-to-order fall guy.

To begin with, Levegh wasn't even his given name. He'd been born Pierre Bouillin, but he took the racing pseudonym of his uncle, who'd been a noteworthy French racer at the turn of the century. This became part of the rickety case against him—that he was so desperate for fame that he adopted the name of a more famous man. Levegh apprenticed as a mechanic and earned a reputation as a performance tuner. Although he was an excellent all-around athlete, he wasn't able to manage his first race—a minor French event in an overmatched Bugatti—until he was 31. But the following year, he convinced Anthony Lago to sell him a Talbot T-150C that he raced at Le Mans (and the enduros at Spa and Reims). And while Levegh was outclassed by the prewar crop of French greats—Raymond Sommer, Jean-Pierre Wimille, Robert Benoist, Philippe Etancelin—he proved himself to be competent and reliable.

Levegh's skills were showcased at Le Mans in 1952. This was the year that Mercedes-Benz had returned to racing, ending its hiatus after World

War II, and the team showed up at Le Mans with a trio of immaculate 300SLs that were immediately declared the odds-on favorites to win the race. But as the hours passed, it was Levegh's Talbot T26GS that remained in the lead. Even more astonishing, Levegh resolutely remained in the car pit stop after pit stop, refusing to give way to his co-driver. After roughly 23 hours, having driven without relief since the start, he was three laps ahead of the closest Mercedes. Then, in sight of Maison Blanche, the crankshaft split, possibly as the result of an over-rev, and the Talbot retired on the side of the road.

Levegh's critics saw this as a modern version of a Greek tragedy—a would-be hero brought low by hubris. But some revisionist historians tell a different story. According to their version of the race, Levegh suspected that the production-based crankshaft of his Talbot engine wasn't robust enough to survive the rigors of Le Mans. During the race, he felt an engine vibration that was later identified as a bolt that had worked its way out of the center crankshaft journal. Levegh was afraid that his inexperienced teammate wouldn't have the delicacy necessary to preserve the compromised crankshaft. So Levegh did his best to nurse the engine, but it wasn't good enough, and Mercedes won after all.

The people who blame Levegh for the tragedy at Le Mans say he received a highly coveted slot in the Mercedes team purely as a public relations sop to ease the French enmity for the German company. At the time, he was 49 years old, and his career had been marked more by failures than triumphs. With its space-frame chassis and desmodromic engine, the 300SLR was the fastest and most sophisticated sports car in the world, and Levegh's detractors claimed that he was in over his head. If Levegh had been more competent, they said, he simply would have steered around Macklin's Austin-Healey instead of crashing into it. But Levegh, they suggested, was distracted by Fangio presence right behind him. More to the point, his Gallic pride couldn't stomach the thought of being passed by his teammate as they flashed past the main grandstands.

This theory seems ludicrous on its face. Levegh was known as "The Bishop," which implies a certain authority and, perhaps, dourness, but which suggests that he was nobody's fool. He'd been around racing long enough to realize there was no disgrace in being passed by a man who'd already won two world championships and who was, even then, regarded as one of the all-time greats. Plus, Levegh was pacing himself to team orders while Fangio was driving at a Grand Prix clip. As it was, he'd lost an average of only seven seconds per lap to Fangio on a four-minute lap, which was nothing to be ashamed of.

Although the Brits ridiculed Levegh for his pace, he was, in fact, as quick if not quicker than any of the Jaguar drivers other than Hawthorn.

The traditional Le Mans start caused cars to bunch up in odd formations, jumbling fast entries with slow ones. Here, in a macabre piece of foreshadowing, Macklin's Austin-Healey (Number 26) briefly leads Levegh's Mercedes (Number 20).
Mercedes-Benz Classic

During testing and practice, he'd also gone slightly faster than Fitch, and while Fitch himself wasn't in the same league as Fangio, Moss, and Hawthorn, he was good enough to be invited by Mercedes to compete at Dundrod later in the year. "Levegh was fully qualified," Fitch says. "He proved it in his lap times. He was a very competent driver." Fangio, in a newspaper interview right after the race, credited Levegh with saving his life by throwing up his hand to alert him to the crash.

Numerous races were cancelled after the tragedy at Le Mans, but French officials dragged their feet investigating the accident. In their defense, one of the three participants was dead. Hawthorn was barely communicative, speaking only when compelled to. And while Macklin was privately livid, he maintained a stoic public face while trying to protect Hawthorn's reputation. Asked at the judicial inquiry whether Hawthorn had caused the accident, he said after a long pause, "In an affair of this kind it is difficult to speak of responsibility. Hawthorn no doubt committed an error, but the real responsibility was the speed of our cars."

The formal findings of their inquiry weren't issued until November 1956, more than a year after the catastrophe. Partially as a result of Macklin's imprecision, the report absolved all the participants of criminal culpability: "Consider that the enquiry has not established any fault of driving, or any infraction of the rule of the road; more especially that the maneuver of Macklin had been unforeseen for Levegh; that Hawthorn seems to have committed no fault in overtaking Macklin and running to the right, then braking; that it has not been established or demonstrated that Macklin was really hindered by Hawthorn's car; nor does it seem to be established that Macklin drove without sufficient dexterity and self control."

Investigators had the advantages of visiting the crash site in person and interviewing the principals shortly after the race. The finely calibrated

The enormous impact of the crash and the terrifying intensity of the subsequent fire—the product, largely, of the highly flammable magnesium bodywork of Levegh's Mercedes—reduced the 300SLR to little more than a skeleton. Mercedes-Benz Classic

language of their report—taken from Christopher Hilton's meticulously researched history, *Le Mans '55*—suggests that they believed the three participants weren't so much equally innocent as they were legally not guilty. Even so, the findings of the inquiry poured oil over troubled waters. Life, and racing, went on as before, and the tragedy of Le Mans was relegated to the history files—until 1958, when William Kimber published Hawthorn's memoir, *Challenge Me the Race*.

The ghostwritten book is sanitized and strangely stripped of emotional content. Reading it, you'd never realize that Hawthorn was one of the great—and polarizing—characters of the postwar racing scene. In the chapter devoted to the 1955 race at Le Mans, Hawthorn downplayed the near-hysteria he displayed immediately after the wreck and laid out his version of events with the deliberation of a defense attorney: "The only car in front of me was Macklin's Austin-Healey and as I came up alongside I worked out whether there was room to pass him and then pull in to the pits. In my view there was, so I kept on and then as the pits drew nearer I put up my hand, put the brakes on and pulled in. I was nearly there, when out of the corner of the eye I saw something flying through the air. It was Levegh's Mercedes."

So Hawthorn's position was clear: He'd done nothing wrong. "What we do know," he wrote, "is that Macklin, taken by surprise, for some reason, pulled over to the left and from that moment Levegh's plight was desperate."

Macklin went ballistic when he read excerpts from Hawthorn's book in the *Daily Express*. From the beginning, he'd blamed Hawthorn for causing the accident by swerving in front of him and then standing on the brakes. He flatly denied that Hawthorn had signaled his intention to pit. Moreover, he'd confronted Hawthorn at the time, and he claimed that Hawthorn had apologized for what he acknowledged was a mistake. Now, Hawthorn was absolving himself of any responsibility for the accident. Even worse, the phrase "taken by surprise, for some reason," intimated that Macklin was to blame for what happened. Enraged by what he considered this stab in the back, Macklin sued Hawthorn for libel. But the case never made it to court. Because in 1959, three months after retiring from racing in the wake of winning the 1958 Formula 1 World Championship, Hawthorn was killed in a traffic accident when he lost control of his hot-rodded 3.4-liter Jaguar sedan on a rain-slick road.

By that time, Macklin had also retired from racing—not because of the Le Mans disaster, he insisted, but after witnessing yet another fatal accident in the Tourist Trophy at Dundrod. For awhile, he sold Facel Vegas in Paris, then returned to England, then moved to New Zealand, then sold real estate in Spain and ran boat charters in the Mediterranean. He no longer had anything to do with racing. But he was still bitter about Hawthorn's betrayal. So in 1975, he placed a call to Mark Kahn, a newspaper reporter who wrote sympathetically about racing. "You don't know me. My name is Macklin," he said. "You know, I was one of the central figures in the Le Mans disaster, and my story has never been told."

Kahn told it, and he told exceedingly well. Although the title—*Death Race*—promises a sensationalistic account, the book was a small gem of fluid and fast-paced storytelling focused on a single dramatic episode. Inevitably, Macklin emerged as the central character, and Kahn sketched his picaresque life with considerable verve. But the core of the book, naturally, was the crash, and Macklin's recollections are worth quoting at length:

"The Jaguar came alongside me. It was Hawthorn. I was delighted that he was clearly leading the race. I thought, Fabulous! Old Mike's doing a great job. . . . Almost immediately Hawthorn overtook me I was surprised when he shot across to the right slap in front of me. I believed that he misjudged the speed of the Austin-Healey. . . . I suddenly saw his brake lights come on twenty or thirty yards—no more—in front of me. I thought, Christ! What the hell is he doing? I had to stand on my brakes as hard as I could to try to avoid running into the back of him. And then I realized that I couldn't stop; that he was slowing faster than I was. . . . One of the front wheels locked and I thought, "Oh Christ, I'm going to hit him!" I could really feel myself going into the back of him. In a last desperate effort to re-pass him, I pulled the car over to the left. It wasn't a swerve. You can't swerve at that speed without spinning or worse. I just managed to ease the car over enough so that I barely got past without touching him. For a moment I felt a flash of elation. Then the car went into a long slide, with all four wheels tobogganing. . . . But I got the thing corrected and pointing straight again with the speed at about 120 mph, although I still wasn't in real control. . . . And then came an indescribable shock. I felt the most almighty BANG! There was a blast of searing heat from an exhaust near my face and my car was catapulted down the road backwards. Out of the corner of my eye I glimpsed a silver shape with the driver hunched over the wheel hurtling through the air ten or fifteen feet above me."

When Macklin jumped out of his crumpled car and made it to the pits, he was met by car owner Donald Healey. "Christ almighty, Lance, what happened?" he demanded.

"That bloody idiot Mike Hawthorn," Macklin snapped. "I don't know what the hell he was up to, but he just suddenly pulled straight across in front of me and clapped his brakes on."

Macklin's recollections were confirmed by his co-driver, Les Leston, who was watching from on top of the Aston Martin pits, which offered the best view of the incident. "As he drew in front of Macklin, [Hawthorn] pulled over to his right violently to stop in his pit," Leston told Kahn. "Lance had to pull over to his left to avoid hitting Hawthorn's car. I think Lance expected him to go whizzing by. Instead of that, he pulls in front of him, stands on everything and Lance has to take immediate and violent action to stop from hitting the Jaguar up the chuff."

A few minutes later, according to the account in Kahn's book, a shaken Hawthorn emerged from the Jaguar pits. He staggered over to Macklin and laid his hand on his old friend's shoulder. "Oh, my God, Lance," he said. "I'm terribly sorry. I bloody nearly killed you, and I killed all those people. I'm really sorry. I'm certainly never going to race again."

Needless to say, this scene doesn't appear in Hawthorn's memoir. But Kahn, no doubt sensitive to the perception that he was trashing a British hero, also gave Lofty England nearly three uninterrupted pages to lay out his case that Hawthorn had done nothing wrong. At the same time, Kahn also quoted several observers who ridiculed Levegh's skills and argued that his ineptitude was the principal cause of the accident.

Despite all the riveting and incendiary material in the book, *Death Race* didn't change many minds. Racing cognoscenti largely ignored it because Kahn was a product of Fleet Street rather than the motorsports fraternity, so his work was considered suspect. Also, the anecdotal evidence in his book was undermined by the rigorous analysis of photos of the crash that had just been published by Belgian journalist Paul Frère in the Austrian magazine *Autorevue*. (It later appeared, translated into English, in Andrew Whyte's indispensable history *Jaguar: Sports Cars & Works Competition Cars From 1954*.)

Besides being a distinguished automotive journalist who wrote for many European magazines and *Road & Track* here in the States, Frère was also a superb race car driver who won Le Mans in 1960. In the infamous 1955 race, he finished second in an Aston Martin, so he was infinitely familiar not

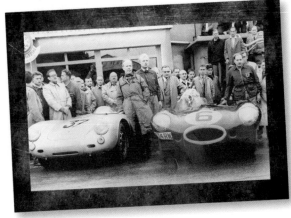

In contrast to the photos published in French newspapers, this image shows a somber Mike Hawthorn—the tall, blond-haired figure wearing a bomber jacket in the center—and mustachioed co-driver Ivor Bueb flanking their D-type Jag during a downbeat victory celebration. Paul Skilleter

only with the track but also with the drivers involved in the crash and the relative performance of their cars. Frère based his commentary on the analysis of nine still photos taken from a brief clip of 16-millimeter film shot by a spectator who was injured by debris from the wreck. The first frame showed Hawthorn just as he swept in front of Macklin. The final frame is a chilling image of Levegh's Mercedes immediately after it struck the Austin-Healey, climbing at a 45-degree angle like a airplane lifting off from a runway.

Frère began by rejecting Macklin's claim that Hawthorn had swerved in front of him. In fact, the sequence of photos accompanying his post-mortem start too late to show this, but Frère wrote that he himself had seen what happened while standing in the Aston Martin pits, waiting to replace co-driver Peter Collins. (For the record, in his racing memoir, *Starting Grid to Chequered Flag*, Frère mentioned nothing about the relative positions of the Jaguar and the Austin-Healey, only "glancing across the track" and seeing "a Mercedes rear up in the air.") Frère was also adamant that Hawthorn started braking early enough to have stopped as planned in the Jaguar pit. This was clearly meant to debunk the claim that Hawthorn overshot his pit stall because he was going too fast to stop. "It is wrong to burden the guilt for this catastrophe on Mike Hawthorn," he wrote.

But now that he'd exonerated Hawthorn, Frère—unlike most other participants in the blame game—felt no compulsion to designate a new fall guy. "One cannot accuse Macklin of not anticipating that the normally much quicker Jaguar would suddenly go slower," he wrote. "And the case of Levegh has great similarity with Macklin's. At most, one could accuse the Frenchman of paying too much attention to his rear." The bottom line, according to Frère? "One cannot burden any of the involved drivers with the responsibility."

Sixteen years later, Chris Nixon—a top-shelf British motorsports historian with a reputation for exhaustive research—seconded Frère's

These still photos taken from a film shot by a spectator show Hawthorn's Jaguar sweeping in front of Macklin's Austin-Healey, which subsequently swerves in front of Levegh's Mercedes. The chilling final frame catches the 300SLR as it vaults over an embankment, precipitating the worst catastrophe in motorsports history. Paul Skilleter

opinion. "Was Mike 'guilty' of causing that disaster?" he wrote in *Mon Ami Mate*, his magisterial dual biography of Hawthorn and Peter Collins. "No. It was, in the truest sense, a racing accident." But he reached this generous conclusion only after clearly painting Hawthorn as the villain of the story.

In addition to quoting extensively from Macklin's account in *Death Race*, Nixon also demolished much of the defense Hawthorn offered in *Challenge Me the Race*. To bolster his case that Hawthorn had swerved in front of Macklin, Nixon then marshaled eyewitness observations from

"The Deadliest Spectacle in Racing"

Thanks—if that's the right word—to the catastrophe in 1955, Le Mans holds the dubious distinction of being the deadliest race circuit in the world. Statistically speaking, the Autodromo Nazionale di Monza, traditional home of the Italian Grand Prix, comes in second. But the most dangerous racetrack in the world? That would be the cathedral of speed known as the Indianapolis Motor Speedway.

Since it opened in 1922, Monza has been the site of more than 70 automobile racing fatalities. But more than two dozen alone were the result of a single incident in 1928, when a car plunged into the crowd. And, of course, Monza is the venue for a wide variety of races, from single-seaters to sports cars, World Championship Formula 1 races to amateur club events, so there are plenty of opportunities for disaster. Indianapolis, on the other hand, was the site of only one race a year—the Indy 500—for most of the past century. Yet despite this extremely limited use, the racetrack has claimed the lives of 66 men and 1 child.

It's not hard to understand why the Speedway has such a gruesome track record. A 2.5-mile paved oval with mild banking, it features a deadly cocktail of high speeds and a dearth of runoff areas. The track opened in 1909 with a three-day festival of races, and before it was over, no fewer than five people were dead—one driver, two riding mechanics, and two spectators. Another driver was killed during private testing in 1910. The next year, in the inaugural Memorial Day race, a third riding mechanic died. From 1929 to 1939, there was only one year that nobody was killed during practice, qualifying, or the race.

Believe it or not, the Indy 500 was so dangerous that, in 1931, it claimed the life of an 11-year-old boy who wasn't even at the track. Defending champion Billy Arnold was miles ahead of the field when he crashed in Turn 4. His car rolled over the wall, and one of the wheels bounced onto Georgetown Road, which runs parallel to the front straight. There, it struck and killed Wilbur Brink while he was playing in his front yard.

several expert eyewitnesses—Macklin's co-driver Les Leston (already quoted in *Death Race*), injured Jaguar works driver Desmond Titterington, and Aston Martin team manager John Wyer. "I've always had the feeling that if there was one person who started the chain of events it was Mike, who was a bit hairy and exuberant when driving into the pits," Titterington said. And as Wyer wrote in his autobiography, *The Certain Sound*: "I must say, with regret but great sincerity, that I believe that the chain reaction was triggered by Mike Hawthorn." But the most damning testimony came from Rob Walker, the Scots heir to the Johnnie Walker liquor fortune and the last private entrant to win a Formula 1 Grand Prix. (He was also *Road & Track*'s longtime F1 correspondent.) Walker tried to comfort Hawthorn shortly after the accident, but Hawthorn was inconsolable. "His first words—and I'll never forget them—were, 'It's all my fault! It's all my fault! I wanted to get into the pits before Fangio came by,'" Walker told Nixon.

That sounds pretty conclusive. But in Hawthorn's defense, he was, by his own admission, near hysteria. The accident had unfolded behind him, and he couldn't have known exactly what happened. All he knew for sure was that something awful had transpired immediately after he moved to the right, and he must have wondered if he'd inadvertently set events into motion.

After the race, Jaguar collected accounts from spectators who saw the accident. As countless academic studies have shown, eyewitness accounts are notoriously unreliable. But Jaguar received one unsolicited letter that's worth quoting. Not only did it dovetail with extraordinary accuracy with the photos studied by Paul Frère, but it was written by an amateur American road racer who worked as an Air Force aircraft accident investigator. "[Hawthorn's] driving at that time was exactly identical to all of the other higher speed cars when they prepared to pit," Maj. Bruce C. Jenney wrote in a letter archived by the British Racing Drivers' Club at Silverstone. "In conclusion, in no way should Mr. Hawthorn or his pit crew be held, even remotely, responsible for the accident at Le Mans 1955."

Despite Jenney's assertion, the question of responsibility for the accident continued to haunt motorsports historians. At a certain point, though, what else could be said about the subject? Every participant and eyewitness had been interviewed. Every document had been scrutinized. All that was left, it seemed, was interpreting material that had already passed into the public domain.

Then Paul Skilleter had a brainstorm.

Skilleter is the British Jaguar authority who cowrote *Golden Boy*, the definitive Hawthorn biography. Many years ago, Lofty England had given him about 57 black-and-white photos, each measuring about 5 by 7 inches, made from the brief film shot by the spectator who was injured by flying debris. (The original movie, which may have been in color, appears to have been lost.) Skilleter sent the photos to a production company that matched them for size and density and strung them together to create a brief video sequence that lasts three seconds. The footage includes the nine photos that Paul Frère used to analyze the accident. But seeing a moving image brings the accident to life in a way that a series of still images can't manage. It also brings several disputed aspects of the episode into sharper focus.

It's clear, first of all, that Hawthorn didn't swerve in front of Macklin. That is to say, there appears to be nothing violent about the maneuver. On the other hand, it was a decisive and aggressive move, somewhat analogous to what's known in sprint car and midget racing as a slide job—where the driver in the bottom lane completes a pass by letting his car slide up into the second lane and impede the driver on his outside. Hawthorn started braking as soon as he cleared Macklin, which suggests that he made the pass as late as possible. Not too late, mind you, because as Frère pointed out, Hawthorn still had room to slow down for his pits. But he must have realized that he'd left it until late in the game. No doubt, he expected Macklin to ease to his left to pass the Jaguar. That still would have left plenty of room for Levegh to get past on the left side of the Austin-Healey. (It was commonplace for two cars to go side-by-side on the front straight while a third car sat in the pits.)

But Macklin didn't pass Hawthorn, and the question is why not? As soon as he saw Hawthorn easing over in front of him, Macklin would have realized that the Jaguar was preparing to slow for the pits since there was no other reason for him to use the right side of the track. Then again, as Leston surmised, Macklin probably thought Hawthorn was roaring off into the distance after passing him, not diving into the pits. As the Jaguar blasted by, maybe Macklin chose that precise moment to check his mirrors to make sure he left room for the two Mercedes that were about to lap him. Then, when he looked up, there was the D-type, smack in front of him, slowing at a sickeningly fierce pace. Or maybe he was simply wrong-footed by Hawthorn's unexpected move. Either way, Macklin had only an instant to choose between turning or braking.

With the 20-20 vision of hindsight, we now know that steering immediately to the left would have been the right call. But immediately nailing the brakes must have been his natural instinct. Unfortunately, Macklin was betrayed by the performance of his car, which was saddled with tiny tires and single-pad discs that had nowhere near the stopping power of the dual-caliper, power-assisted brakes on the Jaguar. How long before he realized that he wasn't going to be able to get the Austin-Healey whoa-ed down in time? A second? Half a second?

That he managed to avoid crunching the rear end of the Jaguar required a masterful piece of driving. Corralling the wayward Austin-Healey after it nearly spun at something like 100 mph was even more impressive. It was just rotten luck that Levegh's Mercedes arrived at the precise moment that Macklin got his car under control.

Of course, rotten luck is a critical element of virtually every major accident, whether it occurs on a racetrack or on an airport runway or even in a suburban backyard. But rarely are these calamities caused by any one single factor. On the contrary, there's usually a cascade of small errors, many of them inconsequential on their own, that have to fit together in precisely the right order for an accident to happen. Take away any of these links and the entire chain collapses. If Hawthorn hadn't left the pass until so late. If Macklin had been paying better attention. If Levegh had been more proactive. If, if, if. All we can say with absolute certainty is that there were three drivers, with three different agendas, driving at three different speeds, arriving at the same place at the same time, and disaster ensued. The wreck was a perfect example of what the NASCAR boys call "one of them racin' deals"—a territorial dispute between a bunch of drivers with more or less equal rights to a single piece of real estate.

Of the three men, Levegh bears the least responsibility for the accident and Hawthorn the most. But none of them was to blame. As for the tragedy that transpired after the crash, this was clearly beyond their control. As Fitch puts it: "The organizers didn't realize that the cars had outgrown the track." The event made such a profound impression on him that Fitch devoted most of his professional life to promoting racetrack and traffic safety. Officials at Le Mans, meanwhile, belatedly upgraded the pits and, eventually, the rest of the circuit. More than a dozen drivers have been killed since 1955, but only three spectators have died, all in a single accident while watching from a prohibited area. Today's cars are three and four times faster than the machines that contested the first race in 1923. But the 24 Hours of Le Mans is safer now than it's ever been before.

VERDICT: False.
The tragedy at Le Mans in 1955 was a racing incident.
–Preston Lerner

THE BLOODY LEGEND OF JAMES DEAN'S DEADLY PORSCHE

LEGEND: The Porsche that movie icon James Dean was driving when he died continued to kill and injure people long after his fatal crash.

The curse of James Dean's Porsche 550 Spyder has all the elements essential to create an enduring urban legend. Iconic celebrity? Check. Macabre death? Check. Inexplicable mysteries? A participant who relentlessly promotes the myth? A loyal group of acolytes willing to believe almost anything? Check, check, check.

Like most legends, the curse of James Dean's Spyder—which he dubbed "Little Bastard"—rests on a solid foundation of indisputable facts. The young actor was killed in a freak accident at the height of his stardom, and reports of a jinx on the car surfaced the year after he died. But because there's no brake on credulity, the myth has taken on a life of its own since then. Consider, for instance, the tale of the two rear tires that were supposedly salvaged from the wreck. As the story goes, they were fitted to another race car—and nearly caused an accident when they simultaneously blew out for no apparent reason. Later, it was said that the blowouts caused the car to flip over. In the most violent version of this tall tale, the driver was killed. If so, that brought the alleged death toll associated with the Spyder to five, in addition to numerous broken limbs, a crushed hip, various gashes, and paralysis. Oh, and one slight case of murder.

"It's pretty difficult for a custom-car designer not to appreciate a $7,000 Porsche Spyder, but there was something strange about that particular car . . . a feeling, bad vibrations, an aura; call it what you will," George Barris, the King of the Kustomizers and the principal mythologizer of the haunted Porsche, wrote in his memoir. "At that time, I was a non-believer in ESP or psychic phenomena, so I didn't want to sound like a 'kook.' It wasn't until after the accident and a whole string of tragedies that followed—all related to that car—that I began to accept psychic sciences. Everything that car has touched has turned to tragedy. It baffled me for years. I've never been able to come up with logical or rational answers to the questions. The only answer seems to be that the car was cursed."

James Dean made his road racing debut in a brand-new Porsche 356 Super Speedster in 1955 at the California Sports Car Club races at Palm Springs. He won going away, beating an F Production field consisting of MGs and other Porsches. Lee Raskin

James Dean has been the object of a cult following ever since his fatal crash on September 30, 1955. He was 24, and he embodied the live-fast-die-young ethos that's been the quickest road to celebrity at least since Achilles faced off against the Trojans in the *Iliad*. Incredibly, Dean's film legacy was limited to starring roles in three movies—*East of Eden*, *Rebel Without a Cause*, and *Giant*—and the last two were released after he died. Because his career ended so prematurely and dramatically, virtually every aspect of his life has been the source of fanatical analysis. His last day—singular—has been the subject of an entire book, various TV specials, and an annual pilgrimage from Los Angeles north to the site of the wreck near the small town of Cholame. And in his definitive book *James Dean: At Speed*, Porsche historian Lee Raskin focused specifically on the actor's passion for fast cars and bikes.

According to Raskin, Dean owned a series of Triumph motorcycles and an MG TD that he'd bought after earning a starring role in *East of Eden*. In March 1955, he traded the MG for a Porsche Super Speedster bought new from Johnny von Neumann at Competition Motors in Hollywood. Although the Speedster was primarily a street car, it was also a popular entry in local road races run by the California Sports Car Club and the Sports Car Club of America. Dean made his racing debut in Palm Springs in March, then competed in the SCCA and Cal Club races at Bakersfield and Santa Barbara during the spring. On the track, he was

Porsche factory mechanic Rolf Wütherich snapped this photo of Dean in his freshly prepped Porsche 550 Spyder at Competition Motors in Hollywood, where he'd bought the car, before they headed north on their ill-fated drive to Salinas. Lee Raskin

quick but wild; his race log included metal-to-metal contact, a clouted hay bale, and an over-revved motor. But like most racers since the beginning of time, he believed a faster car was the answer to his problems. So while he was filming *Giant*—and barred by the studio from racing—he ordered a Lotus Mk IX from Burbank race car dealer Jay Chamberlain. When Chamberlain told him that delivery would be delayed, Dean returned to Competition Motors and traded his Speedster in on a much more sophisticated Porsche 550 Spyder.

Also known as the 1500RS, the 550 Spyder was the first purpose-built race car that Porsche put into production. The car debuted at the Nurburgring in 1953, and prototypes scored impressive class wins at Le Mans and La Carrera Panamericana. After production began in 1955, von Neumann procured five cars for Competition Motors. With its rigid, light-weight frame and exotic horizontally opposed, four-cam Typ 547 engine, the Spyder dominated small-bore racing at both the local and international levels, and it probably did more than any single car in Porsche history to cement the company's reputation as a giant-killer.

Dean's hand-built car was the 55th of 90 Spyders produced by the factory, which gave it the palindromic serial number of 550-055. Dean bought the car on September 19, 1955, and immediately entered it in the Salinas Road Races, scheduled to be run the next week in Northern

California. (He also bought a Ford Country Squire station wagon that he planned to use to tow the high-strung car on an open trailer from race to race.) But first, he wanted to personalize the car, so he took it to the Lynwood shop of Dean Jeffries, whom he'd met through fellow Hollywood racers Lance Reventlow and Bruce Kessler. At the time, the young Jeffries and his friend Kenneth Howard, better known as Von Dutch, were two up-and-coming painters and pinstripers in Los Angeles. Later, Jeffries became a renowned customizer and stunt coordinator whose movie cars included the original Green Hornet vehicle and the Monkeemobile.

Jeffries painted the race number—130—that Dean had been assigned for Salinas in flat black washable paint on the hood, rear decklid, and both doors. At Dean's direction, he also hand-lettered a nickname—Little Bastard, in quote marks—in a stylized script in a permanent black gloss enamel between the rear engine grille and the license plate holder. The precise derivation of the sobriquet is disputed. Raskin says the most likely story is that this is what Jack Warner, head of Warner Brothers, angrily called Dean, and Dean co-opted the insult as a badge of honor. Then again, Dean could just have plausibly been referring to the car itself. By the standards of the day, the Porsche was a mean machine. Dean lore holds that British actor Alec Guinness said it looked "sinister." Then he supposedly told Dean, "If you get in that car, you will be found dead in it by this time next week." Cue spooky music.

On Friday morning, September 30, the Porsche was race-prepped at Competition Motors. The original plan had been to tow it the 300-plus miles to Salinas. But Porsche factory mechanic Rolf Wütherich, who'd been assigned to support the car at the races, thought it would be better if Dean drove it up north, putting some badly needed miles on the new and notoriously temperamental motor. So Dean got behind the wheel of the 550 with Wütherich riding shotgun. Bill Hickman—a legendary stuntman now best known for his driving in *The French Connection* and being pursued by Steve McQueen in the chase scene in *Bullitt*—followed them in the station wagon, towing the unladen trailer.

The two cars made several stops during the trip. But by the late afternoon, while traveling west through hilly terrain on Route 466 (now Highway 46), Dean and Wütherich had left Hickman far behind. At about 5:45 p.m., Dean confronted a 1950 Ford Custom coupe driven by college student Donald Turnupseed turning left across the road in front of them. Dean didn't have time to stop, and there was no room for evasive action. The Spyder struck the Ford nearly head-on, with the driver's side of the Porsche taking the brunt of the impact. The 550 flipped before landing on its wheels in a gully. Dean, entrapped and mangled in the wreckage, was pronounced dead on arrival at a hospital in Paso Robles at 6:20 p.m. Wütherich was thrown from the car but survived critical injuries, including a broken jaw and crushed femur. Turnupseed broke his nose and suffered facial lacerations.

Exactly what happened during the moments just before the crash has been the subject of a remarkable volume of study, speculation, conjecture, and even an accident reconstruction computer simulation. Unfortunately, the actual participants weren't able or willing to shed any light on the matter. Dean was dead. Wütherich, who was psychologically scarred by the accident, didn't remember anything about the wreck. After giving a deposition and granting an interview to a local newspaper, Turnupseed never again spoke publicly about the incident. Some Dean fans claim, implausibly, that Wütherich was driving when the collision occurred. Some devotees also go to great lengths to argue that Dean wasn't speeding at the time of the wreck, implying that Turnupseed bears most of the blame for the accident.

Maybe so. But Dean was known to be a reckless driver. He was behind the wheel of a car that had been designed for racing. He'd already wrinkled the aluminum bodywork of the Spyder during some shenanigans on the streets of L.A., and he'd been cited for speeding by a California Highway Patrol trooper near Bakersfield about two hours before his fatal wreck. Besides being faster than most American cars of the era, the Porsche was also lower and smaller than just about anything else on the road. The bare aluminum skin could easily have been lost in the haze of the late afternoon. (Drivers on that stretch of highway are now required to turn on their headlights to improve the visibility of oncoming traffic.) Turnupseed may not have spotted the Porsche in the distance, and when he finally did, he might have misjudged its speed. Although there was an official inquest, the coroner's jury found that he wasn't to blame for what was ruled to be an "accidental death with no criminal intent."

Dean's death, ending his meteoric career with a literal and figurative bang, was a huge story. It wasn't long before bizarre rumors began circulating. The first and most outlandish, spun out of thin air, was that Dean hadn't been killed at all. But even after this fable was debunked, it was replaced by the legend that Little Bastard had been jinxed. The initial fodder for this tale came from the travails of Dr. William Eschrich, a Burbank surgeon and Cal Club racer who used the motor from the wrecked Porsche in his Lotus Mk VIII. About a year after Dean died, Aline Mosby—a celebrated United Press International correspondent who later interviewed Lee Harvey Oswald after he defected to Moscow—wrote a widely syndicated story about the alleged curse. "Recently, when Eschrich

A final snapshot of Dean and Wütherich sharing a victory pose before leaving Competition Motors. The "130" on the hood—the number assigned to the Porsche for the upcoming road race—was painted by noted SoCal pinstriper Dean Jeffries. Lee Raskin

ran into some gravel and cracked up at the Pomona races, the Dean fans jabbered, 'Jinx,'" she wrote. "The superstitious cries grew when Dr. Troy McHenry was killed in the same race after borrowing two small parts off the Dean motor."

Actually, Eschrich was quoted in a contemporary story in *Pomona Progress-Bulletin* as saying that the pieces were rear swingarms from Dean's car, not engine components. Still, McHenry had been driving in a Porsche 550 Spyder like Dean's, and now he was dead, hence all the talk about a jinx. But Eschrich himself pooh-poohed the supposed curse. "All this superstitious reaction is a lot of baloney," he told Mosby. "The motor had nothing to do with either accident. A machine is a piece of equipment, and that's all. All this morbid interest by fans in his belongings is not normal." Raskin says his research suggests that McHenry's fatal crash was caused by a steering failure unrelated to the salvaged suspension components.

Nevertheless, a couple of other perverse coincidences played into the legend of the cursed Porsche. While working on *Giant*, Dean—dressed in character as ranch hand Jett Rink—had filmed a public-service announcement exhorting young drivers to be careful on the road. "Take it easy driving," he told host Gig Young. "The life you save might be mine." The carcass of the wrecked Spyder later ended up in the hands of George Barris.

A final stop for gas on Ventura Boulevard before leaving Sherman Oaks. Dean also owned the Ford station wagon and open trailer parked behind him but decided to drive the 550 to Salinas to put some time on the new Porsche motor. Lee Raskin

Much of the bodywork had been destroyed in the accident, and several panels had long since been scavenged by other Porsche racers. So Barris used fresh sheet metal to mock up what was presented as the death car and displayed it at car shows all over the country. In Los Angeles, for example, the gruesome-looking car was showcased under a ghoulish placard reading "The Greater Los Angeles Safety Council presents James Dean's last sports car." A headline on another placard in front of the display blared, "This accident could have been avoided."

The larger-than-life Barris has done more than any single person to promote the legend of the cursed Porsche. He's been able to do this largely because he occupies a unique position in the custom car world—as one of its founding fathers and now its self-styled king. It's no coincidence that he and Ed "Big Daddy" Roth were two of the major characters in "The Kandy-Kolored Tangerine-Flake Streamline Baby," journalist Tom Wolfe's memorable *Esquire* feature story about custom car culture. Besides his seminal work in the hot-rod milieu, Barris also produced countless vehicles for Hollywood, from the original Batmobile to the Munster Koach. But with his acclaim, or perhaps because of it, has come controversy. Today, Barris is a polarizing figure whose critics charge that he plays fast and loose with the truth and claims credit for projects that are actually the work of other customizers.

Even if Dean had been wearing a seat belt, he clearly wouldn't have survived the impact of the collision, which was severe enough to send Donald Turnupseed's much heavier Ford careening nearly 40 feet down the highway. Lee Raskin

A case in point is the painting of the Little Bastard. Barris declined to be interviewed for this book. But in an interview with automotive journalist Tom Benford published in 2008, Barris says he befriended Dean on the set of *Rebel Without a Cause*. He claimed that Dean brought the brand-new Spyder to his shop and solicited Barris' advice about painting it. Barris even recounted specific bits of dialogue about their conversation. "I suggested that we put a red stripe on each fender to break things up a bit, and Dean liked that idea," Barris told Benford. While the car was parked in the shop, Barris said, it mysteriously jumped out of gear and smashed into a wall. After this bizarre accident, Barris said that Spyder was striped by Von Dutch, who received a cash tip from Dean after completing the job.

There are a few small problems with this story. Make that a few big problems. First of all, author Lee Raskin, who's a four-decade 356 owner, vintage racer, and serious Porsche-phile, says the racing stripes supposedly masked and painted by Von Dutch were on the car when it was delivered from Germany to Competition Motors. Moreover—and this is the real showstopper—Dean Jeffries insists that he did all the painting in his shop, and he's got the records to prove it. According to Jeffries, Barris wasn't a friend of Dean's and didn't consult on the project. "He never even got to touch the car, and that's the truth," Jeffries says.

DEATH

For better or worse, *Cars of the Stars*—Barris' 1974 biography, written by Jack Scagnetti—is the Bible, Torah, and Koran of the cursed Porsche legend. In it, Barris lays out virtually every element of the myth. In later years, many of the anecdotes were embellished, often by Barris himself. But *Cars of the Stars* is the sacred text for believers in the curse.

In the book, Barris said he bought the Little Bastard from the Dean family. When the car was being unloaded in his shop, it supposedly fell on a mechanic and broke both his legs. Barris subsequently sold the engine to Dr. Troy McHenry, who was killed when he hit a tree while racing a car fitted with the deadly motor. (Later, he claimed that another doctor using a transaxle salvaged from the Spyder was paralyzed in a racing accident.) After Barris reworked the car to display at safety demonstrations, he said it was in a fire in Fresno that destroyed everything in the garage—except the Porsche. A month later, it supposedly fell off a display in Sacramento and broke a teenager's hip. A few weeks after that, while being transported to Salinas, the car fell off the trailer and killed the truck driver.

But wait, there's more! Two years after crushing the hapless trucker, Barris said the car broke in half and fell onto the freeway. (In later accounts, though not according to Barris, the road blockage caused a fatal accident.) That was in Oakland. Then, in Oregon, the car slipped off another truck and smashed into a store. In 1959, while on display in New Orleans, the 550 crumbled into 11 pieces. And in 1968, Barris said that Dean's sole passenger—presumably referring to mechanic Rolf Wütherich—was convicted of murdering his wife.

In later years, Barris added a few more ingredients to the stew. There was, for example, a thief who broke his arm while trying to steal the steering wheel. And there was another mechanic who broke another leg when a door fell off the car. But best of all, Barris told Benford about a souvenir hunter who'd taken a scrap of metal off the car. "He called me up and said, 'I've got to send you this piece of metal—please take it back from me. Ever since I got it off that damned car, everything has gone wrong—I lost my job, I lost my wife, I lost my kid, I lost my house. I'm sick, I'm in the hospital now, *and I'm dying!*'"

Barris' stories are so inventive and entertaining that it seems churlish to challenge them. But after decades of study, Raskin is convinced that most of them are fabrications, and several are demonstrably false. "The only part of the curse that can be proven is the death of Dr. Troy McHenry," he says. "Just about everything else is made up." Warren Beath, the author of *The Death of James Dean* and *James Dean in Death: A Popular Encyclopedia of a Celebrity Phenomenon*, also has subjected Barris' claims to almost micro-scopic examination, and he, too, believes that most of them are fantasies.

After taking possession of the car, renowned car customizer George Barris mocked up a facsimile of the wreckage so it could be displayed at shows around the country. By that point, though, virtually nothing of the original 550 remained except the chassis. Lee Raskin

"There is no curse," he says flatly. "But it's generally believed because it's too good not to be true. And [Barris] keeps it alive."

To begin with, Barris didn't buy the Porsche from the Dean family. Raskin says an insurance company wrote off the wreck and settled with Dean's father, Winton Dean. Dr. Eschrich bought the car for $1,100 from a Burbank salvage yard. He then put the four-cam motor in the front of his Lotus—renamed a Potus—and his son owns the engine to this day. The transaxle was loaned to McHenry, who was indeed killed in a crash, though the gearbox apparently wasn't in the car at the time. It's now owned by Jack Styles, who is the parts manager at Paul Russell and Company in Essex, Massachusetts. Other components of the Little Bastard were parceled out to various Cal Club racers, none of whom were killed or broke any bones or suffered lasting psychological damage as a result.

It's difficult to check most of the other reports of injury and death because Barris provided precious little detail in his accounts—names, for instance. One exception was the mechanic supposedly crushed when the car fell off the trailer. He was identified by Barris as George Barkhuis, or sometimes, by other writers, as George Barhuis. Although this is an extremely unusual name, Beath's search of California newspapers turned up no obituary or coverage of the accident. Raskin unearthed a story in the *Los Angeles Times* about the Porsche being scorched in a fire in Fresno, but it mentioned nothing about the destruction of any other cars, much less an entire garage. As for the claim that Wütherich was convicted of murdering his wife, this isn't true, though the mechanic—whose mental instability may have been related to Dean's fatal crash—apparently stabbed her during a suicidal episode. But in an eerie coincidence, Wütherich was himself killed in a car wreck in Germany 1981.

Most of the claims made in *Cars of the Stars* have been repeated without comment or confirmation by other writers. In many cases, the stories have grown ever more incredible in each new iteration. Thus, minor accidents turn into major ones and injuries morph into deaths. Some writers even apply a twisted brand of logic to extend the curse backward in time to Dean's costars in *Rebel Without a Cause*—Natalie Wood, drowned in a boating accident, and Sal Mineo, murdered in an alley. (Nick Adams, who had a bit part in the movie but later became a modest star, died of a drug overdose.)

On the other hand, Barris tried to demystify one element of his tale. In his book, he said the car vanished from a train while being transported back to California from a show in Florida. "There was never any clue to its disappearance," he wrote, and this statement was cited by others as proof that occult forces were at work. Barris later said that he'd hired J. J. Armes, the celebrated Hollywood private investigator who lost both hands in a childhood accident, to find out what happened. After examining records from weigh stations, Armes concluded that the car had never been loaded on the truck, so Barris surmised that the car had been stolen in Florida. So far, so good. The catch is that, in Barris' book, the Porsche was supposed to have been loaded on a train rather than a truck. And in an interview conducted in 2011, Barris said the Porsche disappeared while it was in New York instead of Florida.

One way or another, Barris left open the possibility that the Little Bastard still exists. So in 2005, to commemorate the 50th anniversary of Dean's death, the Volo Auto Museum in Illinois announced that it would pay $1 million for his car—after it was authenticated by Barris. There was something of an unseemly sideshow quality to the offer. Predictably, nobody came forward to claim the reward. And, in fact, $1 million is pennies on the dollar of the value of the car, assuming somebody actually produced it. As Kevin Jeannette says: "If you could find the remains of that car, you could name your price."

Jeannette, a Porsche specialist who's run professional race teams, operates a shop in Florida that restores and vintage-races historic Porsches. But back in the early 1970s, he serviced and repaired street Porsches out of a garage in Southern California. One Saturday morning, a motorist who'd apparently seen Jeannette's Porsche sign from the highway stopped in.

"Are you into buying old Porsches?" he asked Jeannette. If so, he had a race car to sell. A 550 Spyder, to be precise. That had been wrecked. By a celebrity. By the name of . . . James Dean. "And I thought to myself, 'Why in the world would I want the car that James Dean had been killed in?'" Jeannette says, laughing ruefully.

Back then, of course, most old race cars were considered pieces of junk, little more than obsolete used cars. Porsches always retained some value, but 550s weren't especially collectible at the time. The fascination with celebrity hadn't exploded into a national obsession, and James Dean wasn't yet a cult icon. Jeannette remembers looking at a poster on his wall with line drawings of various Porsches, many of which looked much prettier to his eyes than the Spyder. "If it was an RSK, it would be worth fixing," he told the potential seller. So the alleged owner of the Little Bastard walked out and never returned.

Several variations on this theme have made the rounds over the years. There are also apocryphal stories of the car being locked in a storage unit or secreted away as the ultimate barn find. There's even supposed to be a reclusive owner who's offered to show the remains to big-time collectors—but he cancels the appointments before anybody can see the car. All of which suggests that the survival of the Spyder is as much a myth as the curse purportedly surrounding it. On the other hand, immensely valuable cars that were thought to have been lost forever seem to pop up every year, so who knows?

If the Little Bastard still exists—and that's a very big if—there wouldn't be much left of it. Photos taken after the accident show that the left front corner and most of the driver's side of the Porsche were destroyed. While Eschrich owned the car, it was stripped of its valuable mechanical bits and much of its remaining bodywork. By the time Barris got hold of it, it was essentially a shell. Then again, historically important cars have been "restored" from far less—a tub, some tubing, even a single chassis plate. In this particular case, the original engine and transaxle still exist. If they could be reunited with a reconstructed chassis, the price tag would be almost incalculable. And it might remove the curse from James Dean's 550 Spyder once and for all.

VERDICT: Bogus.
The only certified victims of the curse of James Dean's Porsche were Dean himself and his passenger, Rolf Wütherich. –*Preston Lerner*

THE 300-HORSEPOWER COFFIN

LEGEND: Wealthy Texas/Los Angeles oil heiress/socialite Sandra Ilene West asked that upon her passing, she be buried in her Ferrari, dressed appropriately, and sitting at a comfortable angle.

On the surface, it would have appeared that Sandra Ilene Tara West had it all. She was gifted with exceptional beauty and married wealthy San Antonio, Texas, industrialist Ike West, Jr. Unfortunately, West passed away at just 34 years old in 1968 of not entirely explained circumstances in Las Vegas, Nevada. This left his wife Sandra a beautiful, wealthy widow who settled in Beverly Hills and appeared to be enjoying the life of an entitled socialite.

It wasn't all roses for the unfortunate West, who was said to be battling loneliness, depression, and narcotics (prescribed or possibly otherwise)—an unfortunate fate for a model-beautiful widow only in her mid-30s. She was by then the mother of two children and dropped the use of her middle and maiden names, going by Sandra West in social circles or occasionally still Ilene among some friends.

West was a dazzling dresser, and according to social columns of the day, always made a "grand entrance" wherever she went. She had a stable of flashy cars, including a Stutz Blackhawk neo classic and as many as three Ferraris. Among them, a metallic early '60s Blue Ferrari 330 America most often referenced as Ferrari serial number GT 5055 (or it could have been a 250 GTE model; the two are visually identical).

As you can imagine, Ms. West's will was revised often; however, her 1972 will, or an amendment to it, was very specific as to her instructions for her ultimate burial when that time came. She had no reason to expect this event was in the near offing, but it is common for people of wealth to keep their affairs organized in preparation for their passing. Unfortunately, Ms. West was driving the Ferrari when involved in an automobile accident in November 1976; damage to the car was relatively minimal, but she suffered somewhat serious injuries.

She was believed to be on the road to recovery in early 1977 but was still under her doctor's and nurse's care and often heavily medicated. On

Although this photograph happens to be of a 250GTE model, they wore the same bodywork and are visually identical save for badging. Ferrari constructed more than 300 250GTE models, but only 50 of the larger-engined 330 Americas.

West in a more active stage of her life.

the evening of March 10, 1977, she complained to her nurse of stomach pain and retired to bed. She passed away during the night, at the age of 37.

Her burial instructions in the above- noted 1972 will decreed that she be buried in the Ferrari, in Texas, wearing a favorite evening gown. Her brother-in-law, Sol West III, was charged with carrying out her final wishes. There were also subsequent wills that were determined not to be valid at the time of her passing. Naturally, court cases ensued, but while the whole affair was being straightened out, West was "temporarily interred." The courts held that the 1972 will, and its unique interment request, was

Husband, wife, and Ferrari 330, all together forever. a Simple headstones mark the graves of Ike West, Jr., and wife Sandra; there is no outward indication of what lies beneath. Michael Frazier

Many members of the West family are buried at the Alamo Masonic Cemetery at San Antonio, Texas. Sol West was Ike West, Jr.'s brother—thus Sandra West's virtual brother-in-law—and also the executor of her will. West was once asked about why she chose to be buried in Texas next to her late husband, and she reportedly replied "Well, that's where the money came from...." Michael Frazier

For as beautiful and somewhat flamboyant as Sandra Ilene West was in life, her final resting place is remarkably devoid of ornamentation. Perhaps she felt that being interred in a fabulous blue Ferrari was enough? Michael Frazier

"The Ferrari 330 America"

There's little question that the late Sandra Ilene West's choice of final resting place and burial methodology is unusual, but there's no question she had great taste in coffins.

The Ferrari 330 America that Ms. West is interred in is an outgrowth of a model named 250 GTE, Ferrari's first series production 2+2 model. The 250 GTE is mechanically and architecturally similar with many of the 3.0-liter Ferrari GT models of the day, with a Pininfarina-designed body riding atop a 102.3-inch wheelbase and the multi-carbed, 3.0-liter single overhead cam Colombo series V-12 engine up front. As compared to many of its two-seat stablemates, the 250 GTE's engine was mounted a bit further forward to create more room in the cabin for the rear seating area. The back half of the 250 GTE was relatively roomy for such a sporting car, although it must still be considered a 2+2 in that the rear seats are likely only comfortable for tallish adults on short runs.

Late in the 250 GTE's production run, which spanned parts of 1960 through 1963, Ferrari took the opportunity to insert a larger more powerful engine, this being a nearly 4.0-liter V-12 rated at 300 horsepower; the 250 GTE's 3.0-liter V-12's 240 horses.

What precipitated the name change? It's simple really: In Ferrari-speak, at the time, the number designation most often represented the displacement of one of the engine's cylinders. In cubic centimeters, 250 cc x 12 cylinders meant an engine of 3000 cc, or 3 liters. In the case of the GTE's larger engine, 330 cc x 12 cylinders equals 39600 cc, or approximately 4 liters. Hence the name change from 250 to 330. The GTE designation was dropped, and "America" added. Enzo Ferrari always had great respect for the American automotive marketplace and, given America's penchant for large, powerful engines, perhaps felt that giving the car that country's name might aid its sale there. Just 50 330 America's were built, ostensibly the end of the GTE bodystyles production run. Physical differences were miniscule: the 250 badge on the rear end of the car now read 330 and some cars received "America" badging and some did not. While all early 1960s- era V-12 Ferraris are much prized by collectors these days, the 330 America is more particularly desirable, as so few were made, and because of the substantial power increase.

–Matt Stone

West's unorthodox burial made national news, as newspaper across America carried this photo of her and her crated Ferrari being lowered into the ground at the Alamo Masonic Cemetery in 1977. Once the wooden crate was safely lowered into the ground, it was covered and surrounded in cement to protect it and its occupants.
University of Texas at San Antonio Library

valid, if a bit unusual. Sol West made plans to carry out her dying wishes at the Alamo Masonic Cemetery in San Antonio, Texas.

Family members and the cemetery's management were concerned about the safety of West and her car, buried in what is a relatively open and easy to access facility. They were also mindful of the need to maintain some level of decorum during the actual burial process. The resulting solution was unusual but straightforward. The car, containing West, was to be encased in a large plywood structure that would be lowered into the ground by a large crane. A cement mixer truck was ordered at the ready, and as soon as the crate was safely in its place in the ground, the entire enclosure was then covered in concrete on the sides and on top in order to protect it from would-be curiosity mongers or thieves.

Visitors to the site today will have absolutely no idea of what lies beneath. West, in her Ferrari, inside of a large hand-built plywood crate, encased in concrete, rests next to her husband, the late Ike West, Jr. The scene is marked by a simple marble headstone, denoting "Sandra West 1939–1977."

VERDICT: Absolutely true.
–Matt Stone

The only unusual visual aspect of Mr. and Mrs. West's burial site is that there are no other graves too near them, which makes sense considering what lies just beneath the grass that surrounds their headstones. Michael Frazier

THE DANCER AND THE DEADLY BUGATTI

LEGEND: Modern dance icon Isadora Duncan was strangled when her shawl became entangled in the wheel of her lover's Bugatti.

Isadora Duncan is, paradoxically, a widely celebrated yet largely forgotten figure. A century has passed since her greatest triumphs, and her revolutionary innovations are now taken for granted. She's been lionized as the first great pioneer of modern dance. But if she's remembered at all these days outside the dance world, it's mostly because she died in a macabre accident that was every bit as unlikely and theatrical as her life.

For most people, the most enduring image of Isadora Duncan is the final scene of the 1968 biopic that earned Vanessa Redgrave an Oscar nomination for her performance as the free-spirited dancer. In it, Duncan dances with a dark and handsome young man at a seaside soiree then climbs into a red Bugatti Type 37 fitted with headlights and cycle fenders. While he blasts through the streets of Nice, her billowing scarf becomes tangled around the ears of a knock-off hubcap. As the wheel spins, it yanks the scarf taut and snaps her neck, and she dies bloodlessly with her red hair billowing against the tail of the Bugatti. The scene is played as a fitting capstone to a glamorous and sometimes sordid career.

Of course, biopics are free to play fast and loose with the truth. According to local newspaper reports, Duncan died more prosaically while taking a test ride not in a Bugatti but a much-less-exotic Amilcar. On the other hand, there are also several far more romantic versions of her death. The most popular has her proclaiming (in French), "I go to love!" before climbing into a Bugatti for a tryst with the car's owner, a French race car driver. An even more fantastic scenario invokes a huge conspiracy involving a shadowy Russian lover and an elaborate cover-up designed to shield Duncan's reputation from scandal.

No doubt Duncan would have appreciated all of the attention and speculation her death generated. She was a woman who craved the spotlight, and she spent most of her adult life cavorting in its glare. When she was born in 1877, it took months rather than hours to circumnavigate

During an era when new forms of mass media were creating the first generation of truly international celebrities, Isadora Duncan was among the most famous women in the world, renowned both as an influential artist and as a notorious libertine. Redferns/Getty Images

the globe, and stardom, in the modern sense, tended be provincial. Yet Duncan was a genuinely international celebrity, as renowned in Paris and Moscow as she was in New York and San Francisco, where she'd been born. She was lauded by luminaries ranging from Auguste Rodin and George Bernard Shaw to Edith Wharton and Carl Sandburg. In fact, she might

А. ДУННАНЪ.
726.

Although her choreography would seem unadventurous to contemporary audiences, it was considered not only risqué but positively revolutionary during her lifetime, and she established the foundation for the development of modern dance. Hulton Archive/Getty Images

well have been the most famous woman in the world in the years leading up to World War I.

Duncan's breakthrough was rejecting the formal structure of ballet in favor of a form of dance that was emotional, naturalistic, and improvisational. She scandalized audiences with her innovations, which included baring her breast on stage. But her private life was even more

Vanessa Redgrave, as Isadora Duncan, cavorts in what appears to be a Bugatti Type 37 in the biopic *Isadora* a few moments before her scarf becomes entangled in the left rear wheel and strangles her. AF Archive/Alamy

outrageous. She had affairs with countless men and women, ranging from an illustrious Russian poet and a millionaire industrialist to a World War I flying ace and an anonymous cruise ship stoker. She had two children, both illegitimate, each with a different father. (In a cruel piece of foreshadowing, they drowned in the Seine after their chauffeur neglected to set the handbrake, and their car rolled into the river.)

By 1927, Duncan was past her prime. Although she'd been the subject of a flattering Janet Flanner profile in *The New Yorker* early that year, Duncan was overweight, drinking heavily, and desperate for sexual companionship. Her finances were a mess; debts followed her across Europe like a faithful dog. Her car—a puny Renault—was impounded to settle unpaid bills. Much to her disgust, she was reduced to writing her memoirs for the sole purpose of earning the money the book would presumably generate.

Duncan was living in a modest hotel and renting a studio just off the water on the Promenade des Anglais in Nice. But like a lot of larger-than-life characters, she maintained a coterie of friends who continued to support her. Among the most loyal was an American who'd been born Mary Dempsey but who'd reinvented herself as an Italian aristocrat by the name of Mary D'Este, later changed to Desti. Better known as the loving but less-than-attentive mother of motion picture writer-director Preston Sturges, Desti would become the first and most sympathetic of Duncan's many biographers.

According to Desti, the events that led to Duncan's death were set into motion while they ate at a small restaurant overlooking the water in the fall of 1927. During dinner, Duncan toasted an attractive young man at a nearby table. "Good heavens," Desti said. "That's a chauffeur you are drinking to."

"Oh, Mary, how bourgeoise you are!" Duncan replied. "He's nothing of the kind. Have you no eyes? He's a Greek god in disguise, and that's his chariot out there."

Duncan then pointed to what Desti described as "a lovely little Buggatti [sic] racing car, with red, white and blue circles around the tail."

It's worth noting that, though Desti was Duncan's faithful companion, she may not have been her most trustworthy biographer. "Mary Desti is not merely enthusiastically unreliable, but a good old constructive liar. Starting with herself," British dance historian Nesta Macdonald, a later Duncan biographer, wrote acidly in correspondence archived by The Bugatti Trust. "Every time one reads the lying friend Mary's book, the lies divide like the Red Sea and reveal a germ of truth—but she might just as well have left it out. It was the fashion not to put real names to people, but, in any case, Mary was practically dyslexic about names. (She mixed and muddled even the names of hotels, etc.)"

Another Duncan confidante and biographer, Victor Seroff, offered an alternative version of Duncan's first encounter with the car that would kill her. According to Seroff, he and Duncan stopped in front of an automobile garage during a walk through Nice several weeks before her death. There, she admired a "red Bugatti racing car" that she saw in the window. "I would love to have a ride in a car like that," she told him. So he suggested that either she or Desti call the proprietor of the shop, say they were thinking of buying it, and ask for a demonstration drive.

Although these accounts sound definitive, they're undermined by several problems. First of all, Desti misspelled "Bugatti" throughout her book, which pretty much destroys her credibility regarding car-related issues. Seroff, for his part, seemed profoundly uninterested in high-performance automobiles. (As he put it, "I hated fast and noisy driving in such cars.") Both of them referred to the extremely low-slung two-seater

This stamp from the Republic of Niger depicts a Bugatti Type 35, the most famous and successful of the racing Bugattis. The Type 37 sports car was essentially a Type 35 with a smaller, less sophisticated engine. Bocman1973/Shutterstock.com

as a race car, which it clearly wasn't. They also commented on the cramped cockpit, in which the single passenger sat to the left and slightly behind the driver—extremely uncommon for a Bugatti. Ditto for the red, white, and blue roundels on the tail.

Further muddying the waters, Duncan insisted on calling the driver "Bugatti" even though that wasn't his name. Granted, she had a long history of bestowing pet names upon favored friends. (Thus, her former lover Paris Singer, the blond-haired heir to the sewing machine fortune, was "Lohengrin," after the hero of Wagner's opera.) But she knew very well what a Bugatti was. In her obsessive research into Duncan's death, Macdonald found evidence that Duncan had been seen driving around Nice in a red Bugatti with red, white, and blue rings on the tail for most of the summer. Expatriate American heiress Peggy Guggenheim seemed to confirm this in her memoirs. "She came to visit us as Pramousquier in the little Bugatti car she was so soon to meet her death in," Guggenheim wrote. If so, then why was Duncan so eager to test-drive the Bugatti—if it was a Bugatti—she'd seen with Seroff?

DEATH

In any event, Duncan contacted the driver of the "Bugatti," which was housed elsewhere in Nice at the Helvetia Garage. Desti called him the car's owner. Seroff, who interviewed him a few days after Duncan's death, dismissively referred to him as the shop mechanic. He was later identified in local newspaper reports as garage proprietor Benoit Falchetto. If his published birth date is to be believed, he was 42 at the time that he met Duncan. This doesn't jive with Desti's description of him as "boyish" and Seroff's as "young." Duncan called him a "flying ace," but Macdonald claimed he'd been gassed during World War I, which implied that he was a foot soldier in the trenches rather than a decorated aviator. He later enjoyed a modest racing career driving Maseratis, Amilcars, and, yes, Bugattis. "He was a very good driver," the noted racer and motorsports historian T.A.S.O. Mathieson wrote to Macdonald, "not in the same class as Nuvolari, Caracciola, Varzi and Chiron, but still one of real ability."

According to Desti, Falchetto made two visits to Duncan's hotel, once speaking with her and once with Duncan. They made plans to meet for a test drive on the night of Wednesday, September 14, 1927. After a simple dinner at a nearby restaurant, Duncan and Desti returned to the studio and "danced wildly" as they waited for Falchetto. Desti later claimed that she felt a premonition of catastrophe, which sounds like a romantic fiction. But Desti's misgivings were, in fact, mentioned in several newspaper accounts published the day after the tragedy. "Please, Isadora, don't go into that auto," she pleaded. "My nerves are terribly unstrung; I'm afraid something might happen to you."

"My dear," Duncan said, "I would go for this ride tonight even if I were sure it would be my last."

From their window, they saw Falchetto drive up. As usual, Duncan was wearing the heavily fringed red Chinese shawl that Desti had painted for her. "This shawl was two yards long and sixty inches wide, of heavy crepe, with a great yellow bird almost covering it, and blue Chinese asters and Chinese characters in black—a marvelous, lovely thing, the light of Isadora's life," Desti recalled later. "She would go nowhere without it." Another companion threw a second red shawl, this one made of wool, around Duncan to keep her warm against the cool coastal air.

Desti ran down ahead of Duncan to talk to Falchetto. "I don't believe you realize what a great person you are driving tonight," she told him. "I beg of you to be careful, and if she asks you to go fast, I beg you not to."

"Madame, you need have no fear," he said. "I've never had an accident in my life."

Falchetto offered Duncan his leather jacket, but she refused, instead choosing to wrap her crepe shawl around her neck and shoulders.

"Highway Robbery"

Male celebrities have died in car crashes exponentially more often than their female counterparts. Even more striking than this disparity is the fact that most of the prominent women killed in automobile wrecks were passengers rather than drivers.

Princess Grace of Monaco was one notable exception, though she wasn't to blame: she suffered a stroke while driving to Monaco in 1992. But Princess Diana was a passenger when her Mercedes crashed while being chased by paparazzi in Paris in 1997. So was newswoman Jessica Savitch when she drowned in a canal in Pennsylvania in 1983. Ditto for blues singer Bessie Smith, who died en route from Memphis to Mississippi in 1937.

Jayne Mansfield, a buxom blonde marketed as a poor man's Marilyn Monroe, was killed when the Buick Electra she was riding in slid into and under a truck. Her death prompted the promulgation of new safety regulations.
Hulton Archive/Getty Images

But the incident that seems most similar to Isadora Duncan's was the accident that killed—and reportedly decapitated—blond bombshell Jayne Mansfield.

In 1967, though she was only 34, Mansfield was on the downside of a career that had peaked with a handful of A-list movies. After an evening gig at a supper club in Biloxi, Mississippi, she was driven to New Orleans in a Buick Electra for an early morning television interview. On Highway 90, her car rear-ended and slid under a tractor-trailer. The impact sheared the top off the Electra, instantly killing Mansfield and the two men sharing the front seat with her.

Mansfield died of traumatic head injuries. Police photos of what appeared to be blond hair in the crumpled windshield fueled rumors that Mansfield had been decapitated. In fact, a radio reporter who visited the scene shortly after the accident said that Mansfield had been ejected from the car and that the hair was from a wig that apparently flew off her head.

Shortly after the accident, the National Highway Traffic Safety Administration mandated a so-called underride guard to prevent cars from sliding underneath trucks in rear-end collisions. These devices are often known as "Mansfield bars."

She climbed into the car next to him and theatrically cried (in French), "Goodbye, my friends. I go to glory." This quote isn't in any of the newspaper accounts. And American writer Glenway Wescott, who was a close friend of both women, claimed that Desti later told him that Duncan actually said, "I go to love."

Whatever she said, they were her last words. Seconds later, she was dead.

As Falchetto drove off, Desti noticed Duncan's red crepe scarf hanging out of the car and dragging on the ground. She shouted (in French); "Isadora, your shawl, your shawl, your shawl." Falchetto immediately braked to a stop. But the damage had already been done. The fringe of the shawl had become caught up in—depending on the source—the knock-off hubcap, the drum brake, the spokes, or the axle of the left rear wheel. As the wheel rotated, it fatally tightened the shawl around Duncan's neck, transforming the long scarf into a garrote.

Contrary to the depiction in the movie *Isadora*, Duncan's death was brutally violent. Her body was yanked partly out of the cockpit, and her head was wedged so tightly between the tire and the bodywork that the shawl had to be cut to release her. Her larynx was crushed, her jugular severed and her spine broken in two places. In addition, her nose was ground off by the spokes of the spinning wheel, and a large quantity of blood pooled underneath the car. Duncan died immediately. But after officially being pronounced dead at a nearby hospital, her body was returned to her studio, where Wescott said it continued to ooze blood from various wounds through the nightlong vigil.

The accident was a huge story. *The New York Times* splashed a dispatch from Paris over its front page with lurid headlines. ("Had Premonition Of Death." "Tragedy Marked Career." "Founder of Modern Classical Dance Gained World Fame, but Often Could Not Pay Debts.") All of the major English-language wire services ran long stories about the accident. Naturally, French newspapers offered even more extensive coverage, with the most credible and detailed accounts appearing in the local daily, *Le Petit Niçois.*

In its first-day coverage, probably written under severe deadline pressure, the Nice newspaper identified the car as a Bugatti. But the follow-up story, published the next day, refers to an Amilcar 7CV, with Nice license plate 2318 M9. The same identification was provided by *La France de Nice et du Sud-Est.* These comprehensive accounts are full of times and addresses that could only have come from police investigators or on-the-scene reporting. Other contemporary French articles, though not quite as detailed, referred to the car generically as a "grand sport." This, too, supports the identification of the car as an Amilcar since the two-seat CGS and CGSS models officially used the Grand Sport designation.

The case against a Bugatti is bolstered by several other factors. "CV," which stands for *cheval vapeur*, is the French term for fiscal horsepower—the engine rating used to assess vehicle taxes. A car rated at 7CV would have been quite small. (The Renault 4CV, which was built considerably later, was only 760cc.) At the time, the largest engine found in an sport (rather than a touring) Amilcar was 1.1 liters. The motor in the Bugatti Type 37 displaced 1.5 liters and generated about twice as much horsepower as the Amilcar Grand Sport. Also, virtually every article about the accident mentioned the unusual cockpit configuration as a factor in Duncan's death. Staggered seating wasn't normally a feature of Bugattis. But in an Amilcar Grand Sport, the cockpit was so tight that the passenger sat slightly behind the driver. Oh, and another thing: Amilcars often were customized with red, white and blue stripes down the tail that looked like roundels when viewed from the rear. Bugattis? Rarely, if ever.

Still, it's easy to understand how the cars got confused. The Amilcar Grand Sport came in a CGSS—the extra S stood for *surbaissé*, or lowered—form that looked remarkably like a Bugatti Type 37. Both were roadsters with horse-collar grilles and low-slung torpedo bodies, which is why the Amilcar was often called "the poor man's Bugatti." Neither Desti nor Seroff were car experts, so they may have been using "Bugatti" the same way a modern observer might say "Ferrari" to describe a type of car rather than a specific model. At the same time, the Bugatti was a better fit for Duncan's extravagant life and dramatic death. The modestly priced Amilcar was the early French equivalent of a Mazda Miata—an agile, spirited, and reliable sports car for the masses. A fine car, to be sure, but it lacked the Bugatti's cachet. Duncan dying in an Amilcar would have been like Princess Di being killed in a Toyota Camry rather than an S-Class Mercedes.

Which brings us to Nesta Macdonald's incredible tale of deceit. This recap is drawn from her long correspondence with world-renowned Bugatti expert Hugh Conway, whose collection of books, photos, drawings, letters, and articles formed the basis of The Bugatti Trust archive. Although Macdonald wrote extensively about Duncan, she died before publishing her suspicions about Duncan's death, possibly because she wasn't able to nail down all the particulars. But she spent the better part of a decade investigating it, and she put together a scenario that, like most conspiracy theories, is crafted to fit the known facts and larded with details that can't be verified.

Based on photos and her own research, Macdonald was convinced that the working-class Falchetto was too uncouth, too déclassé and too unattractive to interest Duncan. She found the story of the late-night test drive ludicrous and implied that Desti had confused Benoit Falchetto with the much younger and more celebrated Robert Benoist, who won the Grand Prix world championship in 1927. But Duncan's lover, according to Macdonald, was somebody altogether different—a White Russian artist by the name of Boris. Her sources informed her that he used to squire her around in a Bugatti that had been provided to him by one of his three other mistresses. One night, while Boris was driving her home from a party, she was strangled by her shawl. When he realized she was dead, he panicked and ran off to his nearby apartment.

"The abandoned car may not have been spotted for some time—probably not until the small hours," Macdonald wrote to Conway. "Too late for the morning papers. It might even have been found by people leaving from the same party. The police must have put a stopper on 'news' and very few people can have been involved at that stage. Then, the story was concocted for the evening of the 14th—instead of around midnight [on the] 13-14. Because the owner of the car was the rich Russian woman, Naryshkin, the real car was kept quiet—and the substitute, an Amilcar, which Falchetto had for sale, substituted, and him along with it—for money. No crime, or they could not have done it."

This account is so wildly implausible that it almost seems unfair to start picking it apart. For starters, there's the necessary enormity of the conspiracy, which has to include not only Desti, Falchetto, and the mysterious Boris but also the police, the hospital, and the coroner. The idea that the death of such a prominent figure, in such a public place, could have been covered up for nearly an entire day is preposterous. There's also the inconvenient fact that several newspapers cited a local industrialist—identified by name, profession, and address—who witnessed the accident, helped Desti free Duncan from the Amilcar and then transported the bloody body to the hospital in his car. Oh, and don't forget the friend who recalled seeing Duncan's corpse oozing blood in Desti's studio even though this would have been a full day after her death. And even though Macdonald scornfully describes Falchetto as being mercenary enough to accept a bribe, he also had to be noble enough never to reveal the truth, even to his own family.

No, Macdonald's theory doesn't hold up even to cursory examination. Duncan died as Desti described it, and that was macabre enough. Since then, her life has been the source of perpetual fascination and the subject of countless monographs and biographies, most recently Peter Kurth's excellent *Isadora: A Sensational Life*, published in 2001. But when it comes to Duncan's demise, the last word belongs to her fellow expatriate, Gertrude Stein. "Affectations can be dangerous," she said. Then again, affectation was part of Duncan's genius—in death as well as life.

VERDICT:
Mostly true. The legend of Isadora Duncan's death is largely correct, but the car was an Amilcar rather than a Bugatti. *–Preston Lerner*

6

INSIDE
THE
INDUSTRY

THE NORSEMAN ON THE
ANDREA DORIA

LEGEND: A famous Chrysler Concept car sunk to the bottom of the ocean aboard the *Andrea Doria* cruise liner.

Today most people refer to them as "concept cars." By "them" we mean those one-off dream machines, mock-ups, design studies, and turntable toys intended to dazzle us at auto shows, give potential customers and the media a hint at specific vehicles or automotive design language that's coming in the near future, and possibly even gauge reaction to the same. Virgil M. Exner Sr. used a different name—he called them Idea Cars, because to this visionary designer and design department leader, the power of good ideas was everything. He began his career as an advertising illustrator. As a young design phenom and protégé of GM design boss Harley Earl, Exner ran the Pontiac styling department before leaving to join Raymond Loewy and Associates in 1938, there working primarily on Studebaker projects. Exner was dismissed by Loewy in 1944, only to join Studebaker directly. Even though Loewy gets much of the credit for Studebaker's fresh postwar designs, much of that effort should be more correctly attributed to Exner. Exner left Studebaker in 1949 to join Chrysler's design studio, ultimately to become Chrysler's styling chief and a member of the board.

Exner rightly assessed that Chrysler's early postwar cars were staid and boxy and went to work revolutionizing their look to be more in step with the postwar jet age. He was immediately successful, his new "Forward Look" designs were sexy and exciting, and sales improved dramatically. "Ex" as he was affectionately nicknamed, respected the great work being done by so many of Italy's design houses and automotive bodybuilders, and soon established a friendship and business relationship with one of the best—Luigi Segre ran Ghia in Turin, Italy—and Exner saw the value of a relationship with an Italian *carozzeria* that could turn out high, quality one-offs in relatively little time and at affordable costs. Soon followed a decade-plus-long parade of Idea Cars that enthused the public, the media, and Chrysler management and customers.

In an internally published catalog about Idea Cars, Chrysler stated that they . . . "had to be more than just a show car that was simply a production model with special paint and upholstery. Yet it couldn't be an

The Chrysler Norseman, as photographed before it was crated and loaded aboard the *Andrea Doria*. It was a handsome piece of design and hand-built craftsmanship, these period black-and-white photos not showing the multiple soft shades of green it was painted. Chrysler publicity photo

This profile shows the Norseman's long hood and rear deck, along with its airy glass house and luxurious proportions. Note ultra-think steel rods as windshield posts. Chrysler publicity photo

This elevated three-quarter rear view shows the Norseman's fastback rear deck treatment and elegantly rounded fins; tailfin treatments were of course all the rage in the mid 1950s, although the Chrysler and Ghia design teams managed to make theirs look much different than what would have been found on a Cadillac or Lincoln. Chrysler publicity photo

impractical 'dream car.' It had to have a completely new body that would interest and even startle the casual observer. It had to have new, practical, usable ideas in body styling and passenger accommodation."

The Idea Cars are well known to anyone who is a student of automotive design and include landmarks such as the Chrysler Special, the K-310, Flight-Sweep I and II, the original DeSoto Adventurer and Adventurer II, the GS-1, Plymouth Belmont, several iterations of Dodge Firearrow and many others. Of the 28 vehicles built from 1940 through 1961 that Chrysler identifies as Idea Cars, 24 of them were built in cooperation with Ghia; largely designed by Exner and his staff in the United States, then detailed and built by Ghia in Turin.

Once their days as dazzling turntable toys are over, some concept cars spend a quiet retirement in the carmaker's museum or heritage collection. Over the years, many have been appropriated by design studio chiefs or other corporate executives for use as personal transport. Some are disassembled and the parts reused in the creation of other concept cars. Far too many have been cut into pieces or crushed whole and destroyed.

One of Exner's jet-age concepts, the Chrysler Norseman of 1956, like Luca Brasi of *The Godfather* fame, now "sleeps with the fishes." The Norseman's principle design innovation was the use of a roof section that was cantilevered from the rear and appeared to float over the front half of the car, using no thick, conventional windshield pillars. Exner's main goal with this design was to make the car appear "visually lighter" and to improve the driver's forward visibility without thick "A pillars" to impede the view. In place of the traditional windshield posts, the Norseman employed chromed steel rods at the corners of the windshield to help hold up the roof and support the glass. The Norseman was a good-looking car, combining a sweeping fastback rear end design and Chrysler's own take on a tailfin and bumper treatment. The Norseman also employed hideaway headlamps up front, and a finely detailed chrome grille. The Norseman's cabin design was elegant and filled with chrome and other luxury detailing, including large, thickly upholstered front bucket seats with a wide, padded center console in the middle.

As with most of the rest of Chrysler's Idea cars, Exner and his styling team designed the car and then provided Ghia with a Chrysler chassis and powertrain. The car was built in Turin during the first half of 1956, and completed in the early summer. On July 17, it was loaded aboard the Italian luxury cruise liner *Andrea Doria*, which was preparing to embark for New York. The Norseman, being more than a mere automobile, was specially crated and packed into the *Doria*'s Number 2 cargo hold with great care to ensure it made the 4,000-mile journey to America safely and without suffering any damage.

Sadly, the Norseman never got to strut its stuff and show its innovative design features to the world on the 1957 show car circuit. Because, in one of the worst civilian maritime disasters in history, the elegant *Andrea Doria*, sailing just off the coast of Nantucket and only a few hours from safe harbor in New York, was struck broadside by the SS *Stockholm*, another passenger liner, of Swedish registry, at around 11:00 p.m. on the evening of July 25, 1956. The gravely wounded *Doria* took on water and began listing immediately but somehow stayed afloat well into the next morning, at which time, when her nose was fully submerged, she pointed her tail toward the sky and began a tragic dive toward the ocean bottom with the Chrysler Norseman aboard.

The injured *Stockholm* remained afloat, and even though her ride height had dropped several feet due to the damage to her bow, she was able to assist in rescuing passengers from the *Andrea Doria* and miraculously steamed into New York harbor under her own power.

Naturally, there were numerous inquests as to how this tragedy could have taken place. Given the dark, foggy conditions at the moment of the

"The Ever Graceful Italian: SS *Andrea Doria*"

The SS *Andrea Doria* was an ocean liner owned and run by the Italian Line and is unfortunately best known for its sinking in 1956. Named after the sixteenth-century military admiral Andrea Doria, the ship was rated at 29,100 tons with a capacity of about 1,200 passengers and 500 crew members. It wasn't as large or as grandly fantastic as the *Titanic*, nor did its sinking take nearly so many lives.

Of graceful design and lushly decorated with the Italian artworks, the *Andrea Doria* was an icon of national pride. It was quick and sporty-looking in a large, elegant way, and reputedly safe. It was launched on June 16, 1951, and undertook its maiden voyage in 1953.

Struck in its port side by the SS *Stockholm* on July 25, 1956, the top-heavy *Doria* listed severely to starboard, which left about half of its lifeboats underwater and thus inaccessible. The consequent shortage of lifeboats might have resulted in a more significant loss of life, but amazingly, the ship remained afloat for over 11 hours after being hit by the *Stockholm* before sinking off the coast of Nantucket.

The Italian ship the *Andrea Doria*. Gamma-Keystone via Getty Images

The *Andrea Doria* having a really bad day—July 27, 1956, to be exact. Hulton Archive/Getty Images

collision, it is likely that both ships were traveling slightly too fast, and it's generally accepted that various crewmembers failed to properly read the radar signals showing the other ship's location and direction of travel. It's unfortunate that the two ships failed to contact each other or otherwise communicate their positions, in which case the disaster might have been avoided. Five people aboard the *Stockholm* died, and approximately 46 *Doria* passengers and crewmembers also perished.

Strange though it may sound, the Norseman's fate is, perhaps in some ways, better than the destiny that awaited it in the United States. Chrysler's plan for the car was to tour the 1957 auto show circuit. Then, in order to test the structural rigidity of its unusual roof design, it was scheduled to be crashed at Chrysler's Proving Grounds. The Norseman would surely have impressed show goers had it made it to the United States and safely into Chrysler's hands. But in a way, it is now part of a greater more historic story, and having been aboard the *Andrea Doria*'s final voyage, it avoided the injustice of crash testing and systematic destruction once its days on the auto show tour were done.

Chicago native Joe Bortz has purchased, rescued, and restored many of Detroit's most famous concept cars, including some that have been cut into many pieces and long thought destroyed. One of the world's experts in the area of factory design studies and concept cars, Bortz knew of the Norseman and its unfortunate fate. He wondered, given today's advanced industrial diving techniques, if the car could be located within the ship, extracted, brought to the surface, and restored. After some research a few years back, Bortz was introduced to an industrial diver who claimed he could do the job. Bortz pursued additional research plus discussion with scientists qualified to assess what the car's condition might be after more than 50 years under water. Bortz and company concluded that the ravages of time, pressure, and the corrosive nature of saltwater will have reduced the hapless Norseman to little more than rusty sludge.

Thus, the Chrysler Norseman rests aboard the *Andrea Doria*, which lies on her starboard side, off the cost of Nantucket, Massachusetts, some 250 feet below the ocean's surface.

VERDICT:
Absolutely true.
–Matt Stone

WHEN PINTOS FLY

LEGEND: With a little bit of luck, the Ford Pinto could have been renowned for flying instead of exploding.

Few cars have better credentials for enshrinement in the Automotive Hall of Shame than the Ford Pinto. In 2004, *Forbes* cited it and 13 other stinkers as the "Worst Cars of All Time." *Time* later named it as one of "The 50 Worst Cars of All Time," while MSN anointed it among "The Worst Cars Ever." And *BusinessWeek*, in a clear case of piling on, added it to the list of "Fifty Ugliest Cars of the Past 50 Years."

The principal reason for the lack of love was the Pinto's notorious propensity to explode when hit from behind. Besides turning the car into a morbid joke—"the barbecue that seats four"—this fatal flaw also cost the company millions of dollars in liability lawsuits. In fairness, though, history has shown that the Pinto wasn't significantly more prone to fire than other cars of the era, when gas tanks were commonly located behind the rear axle. By the same token, the car's other supposed engineering and design failures also seem overblown in retrospect. At the time, at least, most Americans didn't find the Pinto objectionable. On the contrary, it was a hit with consumers, and Ford sold nearly 3 million Pintos before the gas tank controversy erupted.

When the car debuted in September 1970, it represented a new direction for American automakers. The popularity of small, cheap imports from Germany and, increasingly, Japan wasn't lost on the executives in Detroit. By truncating the Hornet to create the Gremlin, American Motors became the first American manufacturer to bring a subcompact to market. Ford and Chevy quickly unveiled their all-new Pinto and Vega, respectively. Although all three cars are now mocked as relics of the bad, old days of domestic manufacturing, they sold briskly enough to help Detroit automakers wrest market-share back from foreign competitors until the oil crises forever changed the American automotive landscape.

In greenlighting the Pinto, Lee Iacocca's goal was a car that weighed less than 2,000 pounds and cost less than $2,000. The first television spot for the 1971 model described it as "a little, carefree car to put a little kick in your life." Of course, with a 1.6-liter four-cylinder pushrod lump of iron making a measly 54 horsepower, a little kick was all it could manage. But with a few clever modifications, aeronautical engineer Henry Smolinski was convinced that the car was capable of far more—a top speed of 171 mph, for example, and an altitude of 16,000 feet. Of course, this would have required

This rare color photo of the AVE Mizar being tested at Oxnard Airport shows off the custom graphics created at Galpin Ford. The one-of-a-kind flying car was created by crossing a Ford Pinto with a Cessna Skymaster. Doug Duncan

the addition of wings. And a propeller. And a second engine to turn it, not to mention flight controls and federal certification. But Smolinski was convinced that, with a little bit of development, he could sell thousands of flying Pintos.

The idea was to attach the wings, rear engine, and part of the fuselage of a Cessna Skymaster to a Ford Pinto with four self-locking pins. "Our plan is to make the operation so simple that a woman can easily put the two systems together—or separate them—without help," Smolinski told the media. "We are doing nothing outside the state of the art of flying. In making a car airborne, we feel there are no problems that cannot be solved. The only reason this project wasn't done sooner is that cars were heavier years ago and aircraft was not as advanced as today. Unitized construction of cars, along with a more aerodynamic design plus advances in aircraft, now make it possible to manufacture a flying car."

The flying car concept has been a favorite fancy of would-be inventors for more than a century—longer, in fact, than powered flight. Romanian polymath Traian Vuia received a patent for a flying car four months before the Wright brothers' first flight at Kitty Hawk, and he flew briefly in the primitive machine in 1906. Credit for the first modern flying car is usually given to aeronautical pioneer Glenn Curtiss, whose ungainly looking Autoplane appeared in 1917. Although his "aerial limousine" earned a patent, it was no more successful than Vuia's contraption. Still, Henry Ford famously declared in 1940: "Mark my word. A combination airplane and motorcar is coming. You may smile. But it will come."

With a portion of the fuselage and entire rear propeller assembly bolted to the Pinto, rear visibility was obviously problematic. Airworthiness also proved to be a fundamental and, ultimately, fatal issue. Doug Duncan

He was right, in a sense. The endlessly fascinating Roadable Times website offers details about more than 100 flying car designs. Several of them have made it not only off the drawing board but actually into the air. Nevertheless, the flying car remains a clever idea whose time resolutely refuses to come. Or maybe it's a foolish pipedream that obstinately refuses to die. Despite a century of proselytizing by true believers, flying cars have never generated anything more than idle curiosity among the general public. And engineers generally scorn them as kludges that are neither fish nor fowl. As aviation writer Peter Garrison, himself an airplane designer/builder, put it in *Flying* magazine: "The incompatibilities between automotive and aeronautical engineering are often summarized in the dismissive comment that if it's a good car it can't be a good airplane, and if it's a good airplane, it can't be a good car."

The closest a flying car has come to success was the Aerocar. Built by flying car patron saint Molt Taylor, the Aerocar mated a tiny, fiberglass front-wheel-drive car of his own design to wings and what's known as a pusher prop that could be detached and mounted in a trailer. Taylor built and flew a prototype and four production models. One of them was sold to a Portland, Oregon, radio station for traffic reporting. Another appeared on the set of *I've Got a Secret*. In 1961, Ling-Temco-Vought agreed to build 1,000 Aerocars if Taylor could produce 500 firm orders. Unfortunately, he

Taxiing down the runway at Oxnard Airport. Power was only marginal for an aircraft as heavy as "The Flying Pinto," so both the Cessna's engine and the stock Ford four-banger were used to shorten the take-off roll. Doug Duncan

came up 222 orders short, sinking the deal. In 1970, there was a brief flirtation with Ford Motor Company. But this, too, led nowhere. And by that time, Hank Smolinski was already working on the Flying Pinto, though without any support from the folks in Dearborn.

A native of Cleveland, Ohio, Smolinski was a Southern California aerospace veteran who'd earned a BS in aeronautical engineering from the Northrop Aeronautical Institute. He joined North American Aviation in 1955 as a structural engineer on the FJ-4 Fury fighter-bomber, then worked on the Thor rocket engine at Rocketdyne. He later moved to Daniel, Mann, Johnson & Mendenhall (DMJM), an engineering giant that specialized in transportation. There, among other projects, he did advance design work on STOL (short takeoff and landing) and VTOL (vertical takeoff and landing) programs.

In 1968, Smolinski formed Advanced Vehicle Engineers to create what he originally called the Aircar. His idea was to follow Molt Taylor's template. But instead of reinventing the wheel with scratch-built components, he decided to dramatically reduce development costs by using already proven pieces from existing cars and airplanes. Pretty much any car would do as long as it was light enough. Smolinski reported that there were about 50 cars that met his specifications. Over the years, Advanced Vehicle Engineers (AVE) literature specifically named the Pinto and Vega, and artist's renderings

Test pilot Red Janisse at the controls of the Mizar. Janisse was in the hospital when designer Hank Smolinski took the airplane up for what turned out to be its final flight in 1973. Doug Duncan

pictured a Pontiac Firebird and AMC Javelin. But the airplane requirements were much more exacting. Smolinski's design necessitated a high wing and a pusher prop. So he quickly homed in on the Cessna Skymaster.

The Skymaster was Cessna's quirky attempt to build a twin-engine utility airplane that would be perfectly stable even if one engine failed. Instead of mounting the engines on each wing—the conventional arrangement in a twin—they were placed fore and aft of the cockpit, thereby pushing and pulling the airplane simultaneously. To provide room for the rear propeller blades, the fuselage split behind the cockpit into a pair of P-38-style twin booms that connected to a wide vertical stabilizer. A military variant dubbed the O-2 saw action in Vietnam as the Air Force's primary forward air control aircraft. Later, these airplanes did yeoman duty in aerial firefighting operations.

By 1970, Smolinski had put together a management team. He would serve as AVE president and project leader. Another DMJM alum, computer and marketing maven Hal Blake, was named vice president. (Stanley Moe, a DMJM founder/architect who worked extensively on the space program, served on the board of directors.) Lois McDonald, who was described in press releases and news stories as the mother of five and "an attractive blond pilot," was designated the chief test pilot.

It's a car! It's a plane! It's a flying car! The Mizar flew on numerous occasions out of airports in Oxnard and Van Nuys. Smolinski and company vice president Hal Blake were killed when a wing support failed in flight. Doug Duncan

With this team in place, Smolinski began making the rounds with a "Proposal for Flying a Car." His pitch sought $464,460 in initial financing, with $25,000 as a retainer. His optimistic projections called for first-year sales of 12,000 flying cars. At this rate of production, he estimated that the retail price would be $15,000, which broke down into $4,500 for the car, $5,500 for the aircraft engine and $5,000 for the airframe. Looking back, all of these numbers seem wildly unrealistic, especially since Smolinski didn't account for what promised to be the exorbitant costs of certifying the flying car. But as with any pitch, Job One was finding a taker.

Inevitably, Smolinski found his way to the office of Bert Boeckmann at Galpin Ford. Besides being located a few minutes from the hangar where AVE had set up shop at Van Nuys Airport, Galpin was on its way to becoming the largest-volume Ford dealer in the world. These days, Boeckmann presides over an automotive empire, Galpin Motors, that accounts for $500 million in annual sales. Then as now, one of the secrets of his success was his ability to raise the profile of the dealership with over-the-top promotions. He was also a big believer in installing accessories and making modifications to new cars at the dealership, a process that he called Galpinizing. So funding the development of a flying car based on a Ford chassis was a no-brainer. "Commercially, I didn't know if it would ever take off," he says. "But I thought that it would certainly generate a lot of publicity."

To a certain degree, Boeckmann was investing in Smolinski as much as his product. "The [flying car] was his dream. He believed in it 100 percent," Boeckmann recalls. "I remember him telling me, 'If I have to die, I want to die in my plane.'" Jack Ong, Galpin's marketing and advertising director at the time, was another big fan of Smolinski's. "He was very calm, very cool, soft-spoken, a gentleman with an adventurer's heart," he says. "The way Hank presented it, the whole concept seemed really viable."

Despite his appreciation for the promotional value of a flying Pinto, Boeckmann was also a hardheaded businessman who had no intention of betting the farm on the project. "It was a shoestring deal," he says. "I worried about that sometimes. I didn't want [Smolinski] cutting corners because he didn't have enough money." Although Boeckmann agreed to pay $1 million for the distribution rights for the flying car, this was contingent on the vehicle actually going into production, and that was years down the road. He says he no longer remembers how much he invested in the project, but his total outlay was less than $200,000. (It's often reported that $2 million was spent on developing the flying car, but it's not clear where this figure came from.) Also, according to an agreement executed on December 15, 1970, Boeckmann agreed to provide two 1971 Pintos valued at $3,000 apiece.

The Pinto seemed like a sensible choice since, at less than 2,000 pounds, it was one of the lightest American cars on the market. As an aeronautical engineer with plenty of experience working for major aerospace contractors, Smolinski understood how to put together a development program. He created a meticulously structured calendar that called for the sequential design, construction, and flight testing of six prototypes. P-1 would be unveiled in June 1973. P-6—equipped with a then-novel (and still unusual) airframe parachute—would undergo a 50-hour flight endurance test. Only then would the flying car go into production.

Smolinski acquired a Skymaster and began flying it with the front propeller feathered and various modifications meant to mimic the "dirty" aerodynamic qualities of a Pinto. By 1972, he was confident enough about the project to sell one now-superfluous engine to Peter Garrison. "I paid him $1,100 for the front engine of the Skymaster," Garrison says, "and I remember him being displeased that I interpreted our deal rather generously as including the Dukes electric fuel pump, a pricey bauble itself." The Skymaster was then carved up and mated to the Pinto. When the conversion was complete, Galpin's in-house painter, Orville Dittmann, and his young assistant, Marty Lorentzen, striped the white machine with walnut fire metallic paint.

By 1973, the Flying Pinto prototype was being taxi-tested and hopping briefly into the air at Van Nuys Airport. Although Lois McDonald was nominally the chief test pilot, she didn't have enough experience to develop an experimental airplane with marginal power and questionable aerodynamic qualities. So Charles "Red" Janisse, who'd ferried O-2 Super Skymasters to Southeast Asia during the Vietnam War, was hired to lead the flight-test program. Press releases were sent out to announce that the flying car would be formally unveiled in May. But first, an important milestone had to be achieved. "Up until then, we'd just called it 'The Flying Pinto,'" Jack Ong recalls. "But we decided to give it a better name."

Ong's partner, designer/illustrator Dirk Wunderlich, started researching the names of stars and constellations. Eventually, the two of them chose to rename the Flying Pinto as the Mizar, which had a definite *Star Trek* vibe. (For the record, Mizar is a star near the end of the Big Dipper's handle. Mizar and its binary companion, Alcor, are sometimes referred to as the "Horse and Rider," which tied in loosely to the Pinto's pony car heritage.) As Galpin's marketing and advertising manager, Ong was also determined to get as much publicity out of the Mizar as he could generate. "It wasn't really flyable yet," he says. "But I told Bert, 'This is the time to start shooting a short film, not so much as a documentary but as a sales pitch.'"

The 10-minute 16-millimeter movie—which can be seen on YouTube—made the commercial case for the Mizar: "Simple to operate as an airplane, more convenient than any modern automobile." The film shows a Pinto being driven from a suburban driveway to Van Nuys Airport, backed into a set of wings and then flown along over the endemic traffic of Southern California. Besides producing the film, Ong also wrote the script—and the lyrics for the jingle, "I Wanna Fly." Wunderlich served as the cinematographer and editor. "We flew in the plane twice, two 20-minute flights," Ong says. "We flew out of Van Nuys and got shots of the freeways and the Malibu coastline. I was in the car getting ambient sound and Dirk was strapped in the seat of a helicopter, hanging out while he filmed. We had a ball."

The AVE Mizar made its public debut at Van Nuys Airport on May 8, 1973. "A trip begins and ends at the doorstep!" AVE's promotional material declared. "For long distance trips, ADVANCED VEHICLE ENGINEERS believe the logical approach to point-to-point transportation is to drive an automobile to an airport, attach wings to the car, fly to a desired airport, remove the wings, and complete the journey in the same vehicle."

The Pinto shown to reporters had undergone multiple upgrades ranging from a more robust rear suspension to a large secondary cluster of airplane-specific instrument gauges. The telescoping steering column doubled as an airplane control wheel, operating the ailerons and elevator, and the footwell had been retrofitted with retractable rudder pedals. The Pinto backed into and under the 38-foot-wide wings and partial fuselage of a Cessna Skymaster. The airplane components locked into self-aligning rails on the roof of the car. Additional support for the wings was provided by struts that attached to the rocker panel just ahead of the rear wheels. The engine stuck out behind the rear hatch, and the twin booms and tail extended beyond the propeller. Although both the car and airplane engines could be used together to shorten takeoff rolls, only the Cessna's original unit was necessary. Once off the ground, the Mizar operated like a conventional airplane. It then landed on the rear wheels and rolled to a stop produced by four-wheel disc brakes.

Although the Mizar 210 prototype showed at Van Nuys was equipped with a 210-horsepower Teledyne Continental engine, Smolinski intended to sell production models with larger, more powerful AVCO Lycoming 540-series engines. The Mizar 235, 260, and 300 would max out at 156, 163, and 171 mph, respectively, with the service ceiling rising from 12,000 to 14,000 to 16,000 feet. Retail prices would range from $18,300 to $28,058. Considering the cost of new Pintos and Skymasters, it's not clear how AVE intended to make money at this price point. But the company released an extensive price list for options and accessories. Smolinski also intended to sell a wingless but flight-modified version of the Pinto—called the Runabout—for $5,774. The idea was that only one person in a family or a group had to buy a fully equipped Mizar, and then the wings and aircraft engine could be shared with anybody who owned a Runabout.

The unveiling of the Mizar prompted newspaper coverage from coast to coast, and the flying car eventually was featured in *Hot Rod*. Although most of the stories marveled at the incongruity of a flying Pinto, they accepted the feasibility of the project without much skepticism. A piece in the *Oxnard Press-Courier* quoted Hal Blake as saying that the company had already taken 34 orders and expected to crank out the first production model in late 1974. Meanwhile, a writer for the *Chicago Tribune* was enterprising enough to get a wry comment from a Ford official. "It's a very interesting idea, but I really doubt if we'll be offering propellers and wings as options," Eugene Koch told the newspaper.

In late June, a press release proudly announced that the flight test program had begun at Oxnard Airport in Ventura County. The first flights, it said, "averaged between 30 and 60 feet high [and] were of approximately 90-second duration." On July 1, numerous papers ran Associated Press photos of the Mizar in flight. At first glance, this seemed to be a giant coup. But the caption told a different story: It turned out that test pilot Red Janisse had been forced to make an emergency landing in a field 1.5 miles from the airport after experiencing a propeller problem. Accompanied by a police escort, he drove the undamaged airplane back to the airport "on a road cleared of conventional traffic."

Flight testing clearly demonstrated the Mizar's fundamental weakness. Although it was roughly the same weight as a Cessna Skymaster, it had only half the power. Plus, the flying car had the aerodynamic qualities of a 2 x 4—maybe worse, with the four tires hanging down in the windstream. After watching a Mizar do a low-speed flyby for a BBC film crew, aviation writer Peter Abbott III wrote, "More power would seem well warranted, for Red Janisse flew the course in a somewhat nose-high attitude at what appeared to be a behind-the-power-curve situation."

Since buying the surplus Skymaster engine from Smolinski, Garrison had followed the project "with considerable skepticism." He heard that the AVE team replaced the two-bladed propeller with a three-bladed prop in an effort to produce some more oomph. The promotional movie put together by Galpin Ford showed what he described as "persistent wing rock [and] a flat climb." Looking back, he says, "The thing was probably more or less airworthy, just terribly heavy, and the bigger body may have reduced the stabilizer effectiveness. It certainly increased the drag."

Boeckmann says the AVE team procured a new, more powerful engine. (According to a later newspaper report, it was a 300-horsepower Lycoming—presumably one of the 540-series engines intended for the production version of the Mizar.) When the installation was completed, Janisse happened to be in the hospital, so Smolinski and Blake went to Oxnard to perform taxi tests, and Galpin painter Orville Dittmann accompanied them to do some touchup work. The date was September 11, 1973.

The taxi tests went well. Boeckmann recalls that a shaken Dittmann later told him, "Smolinski was so excited that he said, 'Let's take it up.' My painter said, 'Let me out here'—good for him." Technically, the Mizar wasn't supposed to be flown without first informing airport officials so they could alert emergency crews. It may be that Smolinski didn't intend to make a serious flight, just a quick bunny-hop. But the more powerful engine must've pushed the Mizar faster than usual, and once Smolinski left the ground, he evidently didn't have enough runway to land. Instead, he climbed into the traffic pattern. Two minutes later, disaster struck. "One wing folded," an eyewitness reported in the *Press-Courier*, "then the craft began racing to the ground, parts flying from it."

While a horrified Dittmann watched from the airport, the Mizar plummeted out of the sky with its right wing folded up like a fighter parked on an aircraft carrier. The stricken vehicle clipped the top of a eucalyptus tree about 1.5 miles from the airport and hurtled toward a parked pickup truck owned by Seyto Marso Rillo. "I started to run and got only 10 feet when it plowed into my truck," he told the *Press-Courier*. "He said he was knocked to the ground by the 'exploding impact' and was struck by flying and flaming debris," the newspaper added. "He said he then saw his truck and the plane fully enveloped in fire." Smolinski and Blake were killed by the impact. Both men were 40 years old.

The Internet is full of uninformed speculation that the Mizar was victimized by shoddy workmanship. "I heard a report that the strut had been attached to the sheet metal sill below the car's door with cheap commercial blind rivets or sheet-metal screws, but it seems hard to believe that a professional engineer like Smolinski would use such inadequate fasteners," Garrison wrote in *Air & Space Smithsonian*. The bare-bones National Transportation Safety Board report cited "airframe failure in flight" and listed as probable causes "loose part/fitting," "poor weld," and "poor/inadequate design." According to the NTSB remarks about the accident, the right wing strut failed where it attached to the auto body panel.

After Smolinski's death, San Diego businessman Bill Green floated a proposal to continue work on a P-1B Mizar, but the AVE board of directors decided that the project wasn't commercially viable. During the nearly four decades since then, at least a dozen flying cars have made it off the drawing board if not actually into the hands of consumers. These days, the most promising seems to be a vehicle called the Transition, which was created by a company spun off from the Massachusetts Institute of Technology. Because the Transition is optimized for flying rather than driving, it's referred to as a roadable aircraft rather than a flying car. And maybe that's the way to go. But for better or worse, the dream of putting a production car in the air died with Hank Smolinski and Hal Blake in 1973.

VERDICT:
True, but even if the Mizar hadn't crashed fatally, the Flying Pinto was doomed to become a footnote to both automotive and aviation history. —*Preston Lerner*

"IF I ONLY HAD WINGS"

LEGEND: The 1959 Chevrolet Impala's batwing-styled rear fenders had a dangerous aerodynamic impact on the car, potentially causing the rear end to lift off the ground even at moderate speeds.

Motor Trend Classic magazine's technical director, Frank Markus, didn't buy this premise at all, in spite of several letters published in *Motor Trend* between March 1959 and August 1960, written by readers who claimed to have witnessed this effect. In 2005, Markus and GM designer Mark Florian decided to put the notion to the test, using Florian's own '59 Impala sedan and GM's world-class, full-scale wind tunnel. It took many months of negotiating to secure the needed hours of wind tunnel time to test the premise, but Florian and Markus got the job done, rolling Florian's blue and white Impala sedan into the GM wind tunnel, with Markus looking on, and photographer David Freers on hand to document the action.

The group performed a battery of tests intended not so much to measure the overall aerodynamic properties of the entire car, but to convict or exonerate the rear fins of the accusations of dangerous aerodynamic lift, which, if true, could cause the rear end of the car to get light or even lift off the ground. The car was ballasted to simulate the weight of two passengers and a full tank of gas, per Society of Automotive Engineers standards. The battery was disconnected and the brakes locked, in the name of added safety, and the tests began.

The notion may have seemed unlikely from the beginning; wouldn't GM have aerodynamically evaluated the shape of this car before its design was put into production? It may or may not have done so mathemamatcially on paper, but it could not have done so in practical application, since GM's wind tunnel wasn't built until 1980. Smaller-scale wind tunnels existed in other parts of the world in the late 1950s, but according to Markus, the radical batwing fender shape was designed and approved without any real-world aero testing.

The tunnel's massive wind generators were spooled up to near 50 mph, with various areas of the car blocked off by foam core panels in an attempt to isolate the aerodynamic effect of the rear fender wings only. The car was

El Camino and 1959 Chevy stationwagon models even boasted the big rear fins, yet *Motor Trend's* wind tunnel test absolved them of creating enough lift to make the cars fly or lift off the ground. GM publicity photo

If the bat-wings caused any aerodynamic problems, most likely they would have showed up here, on NASCAR's super speedways. Getty Images

pointed straight into the wind, and then turned in various directions to determine if side winds would be a factor.

Prior to any scientific testing of this nature, the car's design had already been largely vindicated on the high-banked tracks in NASCAR stock car racing. NASCAR legend Junior Johnson won the 1960 Daytona 500 in a '59 Chevrolet; in fact there was some concern at the time that the rear fender design gave him an unfair advantage. This notion was quickly

This 1959 Chevrolet Impala stands tall and proud in the General Motors Wind Tunnel, ready to prove that its distinctive "bat fin" rear fenders won't make the car fly, as was alleged by some back in the day. Motor Trend Classic Magazine and David Freers Photography, LLC

dismissed, and Johnson's win has stood the test of time uncontested. Johnson raced the same car at various high banked NASCAR tracks for the rest of the 1960 season, winning often and convincingly.

The wind tunnel and Markus' conclusions were clear: "At long last, the computers spit out definitive proof vindicating the fins. According to the most sophisticated instruments in the business, they contribute a miniscule amount of downforce. There's 64.4 pounds of lift in front and 1.2 pounds of downforce in back (lift coefficients of 0.416 and -0.008 respectively). They lift a bit in a side wind, but front lift goes up as well maintaining the same general vehicle attitude. The only way we were able to coax those fins into producing more lift than the front end does was to point them directly into the wind at 50 mph, and at that speed in reverse, oversteer is a problem in every car. Tell your fellow 1959-o-philes that they can hammer down the highways with confidence."

VERDICT:
The myth is simply untrue.
The shape of the '59 Chevy's rear fender fins might lead the untrained eye to think that they could act as wings, but *Motor Trend Classic's* well-considered scientific wind tunnel test proved that these rear fenders have no meaningful aerodynamic impact on the car's road manners and definitely will not make the rear end of the car rise or fly. –*Matt Stone*

WHO KILLED THE ELECTRIC CAR?

LEGEND: General Motors, the United States Government, and several major oil companies conspired to "kill" the electric car.

In his 2006 op/ed documentary, titled *Who killed the Electric Car,* filmmaker Chris Paine describes a scenario implicating General Motors, President George W. Bush (and others), and big oil in the death of the electric car. In his follow, up film, *Revenge of the Electric Car,* of 2011, Paine works hard to undo that notion, (primarily) chronicling the development of the Tesla, the Chevrolet Volt, and the Nissan Leaf. These are cars that, as of this writing,

GM's two most notable-modern, era electric cars. The EV1, foreground, was the fore-runner of General Motors' current electric car movement. Behind is the newer Chevrolet Volt, which isn't a pure electric in that it also has a gasoline-powered on-board range-extending generator, which recharges the batteries once the plug-in charge has been depleted. General Motors publicity photo

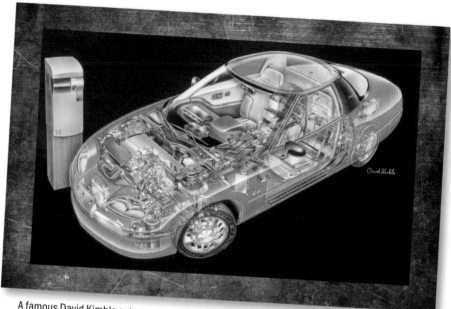

A famous David Kimble cutaway drawing of the revolutionary EV1. The car worked so well that EV1 lessees didn't want to give them back and even staged funerals and protests in objection to GM's ending of the program. General Motors publicity photo

are alive and well in the marketplace, so the purpose and content of the second film ultimately repudiates the premise of the first.

Who Killed the Electric Car chronicles the development and roughly 10-year life of the General Motors EV1, which, at the time of its joining the marketplace in 1996, was the first modern fully electric car produced by a major automotive corporation since prior to World War II. While the EV1 was a full-scale production automobile, the program was built around a limited, controlled supply volume from the beginning. GM had given it a finite life from birth, in that it was more intended as a long term "proof of concept" program to test the viability of modern electric cars for everyday use, and for the development of the technology required for that job, while meeting government regulatory and safety requirements. General Motors didn't sell EV1s; it leased them for a specific period of time and serviced them only at select Saturn dealers. The EV1 was not offered in all markets, although after its initial launch in Los Angeles, the EV1 was made available in other populous locales.

GM built the EV1 in part to do research into the feasibility of electric vehicles, but also in part to generate publicity. Thanks to the uproar surrounding the end of the EV1 program, the company got more publicity than it might have wanted. AFP/Getty Images

GM put a total of 1,117 EV1s into circulation, and the real ruckus began when the company felt they had served their purpose and began to reel them in as the leases expired. Conspiracy theorists had a field day with the winding down of the program as the cars were systematically retrieved from circulation and ultimately crushed. Loyal lessees and many others charged that GM, the government, and Big Oil killed the car off for political and a variety of greed-motivated reasons. On one hand, it makes sense that an electric car would be at odds with the business model and profit motivations of international oil companies, who produce and sell many billions of dollars of conventional gasoline and diesel oil fuels—cars costing just a few dollars worth of electricity to charge and keep on the road don't need gas! Many people criticized President George W. Bush as having a hand in the conspiracy, in as much as he hails from the state of Texas and has oil interests of his own, but this seems unwanted, given that the project was cancelled more than a year before Bush was elected. No matter, GM steadfastly defended its position that the EV1 was its program, the experiment was over, and the company had every right to wind the program down and destroy the vehicles as it saw fit. Another aspect of the backstory is that the EV1 was expensive to build, and given the state and cost of battery technology at the time and in the foreseeable future, GM would lose money on a full scale EV1 production program. And there's no law that says any carmaker needs to build and sell unprofitable cars—in fact, it's bad for business to do so.

The last EV1s were built for the 1999 model year, and then car owners and conspiracy theorists took their message very public. They staged dramatic (some would say melodramatic) mock funerals for the EV1 and staged protests at the facilities charged with scrapping them. Nearly a decade after his first film, writer/director/producer Paine elected to take another—and far different—bite of the electric car apple. In fact, he switched his tone completely, embarking on a new project named *Revenge of the Electric Car*, this time focusing on electric car development and production efforts that worked—or appeared to be working. In a move that some saw as Paine giving GM a chance to right its wrongs or defend itself, he chose to follow the development of the Chevrolet Volt—an electric car that employs some of the computer and battery controller technology developed by GM for the EV1. The trials and tribulations of technology millionaire Elon Musk's Tesla car company are also shown in positive and occasionally negative lights. The film also shadows charismatic and hard-charging Nissan and Renault CEO Carlos Ghosn during the development and introductions of the pure electric Nissan Leaf.

The long-term success or failure of these three automobiles is yet to be determined, but it is clear that many of the world's drivers want non-petro-dependent, emissions-free electric cars, and ready or not, carmakers will continue to develop them.

VERDICT:
False. So, who killed the electric car? Nobody—because it's not dead. *–Matt Stone*

UNINTENDED ACCELERATION

LEGEND: Unintended acceleration results from intermittent electronic glitches that caused—and continue to cause—Audi 5000s, contemporary Toyotas, and countless other cars to speed out of control.

Shortly after 7 o'clock on Sunday evening, November 23, 1986, roughly 20 million viewers tuned into *60 Minutes* and saw bearded correspondent Ed Bradley at his magisterial best as he introduced what would become one of the program's most notorious episodes. "What we're talking about is the sudden rocketing of a car out of control after the driver switches gears from park into either drive or reverse," he intoned in his mellifluous voice. Then he set the scene for the incident that inflamed the nation, launched countless lawsuits, and nearly drove Audi out of the American market: "Six-year-old Joshua Bradosky liked to open the garage door when he drove home with his mother. The Reverend and Mrs. Bradosky told us what happened after she let the little boy out of the car to open the garage."

Kristi Bradosky was young, attractive, heart-rending, and understandably tearful. "I got back into the car [a 1985 Audi 5000] and put my foot on the brake to put it in drive, and the car surged forward, and I saw that I was going to hit him," she said. "So I put my foot on the brake, but it didn't stop the car. It pushed him through the garage. And we had a panel partition, and it went through the partition. He went through it."

Her son died in the accident. Neither Audi nor police investigators found anything wrong with the Audi's throttle or brakes. But engineer Paul Ast told Bradley that the problem—a mysterious malady known as sudden or unintended (or sudden unintended) acceleration—had been caused by an intermittent electronic glitch. "It'll cause a transient malfunction in the computer," he said, "and it may not happen for the next 10 years."

Happily, *60 Minutes* was able to reproduce the malfunction on demand for its viewers thanks to William Rosenbluth, another engineer who often testified as an expert witness in automotive cases. Rosenbluth told Bradley that the Audi 5000 was prone to "unusually high transmission pressure" that could cause the car to take off on its own. Allan Maraynes, the producer of the segment, provided him with an Audi that had already been involved in two previous sudden-acceleration incidents. For the camera, Rosenbluth demonstrated how the car launched itself even though

Although it was blessed with a groundbreaking shape, the 1986 Audi 5000 was also cursed with an unwarranted reputation for unintended acceleration. A *60 Minutes* hatchet job about the car nearly drove Audi out of the United States. Audi of America

he wasn't pushing the pedal. "Again," Bradley reported, "watch the pedal go down by itself."

Audi was represented on the broadcast by a pair of overmatched executives, Bob Cameron and Philip A. Hutchinson. Filmed in extreme close-up and grilled unmercifully, they were classic *60 Minutes* targets, unable to escape Bradley's crosshairs. Hutchinson and Cameron didn't want to blame the car owners, who were, after all, their customers. But since Audi hadn't been able to identify any systemic problem with their cars, Bradley skeptically theorized that driver error might have been the cause of these low-speed accidents. "Maybe you ought to have a special course to teach these articulate, well-educated people who buy the Audis the difference between the gas and the brake," he scoffed.

Although the Bradosky case was the most damning evidence against Audi, it was by no means unique. "Why are people landing on diving boards?" one victim demanded. "Why are they leaping over marina walls? Why are they going down elevator shafts? Why are they driving through people's buildings and landing on their beds?" Said another, "The foot was on the brake so hard, Mr. Bradley, that I had a shin splint. The entire foot was black and blue from pressing so hard on the brake." The volume and severity of complaints prompted Bradley to declare, "The sheer number of incidents involving the Audi 5000 alone would make it the most frequently occurring serious defect in automotive history."

The segment—which was rerun less than a year later—had a catastrophic effect on Audi of America. The company mounted a massive public relations campaign and sent general sales manager James Wolter around the country to rehabilitate Audi's reputation. "If there is anything we wish we could recall, it's the statement 'driver error,'" he said. "The intent was not to blame the drivers. The intent was to say that we can't find anything wrong with the cars. To come to our own logical conclusion that it was driver error was a mistake."

This remarkable mea culpa didn't help. Neither did a recall to install a shift lock—now standard on all cars—that prevented drivers from engaging Drive without having their foot on the brake pedal. Members of the newly formed Audi Victims Network filed multimillion-dollar lawsuits while the Center for Auto Safety—a consumer advocacy group founded by Ralph Nader—agitated for a National Highway Traffic Safety Administration (NHTSA) investigation. Thanks largely to the groundbreaking aerodynamic styling of the Audi 5000, Audi's American sales had peaked at nearly 75,000 cars in 1985. By 1991, they'd plummeted to slightly more than 12,000. It took the company nearly a generation—and axing the Audi 5000 nameplate—to recover.

Eventually, Americans forgot about the scourge of unintended acceleration. Oh, there continued to be occasional reports, a few hundred a year. Car wash owners complained vociferously about certain models of Jeeps, which they claimed had a mind of their own. But there was no longer an epidemic. The shift lock prevented what had been the most common unintended acceleration scenario—a car that took off like a dragster even though the driver was standing on the brake pedal—and the fear that cars acted as though they were possessed was limited to a world imagined by novelist Stephen King.

And then, on the evening of August 28, 2009, came the nightmarish and seemingly inexplicable accident that claimed four lives near the San Diego suburb of Santee. Off-duty California Highway Patrol officer Mark Saylor was at the wheel of a 2009 Lexus ES 350 sedan—a loaner he was driving while an El Cajon Lexus dealership serviced his car. Riding with him were his wife Cleofe, 13-year-old daughter Mahala, and Cleofe's brother-in-law Chris Lastrella. They were heading north on State Route 125 to take Mahala to soccer practice. Several witnesses later told police that the car appeared to be behaving erratically, sometimes going slower

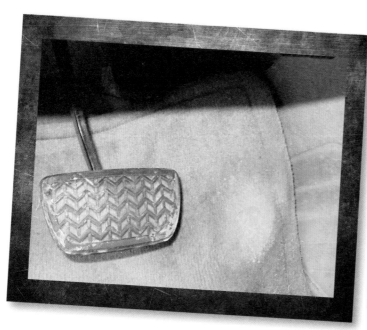

Investigators examining claims of unintended acceleration in Toyota and Lexus vehicles found that improperly installed floor mats were often the cause of the problem. Here is a floor mat that was not merely blocking but completely covering the accelerator pedal. Toyota Motor Corporation

than the flow of traffic, then pulling off the side of the road, then racing along at speeds up to 120 mph. There were reports that smoke and/or fire was emanating from under the front of the car.

Around 6:35 p.m., as the Lexus approached the major intersection at Mission Gorge Road, a local 911 dispatcher received a cell phone call from a man later identified as Chris Lastrella. "We're going north 125 and our accelerator is stuck," he said. "We're going 120 [miles per hour]! Mission Gorge! We're in trouble—we can't—there's no brakes. Mission Gorge— end freeway, half mile."

"Okay," the dispatcher broke in. "You don't have the ability to, like, turn the vehicle off or anything?"

"We are now approaching the intersection," Lastrella said. "We're approaching the intersection. We're approaching the intersection."

"Hold on, guys," came another voice from the car. "Pray."

"Oh, shoot," Lastrella said. "Oh . . . oh."

Then a woman screamed, and the call ended.

At Mission Gorge Road, the Lexus rear-ended a slow moving Ford Explorer at a speed estimated at 100 mph. One witness said the Lexus seemed to accelerate *after* the collision. It went airborne, smashed through a wood fence and crunched heavily into a raised dirt embankment. The medical examiner concluded that this was most likely the cause of the "blunt impact injuries" that killed all four occupants. The car cartwheeled violently and landed on its wheels in a riverbed. Intense heat, probably

The furor over allegations that Toyotas were beset by electronic glitches that caused unintended acceleration was ignited when four people died in the crash of a 2009 Lexus ES 350 driven by California Highway Patrol trooper Mark Saylor. Toyota Motor Corporation

from the overworked brakes, ignited the nearby brush, and the Lexus was engulfed in flames.

Naturally, the story was big news locally. Police blamed the accident on an incorrect and improperly installed floor mat that trapped the gas pedal and kept it depressed. A month later, Toyota—Lexus' parent company—announced a recall of 4.2 million vehicles and advised owners to remove their floor mats and place them in the trunk. A few days after that, Toyota president Akio Toyoda expressed remorse and publicly apologized to the Saylor family. This, too, was big news. But the Saylor incident didn't ignite a national firestorm until October 18, when the *Los Angeles Times* belatedly weighed in on the accident.

Although they waited nearly two months to write about the Saylor crash, reporters Ralph Vartabedian and Ken Bensinger used the incident as a launching pad for what turned out to be a barrage of articles about Toyota safety issues. Their first story, which ran on the front page, suggested that floor mats were a smokescreen that obscured more serious problems. In fact, even before mentioning the floor mat explanation, in the paragraph containing the nut of the story, they wrote: "The tragedy Aug. 28 was at least the fifth fatal crash in the U.S. over the last two years involving runaway Toyota and Lexus vehicles made by Toyota Motor Corp. It is also among hundreds of incidents of sudden acceleration involving the company's vehicles that have been reported to Toyota or the federal government, according to an examination of public records by *The Times*."

Vartabedian and Bensinger grudgingly acknowledged that none of the nine federal inquiries into allegations of sudden acceleration in a Toyota had uncovered any mechanical or electronic flaws. Nevertheless, their story raised the possibility that sudden acceleration could be caused by "unknown defects in the electronic control system, as alleged in some lawsuits." This hypothesis was developed more explicitly the following month in an in-depth story—"A *Times* Investigation"—that ran on the front page under a dramatic headline: "Data points to Toyota's throttles; The automaker cites floor mats, but reports of acceleration trouble shot up after the move to electronic control."

Coincidentally, Toyota also had to deal with unrelated problems with throttle pedals that failed to return properly to idle. Although these so-called sticky pedals didn't cause any accidents, they prompted another recall. By the end of February 2010, Toyota had recalled nearly 8.5 million vehicles in six months—a humiliating development for a company that prided itself on its exemplary quality control. Neither the pedal nor the floor mats were systemic electronic issues, but this distinction was blurred in the public mind as the media fixated on the complex electronics and on-board computers that kept modern automobiles running. In addition to the stories in the *L.A. Times*, ABC investigative reporter Brian Ross jumped on the "runaway Toyotas" bandwagon. The tenor of his stories was captured by a headline on the ABC website: "Terror on the Roads."

Before long, the ghost-in-the-machine meme went viral, and Toyota lost its fragile grip on the story. In a line so damning that Toyota's worst enemy couldn't have scripted it, Transportation Secretary Ray LaHood told reporters, "My advice is, if anyone owns one of these vehicles, stop driving it, take it to a Toyota dealer." Then, at a congressional hearing primarily convened, it seemed, to administer a public flogging of Toyota, retired social worker Rhonda Smith testified that her Lexus ES 350 sped up to 100 mph even though she braked and shifted first into neutral and then into reverse. "I thought it was my time to die," she said. "Today, I must say, shame on you, Toyota, for being so greedy. Shame on you, NHTSA, for not doing your job."

The maelstrom of dreadful publicity prompted countless anti-Toyota diatribes and not one but two federal investigations: NHTSA looking at the general issue of unintended acceleration and NASA drilling down into the sophisticated electronic throttle control (ETC) that was widely thought to be the root cause of the problem. But a funny thing happened on the road to perdition. Both reports gave Toyota a clean bill of health.

"After conducting the most exacting study of motor vehicle electronic controls ever performed by a federal agency, NASA did not find that the ETC electronics are a likely cause of large throttle openings in Toyota vehicles as described in consumers' complains to NHTSA," the report concluded in February 2011. "NASA's study confirmed that there is a theoretical possibility that two faults could combine under very specific conditions to affect the ETC systems so as to create an unintended UA but did not find any evidence that this had occurred in the real world or that there are failure mechanisms that would combine to make this occurrence likely."

NHTSA then turned its attention to the worst-case scenario allegations—the 75 Toyota-related unintended acceleration complaints that supposedly had killed 93 people since 2000. These were the terrifying numbers that had damned a company increasingly perceived as arrogant and tone-deaf. But after investigating each accident, NHTSA found only one that could conclusively be attributed to a vehicle fault. And the problem wasn't the dreaded ghost in the machine. On the contrary, it was a pedal trapped by a floor mat in the Saylor accident near San Diego. As for the hundreds of claims of standard-issue low-speed unintended acceleration, the reported stated, "NHTSA believes that these incidents are very likely the result of pedal misapplication." In other words, driver error.

Although NHTSA's report confounded conventional wisdom circa 2011, it sounded like old news to the people who'd paid close attention to the charges made against the Audi 5000 a quarter-century earlier. Three years after the inflammatory "Out of Control" segment ran on *60 Minutes*, NHTSA issued its first comprehensive report on unintended acceleration. Its findings? "For a sudden acceleration incident in which there is no evidence of throttle sticking or cruise control malfunction, the inescapable conclusion is that these definitely involve the driver inadvertently pressing the accelerator instead of, or in addition to, the brake pedal." That is, driver error.

Upon closer examination, it turned out that the most notorious allegations of unintended acceleration had prosaic explanations that had nothing to do with, well, unintended acceleration. For example, Kristi Bradosky, the young mother featured in the *60 Minutes* episode, told a police investigator immediately after the accident that killed her son that her foot had slipped off the brake and onto the gas pedal. Moreover, the only reason that an Audi 5000 appeared to accelerate on its own during the broadcast was because engineer William Rosenbluth had rigged a

Toyota Motor Corporation President and CEO Akio Toyoda, left, and Toyota Motor North America CEO Yoshi Inaba testify before the House Oversight and Government Reform Committee hearing on Capitol Hill in 2010. Getty Images

hose to shoot air into the transmission to produce just this special effect. The fraudulent road test later surfaced as one of the highlights of the book *Galileo's Revenge*, Peter Huber's scathing demolition of junk science. These days, the Audi broadcast is considered one of the worst blemishes on the generally illustrious reputation of *60 Minutes*. As Audi's Phil Hutchison puts it: "If the issue had been presented fairly, we would have been vindicated. Our mistake was thinking that they were journalists."

In the Saylor case, like all of the Audi cases, no electronic fault was identified. In the course of her rigorous investigation, San Diego County Sheriff's Deputy Janine Alioto discovered that the loaner Lexus involved in the accident had been driven the day before by another one of the dealership's customers. He, too, had experienced unintended acceleration, but was able to brake firmly to a stop. He told Alioto that when he checked the footwell, he realized that the floor mat—the wrong model, it turned out, and improperly installed—had wedged the gas pedal down and prevented it from returning to idle. Alioto concluded that this is what happened to Saylor. "The accelerator pedal became trapped either in the grooves of the mat or underneath it, causing V1 [Saylor's Lexus] to reach speeds greater than 100 MPH," she wrote in her 29-page report. "The brakes most likely failed due to over burdened, excessive, and prolonged application at high speed."

Audi of America general sales manager James Wolter drives his Audi 5000 in San Francisco during a nationwide tour in 1987 to deflect criticism that the car was susceptible to unintended acceleration. The public relations campaign failed miserably. Associated Press

As for Rhonda Smith, the unintended acceleration poster child who testified before the House Energy Committee, NHTSA investigators found evidence of another floor mat problem. Moreover, they claimed that when they showed Smith how her pedal had gotten trapped, she seemed to accept their explanation. Her runaway Lexus was bought by another consumer who drove it 33,000 additional miles without any problems. NHTSA subsequently recovered the vehicle and found nothing wrong after testing it extensively. In a crowning irony, Smith later bought a—wait for it—Toyota Tundra.

It's important to understand that the scary numbers regularly quoted in the media about thousands of accidents and hundreds of fatalities come not from NHTSA or any other official source but from Vehicle Owner Questionnaires, or VOQs. These are complaints filed by consumers. They aren't refereed or verified. It's true that you can't prove a negative, and the old adage holds that where there's smoke, there's fire. But the fact remains that despite the huge volume of VOQs, NHTSA's Office of Defects Investigations (ODI) hasn't been able to verify a single case of a car accelerating out of control because of some mysterious ghost in the machine. Not one. Zero. Zilch. Nada. Zip. A big, fat goose egg.

One reason, retired NHTSA attorney Allan Kam suggests, is that ODI officials wholeheartedly embraced the Audi 5000 report—known as the Silver Book because the cover was silver—that blamed most cases of unintended acceleration on drivers rather than cars. "The report was treated like gospel at ODI," he says. "After it was issued, there developed an institutional bias that all complaints of unintended acceleration were assumed to be pedal misapplication."

Safety advocate Sean Kane is convinced that NHTSA's culture blinds its investigators to alternate causes of unintended acceleration. "I'm not saying that driver error doesn't play a role," he says. "It most certainly does. But I get concerned when I hear them blaming stupid drivers." Kane, who started his career at the Center for Auto Safety, now runs Safety Research & Strategies, which is the most effective and strident proponent of an electronic explanation for unintended acceleration—and one of the most painful thorns in Toyota's side. He raises several valid points about flaws in NHTSA's methodology and suggests that agency officials are guilty of cronyism that undermines their objectivity when evaluating claims against automakers. He also argues persuasively that NHTSA is stronger on old-school mechanical engineering than it is on cutting-edge software and electronics technology. "These days, systems in cars communicate with each other," he says. "The idea that the brakes are separate from the accelerator is ancient history. But a lot of things have become mythologized there [at NHTSA]. They come at the issue from a belief system that drivers are the cause of unintended acceleration."

For many people, to be sure, unintended acceleration has become a religion—a matter of faith rather than a question of evidence, and those who believe most fervently in the phenomenon see signs of it everywhere. That said, they recognize that skeptics will never accept their truth without evidence. So, even for the true believers, the Holy Grail is incontrovertible proof that demonstrates the existence of unintended acceleration just as surely as a medieval proof established the existence of God.

Michael Pecht, a professor of electrical engineering and applied mathematics at the University of Maryland, says he managed to do just that in his lab several years ago—creating an error in a cruise control module that didn't throw a diagnostic trouble code, or DTC, which means it wouldn't have been caught after the fact by anybody looking for evidence of a problem. This is a far cry from replicating unintended acceleration in an actual car. But Pecht's point is that the issue isn't as cut and dried as NHTSA claims. "These are complex systems," he says. "The world of electronics is fraught with intermittent problems that can't be replicated. The diagnostics and test equipment aren't good enough to catch everything."

The closest that unintended acceleration believers have come to unearthing a smoking gun was the research of David Gilbert, an associate professor at the Southern Illinois University, Carbondale. Working in his lab, Gilbert said he was able to induce a fault that caused an electronic throttle control to open without throwing a DTC or ordering the vehicle into limp-home mode. Gilbert testified before Congress about his findings and later was featured prominently on one of Brian Ross' investigative pieces on ABC. But Toyota insisted that there was no cause for concern because the number and precise sequence of errors needed to produce the problem in the real world were astronomical. "The chances are about the same as a shark attacking you in the desert," says Gary E. Smith, Toyota's corporate manager for quality assurance and technical support.

If unintended acceleration existed in the real world, logic suggests that evidence would be found in the so-called event data recorders, or EDRs, that are standard equipment on, modern cars. These EDRs, like the black boxes in airliners, record a host of vehicle data—throttle position, brake application and so on—immediately prior to what's known as an airbag deployment event. EDRs aren't infallible, and the data they record is sometimes corrupted. But none of the dozens, if not hundreds, of EDRs examined by NHTSA has ever supported a finding of electronically uncommanded acceleration. On the contrary, in most cases, the data logged by the EDR suggested that pedal misapplication had been the cause of the incidents.

Some people, no doubt, will continue to believe in unintended acceleration no matter what the evidence shows—or doesn't show. They see their computers crash for no apparent reason, so why, they reason, shouldn't the same thing happen in their cars? And it's possible, of course. But even if the engine were to race out of control, the brakes are always powerful enough to overcome it. *Car and Driver* and *Motor Trend* have both demonstrated in instrumented tests that even cars traveling at high speed with the throttle wide open will come to a stop—in some cases in virtually the same distance as when the throttle was closed—as long as the driver brakes *hard*. In fact, the standard practice for launching a street car with an automatic transmission off the line at a drag strip is to firewall the gas pedal while standing on the brake to keep the car from creeping.

So the classic case of unintended acceleration requires not one but two system failures—throttle and brake—and they have to occur simultaneously. Many unintended acceleration complaints also allege that the problem was somehow related to the cruise control, so that's a third system that has to fail at precisely the right time. In the case of Rhonda Smith, whose car supposedly continued to speed along even after she shifted into neutral and then reverse, the transmission also must have failed. What are the chances that all of these highly unlikely occurrences would occur at the same time?

Those who believe in an electronically induced form of unintended acceleration acknowledge that the odds against a perfect storm of failure are extremely long. But, they point out, there are millions of drivers on the road. They drive billions of miles a year. Considering the sheer size of the automotive universe, they argue, is it really so hard to imagine that things occasionally go wrong in what otherwise might seem to be highly implausible ways?

Back in 1950, Nobel Prize–winning physicist Enrico Fermi asked himself a similar question. Not about cars. About UFOs, actually, but the statistical issue was the same. He and some fellow physicists at the Los Alamos National Laboratories were talking casually about a spate of recent flying saucer sightings. Being scientists, they began speculating about the odds that they might spot an object moving faster than the speed of light— an alien spaceship, for example—during the next 10 years. Considering the immense size and almost unfathomable age of the universe, Fermi thought it was unthinkable that Earth could be the only place where intelligent life had developed, and he placed the odds at 10-1. The conversation moved onto other subjects. Much later, over lunch, Fermi blurted, "Where is everybody?" Meaning that if there were other forms of intelligence life in the universe, as statistics suggested, we should have seen some signs of them over the past 100 billion years.

That's where things stand with unintended acceleration. Theory says that it could happen. Statistics say that it should have happened. So where is the proof? Or is the lack of proof all the evidence we need?

VERDICT:
Still out. It doesn't seem to be beyond the realm of possibility, but as it stands, electronically induced unintended acceleration is a hypothesis rather than a fact. –Preston Lerner

BLACK IS BEAUTIFUL

LEGEND: Henry Ford is often quoted as having said, "The Ford Model T customer may have his car in any color he wishes, so long as it is black."

The underlying presumption is that that Ford Model Ts could only be had in black. Strangely enough, not only were many colors offered over the years, but there was even a period of time, early on in Model T production,

The great-grandson of Henry Ford, Ford Motor company founder, is William Clay (Bill) Ford, Sr. and he seems very proud of these Model T color combos as he poses with them in front of the Ford World Headquarters building in Dearborn, Michigan. Ford publicity photo

that black was not available from the factory. To get the real story, we contacted Model T owner and expert Jonathan Klinger.

According to Mr. Klinger: "Color options were available early on (1909 to somewhere around 1914), and then colors were again offered the last two model years (1926 and 1927). Ironically, black wasn't even offered until 1915. The reason Henry declared in 1915 that all Model Ts will come in only one color was because he discovered a formula of black paint that dried quicker than any other color so this added to his constant quest of continually speeding up the production time." Another oft-cited reason for the ever-frugal Mr. Ford's penchant for black paint is that it was likely cheaper than color-pigmented paints.

continued on page 252

Born to Be Painted Black

Now that we've established that not all Model Ts were painted black, it's interesting to note that certain cars have always been painted black and were never intended to be presented in any other hue. In the case of the three cars noted here, the black paint job was likely meant to enhance their menacing shape, demeanor, or purpose. Really—how could a car named the *Black Beauty* be painted any other color? *—Henry Ford: Mass Production, Modernism and Design*

The Phantom Corsair

Rust Heinz was a wealthy young member of the Heinz food family. Heinz decided he wanted to produce a high-tech, aerodynamic automobile, and he did so in concert with custom coachbuilder Bohman & Schwartz. Heinz and Schwartz's car was called the Phantom Corsair, an appropriate name for its super-streamlined, somewhat evil-looking shape, leading one wag to call it "the world's largest drop of Marvel Mystery Oil." The look was decidedly advanced, especially for 1938, when one of the most aerodynamic automobiles around was the mass-produced Chrysler Airflow. The Phantom's prototype steel and aluminum body was built by hand, sat on a Cord 810 chassis, and employed the Cord's powertrain, including its 287-cubic-inch flathead Lycoming V-8 engine, one of the best of the day. The Corsair dripped in luxury and advanced technological features, including full fender skirts, front-wheel drive, and an elegant, art deco–inspired cabin that seated six. Heinz planned to put the car into limited production and had sales brochures designed and printed. Unfortunately, Mr. Heinz's untimely death in a 1939 car accident put an end to the entire plan. Speculation is that the car would have likely cost between $12,000 and $13,000 had it made it to the marketplace. There exists one photograph of the Phantom Corsair wearing a lighter color, but this appears to be primer applied prior to the final coat of glossy black paint. *—Ford: The Men and the Machine*

249

The Original Barris Batmobile

Automobile company concept cars and design studies seldom make their makers grasp. They often end up in the company museum—or the crusher. One such turntable toy went on to a much bigger life after the conclusion of its auto-show circuit career. By the mid-60s, the Lincoln Futura concept car of 1955 was living in quiet retirement in a Ford warehouse in Dearborn, Michigan, and was offered to Kustomizing King George Barris as a foundation on which to build the Batmobile for the new-for-'66 television series *Batman*. A fair amount of the look that Barris envisioned was already in place, including an open bubble-top canopy and wing-like rear fenders. Barris resculpted some of the body panels, keeping much of the Futura's basic look and proportions in place, and of course he added all of the trademark Batman and Robin weaponry, assorted geegaws, and identification prior to spraying the whole job in black with red trim for just the right Bat-inspired crime-fighter look. There was but one original Batmobile built for use in the TV series, but the car has since been replicated many times, at least once by Barris, and numerous times by others who built their own unofficial Batmobile tribute replicas. The original? Still shiny black, of course, and still owned by Barris.   –The Henry Ford Museum

The Green Hornet's Black Beauty

Renowned customizer/pinstriper/carbuilder Dean Jeffries is justifiably proud of designing and building the original Black Beauty for the '60s comic book hero-inspired television show *The Green Hornet*. He well remembers the day when producer William Dozier called and said, "Chrysler will be providing the cars for *The Green Hornet*, so we're sending you a new '66 Imperial, and it needs to become the rolling fortress for good guys Green Hornet and Kato."

Jeffries says, "I had a pretty free hand in what the car was to look like, but didn't have a big budget for the project, or a lot of time in which to get it done." He wanted the look to resemble that of a "sporty limousine," but didn't want to cut and lengthen the body and chassis, so he built a false roofline at the rear of the Imperial's factory roofline and substantially decreased the size of the rear window opening. It all adds to a stealthier look, as does a virtually complete dechroming job; Jeffries removed most of the exterior chrome trim, including the door handles, which were replaced by hidden electric switches operating solenoids to open the doors. The factory chrome bumpers also bit the dust. The front and rear ends were entirely redesigned, incorporating a variety of weaponry, glinting green headlights, and a reshaped trunk and taillight treatment. The windows were tinted, a variety of switchgear installed in the interior (plus a telephone), custom wheels were added, and the whole job was finished off in what seems like acres of glossy black paint. Jeffries ended up building a second Black Beauty so the two could appear opposite each other in one episode of the show. The original, "Beauty 1," is owned by the Petersen Automotive Museum in Los Angeles.   –*The Press* newspaper, Ford Motor Company

Two more Model Ts showing off the fact that Model could indeed be had in colors other than black. Ford publicity photo

Partially assembled Model Ts await completion at one of the many Ford assembly plants in which they were built. Even though this period shot is a black-and-white photograph, there doesn't appear to be cars here of any other color other than black. Ford publicity photo

YEAR	FORD COLOR
1909-14	Red
1909-14	Green
1909-14	Gray
1909-14	Blue
1915-1926	Black
1926	Channel Green
1927	Windsor Maroon
1927	Commercial Green
1927	Channel Green
1927	Drake Green
1927	Highland Green
1927	Phoenix Brown
1927	Gunmetal Blue
1927	Moleskin
1927	Royal Maroon
1927	Fawn Gray

continued from page 249

"I've been told that many different formulas of black were used throughout the span of Model T production. Toward the end of the production run of the Model T, Henry was feeling the heat from his competition that was finally catching up to him. Despite the fact that Model Ts were the best value for your money on the market, they were very outdated compared to the competition. He reintroduced color options in 1926 to add a little flavor to the Model T until the Model A came out. Black was not an option on the first year of production for the Model A.

"[The years] 1915 to 1925 were the peak production years of the Model T, which is why 95 percent of the Model Ts you see at shows are the famous black."

VERDICT:
False. While false, it is true 95 percent of the time.
–Matt Stone

BIBLIOGRAPHY

The 1911 Indianapolis 500
500 Miles to Go by Al Bloemker, 1966,
Coward-McCann

*Autocourse Official History of the
Indianapolis 500* by Donald Davidson and
Rick Schaffer, 2006, Crash Media Group

Blood and Smoke by Charles Leerhsen,
2011, Simon & Schuster

Indy by Rich Taylor, 1991, Robert McCord

1933 Tripoli Grand Prix
Enzo Ferrari by Brock Yates, 1991,
Doubleday

Grand Prix Tripoli by Valerio Moretti,
1994, Automobilia

Nuvolari by Christopher Hilton, 2003,
Motorbooks International

*A Record of Grand Prix and Voiturette
Racing, Volume III* by Paul and Betty
Sheldon and Duncan Rabagliati,
1992, Sheldon

Speed Was My Life by Alfred Neubauer,
1960, Barrie and Rockliff

The 1955 Le Mans Tragedy
Adventure on Wheels by John Fitch
with William Nolan, 1959, Putnam

Challenge Me the Race by Mike
Hawthorn, 1959, Kimber

Death Race by Mark Kahn, 1976, Barrie
& Jenkins Limited

Fangio: My Racing Life by Juan Manuel
Fangio with Robert Carozzo, 1990,
Patrick Stephens

*Jaguar Sports Racing & Works
Competition Cars from 1954* by Andrew
Whyte, 1988, Haynes Publications

Le Mans '55 by Christopher Hilton,m
2004, Breedon Books

Mike Hawthorn: Golden Boy by Tony Bailey
and Paul Skilleter, 2008, PJ Publishing

Mon Ami Mate by Chris Nixon, 1991,
Transport Bookman Publications

Starting Grid to Chequered Flag by Paul
Frère, 1961, B.T. Batsford

Dale
The Dale Automobile by Richard Smith,
2008, Froggy Press

Edsel
Disaster in Dearborn by Thomas E.
Bonsall, 2002, Stanford University Press

The Edsel Affair by C. Gayle Warnock,
1980, Pro West

*The Fate of the Edsel and Other Business
Adventures* by John Brooks, 1963, Harper

Make 'Em Shout Hooray by Richard H.
Stout, 1988, Vantage

Isadora Duncan
Isadora by Peter Kurth, 2001, Little,
Brown

The Real Isadora by Victor Seroff, 1971, Dial

The Untold Story by Mary Desti, 1929,
Horace Liveright

James Dean
Cars of the Stars by George Barris and
Jack Scagnetti, 1974, Jonathan David

James Dean: At Speed by Lee Raskin,
2005, David Bull

Porsche Legends by Randy Leffingwell,
1996, Motorbooks International

JATO Rocket Car
The Call Me Mister 500 by Andy
Granatelli, 1969, Henry Regnery

Jocko Flock
Tim Flock, Race Driver by Larry
Fielden, 1991, The Galfield Press

Fast as White Lightning by Kim Chapin,
1981, Dial Press

Paul Newman
Winning by Matt Stone and
Preston Lerner, 2009,
Motorbooks International

Rodney King
Official Negligence by Lou Cannon,
1999, Westview

Presumed Guilty by Stacey C. Koon,
1992, Regnery Gateway

Smokey Yunick
Best Damn Garage in Town by Smokey
Yunick, 2004, Carbon Press

Cheating by Tom Jensen, 2004,
David Bull

Unintended Acceleration
Galileo's Revenge by Peter W. Huber,
1991, BasicBooks

Toyota Under Fire by Jeffrey K. Liker
and Timothy N. Ogden, 2011,
McGraw-Hill

INDEX

INDEX